Mastering Financial Mathematics
in Microsoft® Excel

Mastering Financial Mathematics in Microsoft® Excel

A practical guide for business calculations

Third Edition

ALASTAIR L. DAY

PEARSON

Harlow, England • London • New York • Boston • San Francisco • Toronto • Sydney
Auckland • Singapore • Hong Kong • Tokyo • Seoul • Taipei • New Delhi
Cape Town • São Paulo • Mexico City • Madrid • Amsterdam • Munich • Paris • Milan

PEARSON EDUCATION LIMITED

Edinburgh Gate
Harlow CM20 2JE
Tel: +44 (0)1279 623623
Fax: +44 (0)1279 431059
Website: www.pearsoned.co.uk

First published in Great Britain in 2005
Second edition 2010
Third edition 2015 (print and electronic)

© Pearson Education Limited 2005
© Systematic Finance Limited 2010, 2015 (print and electronic)

ISBN: 978-1-292-06750-6 (print)
        978-1-292-06752-0 (PDF)
        978-1-292-06751-3 (eText)
        978-1-292-06753-7 (ePub)

British Library Cataloguing-in-Publication Data
A catalogue record for this book is available from the British Library

Library of Congress Cataloging-in-Publication Data
A catalog record for this book is available from the Library of Congress

10 9 8 7 6 5 4 3 2 1
19 18 17 16 15

Print edition typeset in Garamond 11.5/13.5pt by 76
Printed in Malaysia, CTP-PJB

NOTE THAT ANY PAGE CROSS REFERENCES REFER TO THE PRINT EDITION

Contents

Acknowledgements

I would like to thank Angela, Matthew and Frances for their support and assistance with the completion of this book. As in all the previous projects, Pearson Education have provided excellent support and backing for this project.

About the author

Alastair Day has worked in the finance industry for more than 30 years in treasury and marketing functions and was formerly a director of a vendor leasing company specialising in the IT and technology industries. After rapid growth, the directors sold the enterprise to a public company and he established Systematic Finance as a consultancy specialising in:

- financial modelling – educate, design, build, audit and review;
- training in financial modelling, corporate finance, leasing and credit analysis on an in-house and public basis throughout Europe, the Middle East, Asia, Africa and the Americas;
- finance and operating lease structuring as a consultant and lessor.

Alastair is author of four modelling books published by FT Prentice Hall, namely *Mastering Financial Modelling*, *Mastering Risk Modelling*, *Mastering Financial Mathematics in Microsoft Excel* and *Mastering Financial Mathematics in Excel*, apart from a range of other books and publications on financial analysis and leasing.

Alastair has a degree in Economics and German from the University of London and an MBA from the Open University Business School.

Conventions

- The main part of the text is set in Garamond, whereas entries are set in Courier. For example:

  Enter the Scenario Name as `Base Case`

- Items on the menu bars are also shown in Courier. For example:

  Select `Data, What-if Analysis, Goal Seek`

- The names of functions are in Courier capitals. This is the payment function, which requires inputs for the interest rate, number of periods, present value and future value:

  `=PMT(INT,NPER,PV,FV,TYPE)`

- Cell formulas are also shown in Courier. For example:

  `=IF($C$75=1,IF($B25>C$22,$B25-C$22-C$23,-`
  `C$23),IF($B25<C$22,C$22-$B25-C$23,-C$23))`

- Equations are formed with the Equation Editor and are shown in normal notation. For example, net present value:

$$NPV = \frac{(CashFlow)^n}{(1 + r)^n}$$

- Genders. The use of 'he' or 'him' refers to masculine or feminine, and this is used for simplicity to avoid repetition.

Overview

WHO NEEDS THIS BOOK?

More than 25 years ago I used an early Hewlett Packard 38C to calculate interest rates and analyse cash flows and then progressed to the 'state of the art' programmable HP 41C with a printer, magnetic strip reader and plug-in finance and mathematics packs. This was an early alphanumeric calculator, which gave me the opportunity to program lease versus purchase or lessor lease evaluation cash flows and structure more complex lease transactions. This was before IBM launched the personal computer in the early 1980s.

Since that time I have used and programmed other calculators, such as the HP 12C, HP 17BII, HP 19B and TI BAII Plus, which all provide dedicated user screens and allow you to undertake financial mathematics. While calculators are much easier to use than tables or earlier methods they can be difficult to use without making simple errors. When I run training courses on the basic financial calculations the main drawback is only too obvious: you cannot see your inputs or check the interim calculations, and therefore delegates always want to see a map of the variables to understand the answer.

While I have continued to use financial calculators, which have now been augmented with applications on mobile phones using Apple IOS or Android, and have in the past created programs in Basic, the most comprehensive medium for financial mathematics has grown to be spreadsheets such as Microsoft Excel. I first used Lotus 1-2-3 in 1988 and Excel 3.0 in 1990, and through various upgrades Excel grew into the latest Microsoft Office, which remains little changed in the core financial functions through to today's versions.

Given that almost everybody engaged in finance functions has Excel on their desktops, and increasingly on their laptops, mobile phones or tablet and notebook computers, the objective of this book is to explain the basic calculations for mathematical finance backed up by simple templates for further use and development, together with examples and exercises. If you work through each of the chapters in the book, repeating the models and trying the exercises, you will improve your Excel skills and obtain a better grasp of the underlying financial concepts.

My other modelling books published by FT Prentice Hall, *Mastering Financial Modelling*, *Mastering Risk Modelling* and *Mastering Cash Flow and Valuation Modelling*, provide alternative models for some of the topics in this book. These combine financial theory with model design, using ideas of best international practice coupled with tried and tested methods of auditing and testing. This book adheres to systematic spreadsheet best practice and adopts the same standards, method and layout.

The key objectives for this book are to:

■ provide an explanation of key financial formulas and subject areas;

■ show the use of the formulas using straightforward Excel templates;

■ introduce examples and exercises for extension work;

■ provide a library of basic templates for further development.

This book aims to assist two key groups:

■ practitioners who want a manual of financial mathematics from which they can gain immediate use and payback;

■ business students who need a textbook which is more geared to Excel solutions than some college manuals.

The areas of responsibility where the book should be of interest are:

■ CFOs and finance directors;

■ financial controllers;

■ financial analysts and executives;

■ accountants;

■ corporate finance specialists;

■ treasury managers;

■ risk managers;

■ academics, business and MBA students.

Therefore, people interested in this book range from a company accountant who wants a reference book to academics and business students who need a financial mathematics manual in Excel. The book has an international bias and provides examples which are relevant to the UK and overseas.

HOW TO USE THIS BOOK

- Install the Excel application templates using the simple **SETUP** command. The files will install automatically together with a program group and icons. There is a key to the file names at the end of the book.
- Work through each of the chapters repeating the models and examples.
- Use the manual, spreadsheets and templates as a reference guide for further work.
- Practise, develop and improve your efficiency and competence with Excel.

Alastair L. Day
Email: aday@system.co.uk or Internet: www.financial-models.com

Warranty and disclaimer

The financial models used in the book have not been formally audited and no representation, warranty or undertaking (express or implied) is made and no responsibility is taken or accepted by Systematic Finance Limited and its directors as to the adequacy, accuracy, completeness or reasonableness of the financial models and the company excludes liability thereof.

In particular, no responsibility is taken or accepted by the company and all liability is excluded by the company for the accuracy of the computations comprised therein and the assumptions upon which such computations are based. In addition, the reader receives and uses the financial models entirely at his own risk and no responsibility is taken or accepted by the company and accordingly all liability is excluded by the company for any losses which may result from the use of the financial models, whether as a direct or indirect consequence of a computer virus or otherwise.

Microsoft, Microsoft Excel and Windows are either registered trademarks or trademarks of Microsoft Corporation in the United States and/or other countries. Screen shots reprinted by permission from Microsoft Corporation.

1

Introduction

File: MFMaths3e_01.xls

OVERVIEW

The book begins with an explanation of cash flows, returns and compounding a present value to a future value and then develops the calculations into net present values and internal rates of return. In subsequent chapters the methods develop these formulas to analyse fixed income products, derivatives, foreign exchange, equities and leasing.

Since Excel can display the layout of each stage of a complex calculation, it is better suited to automating and displaying the results than traditional programming languages which use a 'black box' approach. Here you enter the inputs and an answer is displayed without showing the methodology. Many users do not use the full functionality of Excel, and although this is not a book on pure financial modelling the models use a combination of Excel features and techniques. This conforms to the Systematic Design standards set out in *Mastering Financial Modelling*, *Mastering Cash Flow and Valuation Modelling* and *Mastering Risk Modelling*. This method uses standardised layouts and structures to use Excel primarily for analysis, decision making and communication rather than simple mathematics. The objectives in financial modelling should be:

- a reduction in the amount of development time needed;
- decreased repeat or extended calculations;
- prevention of coding, logic and other errors;
- easier updating, development and maintenance;
- clear communication through charts, tables, dashboards and summaries.

The widespread use of Microsoft Office means that most people (like you) have Excel as part of their desktop. However, consider the following:

- Many companies do not appear to offer specific training in applied financial modelling and solving problems in Excel.
- Basic financial modelling courses often seem to show functions and methods without demonstrating how a series of methods and techniques can be combined to make more powerful and informative models.
- Few business schools teach Excel as a core part of their curriculum, yet many junior analysts and corporate finance executives need the expertise in their first job placements.
- Most corporate finance textbooks rely on calculator solutions rather than providing instruction on how to write simple spreadsheets to solve the problems.

With enough practice, people eventually achieve a certain standard in modelling through trial and error; however, this means that many spreadsheet models often:

- are incomprehensible except to the author;
- contain serious structural errors which remain undiscovered;
- cannot be audited due to the lack of structure and standards;
- are not maintainable or flexible enough to be developed further due to poor structure and basic errors;
- ultimately fail in their key objectives.

The inherent simplicity of Excel means that models can be written 'on the fly' with no thought to any of the above problems; however, Excel is a sophisticated tool only if used properly. Given the importance of financial analysis, the use of Excel should be a core skill for managers to enable them to produce clear, maintainable applications and be proficient in spreadsheet design.

COMMON EXCEL ERRORS

There have been many studies of spreadsheets in use by organisations and here are some questions that you could ask about your own or colleagues' spreadsheets. If you can answer 'yes' to any of the questions then you could examine the structure and some of the coding using the simple rules in the chapter.

- Have you ever found an error in a spreadsheet long after it was finished?
- When you receive spreadsheets from others, do you find it hard to understand the structure or know what to do next to obtain alternative answers?
- If you want to add extra functionality to a spreadsheet, do you have to undertake major redesign?
- Do you wish that a spreadsheet could answer more complex problems?
- Have you or others ever doubted the accuracy of the spreadsheets you developed?

Since the majority of people using Excel are really amateur programmers, there is a wide range of errors that can be categorised, ranging from high-level conceptual errors to lower-level coding and method errors. Spreadsheets can be quick and dirty for individual use; however, models for corporate use need to adopt different standards. Many applications are used for critical corporate decision making and need to be reviewed or used by others.

Types of spreadsheet models that appear to be used are:

- unplanned and uncontrolled with code leading in all directions;
- technical applications that are over-complex, often with minimal documentation;
- single user application what-if, risk, decision tree, probability and simulation models;
- database and data analysis;
- 'turnkey' applications.

Nevertheless, both experienced and new users make mistakes in Excel. Whether there are time pressures or a lack of thought about design, it is too easy to make simple errors. Here is a selection of common input errors:

- No clear layout with code split into inputs, calculations, outputs, reports and explanation. Where calculations and inputs are mixed, it is hard to understand how to change inputs easily.
- No specific colour or marking for inputs, calculations and answers. My spreadsheets use a blue, bold font with a turquoise background, and many other people do too.
- No styles, borders or shading to mark the different areas of the model.
- No use of more advanced features, such as validation, names, comments, views and protection.

Where there is no organisation in a file, it makes it difficult to understand and maintain. Similarly, there are typical calculation problems which, if present, can reduce confidence in the answers. Here are some examples:

- Cell formulas are overwritten with numbers and hard coded so that users cannot be sure that changes will cascade through a model. A lack of consistency means that, from experience, there are likely to be more errors in a model.
- Mixtures of number formats with no consistency in percentages or numbers of decimal places. Cells contain a mixture of numbers and formulas. For example, hard-coded corporate tax $= C5 * 0.20$. You could change the tax rate by performing an edit replace through the file, provided that somebody has not changed 0.20 to another number such as 0.21. The 0.20 should be variable in an inputs area and this reference used in all the formulas.
- Where there is more than one formula per line, this can also cause confusion. For example, the columns for January, February and March contain one formula and then the formula inexplicably changes in April and back to the original formula in May. Sometimes users make formulas impossibly complicated as if it is some kind of competition, where it could be advantageous to show workings not shown separately or break down the calculations.

- There is a wide range of built-in functions and procedures in add-ins such as the Analysis ToolPak, and it is usually preferable to use the functions in order to reduce the volume of required code. Since Excel is an analysis tool, some users do not take advantage of the procedures to obtain clearer management information.

- Techniques such as data tables, sensitivity analysis, scenario manager, report manager, custom views, advanced charting, pivot tables, database queries and Microsoft Office connectivity can reduce the use of unplanned macros and improve the quality of information.

- Many users do not document their work or provide some explanation of how to use the model or the range of permitted results.

This is not an exhaustive list of Excel errors, but it shows the weakness of an unplanned approach with the consequent sub-optimisation in the eventual spreadsheet model.

SYSTEMATIC DESIGN METHOD

There are many ways of designing spreadsheets, with no right or wrong answer. While the previous section includes practices that many users would agree produce weak and error-prone models, there is no accepted method adopted by the majority of spreadsheet users. Some modelling methods use complicated rules; however, the objective should be a distinctive, simple, repeatable style that can be utilised in every model and maintained efficiently. The basic method used in this book is one that I have developed over the last 25 years. I have found that it works so that models can be developed rapidly while reducing the incidence of errors.

Some aspects are:

- defined colour coding of cells;
- specific areas for inputs, calculations, outputs, summaries, etc.;
- style guides to simplify the colours and formats on each sheet.
- simplicity with no long formulas or nested IF statements;
- as little hard code as possible with formulas cascading through workbooks;
- one formula per row or column across sheets;
- no mixed formulas and numbers in cell formulas;
- standard number formats, for example, negative numbers in brackets and in a red font;
- formulas refer to cells to the left or above, like in a book rather than an illogical flow of information;

- multiple sheets with a modular design rather than sheets with multiple reports or sub-schedules;
- standard schedule and model layouts with menu sheets, version numbers, author names and full explanation and documentation.

The simplest way of showing the difference is to take a poor model and demonstrate the difference in the model when properly formatted. This is a simple cash flow and discounting valuation model where cash flows grow each year for five years. At the end of the period, the company is valued at a multiple of the earnings before interest, tax, depreciation and amortisation (EBITDA) (see Figure 1.1). The cash flows are then discounted at 10 per cent to a present value. The methodology is covered in more detail in later chapters; however, the model is difficult to understand since all the variables are hard coded into the cells. If you want to increase the growth rate or reduce the discount rate it is hard to know what to do next.

Initial model

Figure 1.1

◢	A	B	C	D	E	F	G	H
4								
5			-	1	2	3	4	5
6		EBITDA		75.00	79.50	84.27	89.33	94.69
7		Free cash flow		100.00	105.00	110.25	115.76	121.55
8								
9		Terminal value						473.43
10								
11		Discount factor		0.91	0.83	0.75	0.68	0.62
12								
13		Net cash flow		90.91	86.78	82.83	79.07	75.47
14		Net terminal value						293.96
15								
16		Net present value	709.02					

If you go to Formulas, Formula Auditing, Show formulas you can show the formulas quickly (or Control +' or use search Help for Formula Auditing Mode). Figure 1.2 reveals the mixture of numbers and formulas in the cells.

Show formulas

Figure 1.2

Figure 1.3

Pattern match

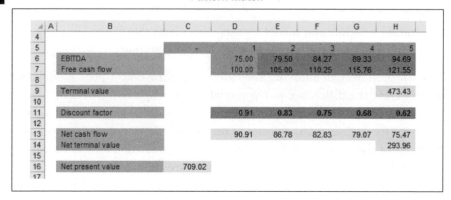

An alternative method using third-party audit software produced by Systematic Finance (www.financial-models.com) is to match patterns in the cells by use or function (see Figure 1.3). The colour scheme is visible on the Excel model and the key to the function is:

■ Blue denotes text cells or labels (cell B6).

■ Crimson marks numbers cells (cell C5).

■ Beige shows all formulas (cell H9).

■ Orange is reserved for mixed formulas which require attention since mixed formulas can be difficult to maintain (cell E6).

■ Green cells show complex formulas with more than a defined number of characters.

■ Bold is used to mark row differences where a formula changes across a line (cell E11).

■ Turquoise shows errors such as DIV/0

■ Patterned blue bold marks unlocked cells (there are none in this initial model).

The solution to this simple model is to extract all the inputs and rework the model into sections with colour coding (see Figure 1.4). This means that any user can immediately see all the inputs and follow the information flow through to the answer and summary. As a model grows in size, these small sections would be developed as separate sheets; however, a user can understand a model more quickly if there is a consistent style and approach.

Using Styles in Excel can facilitate faster coding and instil consistency in spreadsheets. The files in this book all use a standard Systematic Finance style guide which sets out how an input, total, title, etc. should be displayed. This means that spreadsheets are easier to understand since they all look the same. Styles are at Home, Styles (shortcut Alt HJ). Figure 1.5 shows the different styles, and you should modify one of these templates

Revised model layout

Figure 1.4

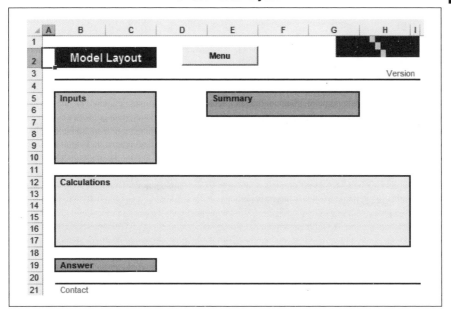

Style sheet

Figure 1.5

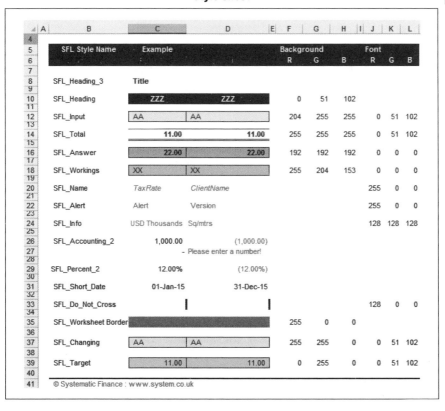

Figure 1.6   **Revised model**

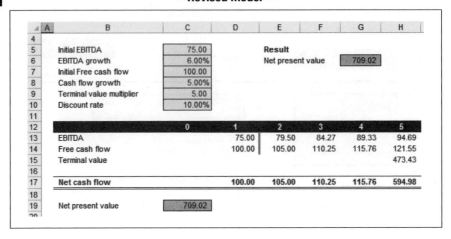

to produce your own style sheet. The numbers on the right display the Red/Green/Blue numbers for backward compatibility to Excel 2003, but you could replace these with the numbers from your corporate Pantone colours.

The revised model (see Figure 1.6) follows this approach. The individual factors are replaced with a single function and a management summary is available near the inputs. More techniques or layers are possible since a user can have confidence that the inputs flow directly through the calculations to the answer. If sensitivity, scenario analysis or some form of optimisation or simulation technique is required, this can be added efficiently as an extra module without fundamental redesign.

The pattern matching reveals the consistency with the removal of mixed formulas and the marking of formula column changes. The input cells are the only unlocked cells on the sheet and the inputs are used in the calculations in Figure 1.7. This is a simple example; however, the same methods are used in all the models developed for this book.

AUDITING

While it is important to set out the models correctly, model auditing is often ignored or performed inadequately. Simply looking at the model will not find the errors, and it is important to assume that there are errors in a model and apply consistent auditing and checking methods. A systematic, organised approach is required. There are a few initial tests that can be run to try to understand the reliability of the output. You can use

Revised pattern match

Figure 1.7

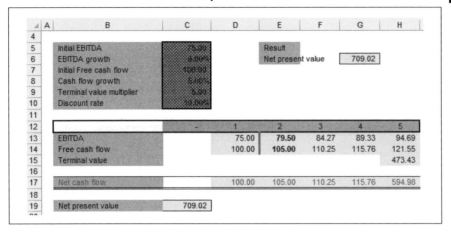

these tests to understand the spreadsheets in this book. Instances that need to be checked carefully include:

- formulas not copied correctly across multiple ranges;
- inconsistent references used in formulas;
- sum over wrong range;
- mixed numbers and formulas;
- long formulas using multiple or nested functions;
- relative and absolute references with cell locking (F4) not applied correctly;
- unit errors where percentages and numbers are used interchangeably;
- functions such as LOOKUP, MATCH and INDEX can produce errors if the ranges are not carefully chosen.

Some initial methods for checking the spreadsheet in this book include:

- Manual review looking at the reasonableness of the answers and interim calculations. For example, you can always select a range and press Alt F1 or F11 to produce a chart directly. If you expect a downward or linear relationship, charting can assist in showing errors.
- Showing formulas or the formula auditing mode used earlier (Formulas, Formula Auditing) helps to demonstrate consistency and also provides a visual 'quality score' on the spreadsheet.
- Audit toolbar (see Figure 1.8) allows you to trace precedents and dependents to a specific cell or range. An alternative is to use Control + [or Control +] to show immediate precedents and dependents or Control Shift with the brackets to show all links on the sheet.

Figure 1.8

Audit trace arrows

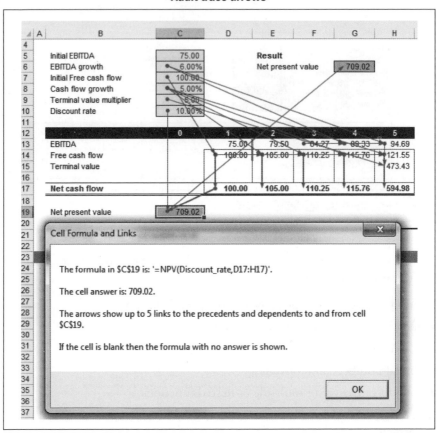

The arrows show the cells that build up the answer in cell C19 by clicking the second left-hand icon for each stage. The next arrow allows you to hide each stage. The next two arrows do the same for dependents and the icon with three arrows removes all arrows. Other icons allow you to display formula watches similar to other programming languages or evaluate formulas (see Figure 1.9).

As you click Evaluate, each number or formula is transformed to its interim result. This is especially useful for working through nested IF statements where you are not sure of the progress of the logic.

■ Other extras include options such as Formulas, Formula Auditing, Error Checking. Figure 1.10 lists the rules that you either accept or unclick. You can then run tests on a sheet using commands under Office Button, Excel Options, Formulas. While this method will find many errors, you cannot rely on it to find all the mixed or inconsistent formulas.

Evaluate formula

Figure 1.9

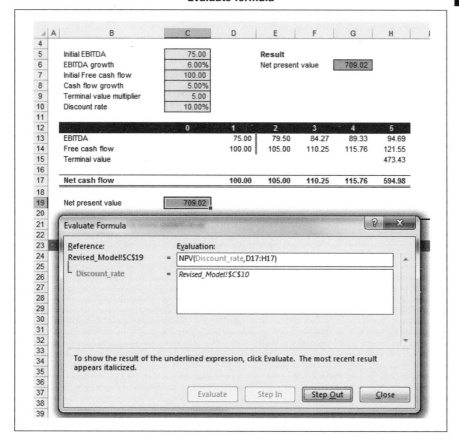

Excel error checking

Figure 1.10

Error Checking

☑ Enable background error checking

Indicate errors using this color: 🎨▾   [Reset Ignored Errors]

Error checking rules

☑ Cells containing formulas that result in an ⓘ
error

☑ Inconsistent calculated column formula in ⓘ
tables

☑ Cells containing years represented as 2 ⓘ
digits

☐ Numbers formatted as text or preceded by ⓘ
an apostrophe

☑ Formulas which omit cells in a region ⓘ

☑ Unlocked cells containing formulas ⓘ

☐ Formulas referring to empty cells ⓘ

☑ Data entered in a table is invalid ⓘ

SUMMARY

The following chapters outline financial mathematics in Excel and try to make the models more understandable by using a specific design method. It may be easier to produce unstructured models in Excel but in the long run these end up costing time, money or both. This chapter sets out a few pointers to design, such as layout and colour coding, and shows the advantages of this consistent approach. By repeating the same standard design method the quality and reliability of models improve and this reduces development and audit time.

Basic financial arithmetic

File: MFMaths3e_02.xls

Basic financial arithmetic

This chapter deals with the basic concepts of financial mathematics which underpin investment analysis, bonds, derivatives, leasing and many other examples. Companies and individuals face the problem of investing today in the hope of some financial gain or reducing expenditure. Investing is risky, so companies expect a suitable return for both known and unknown risks. Similarly, investors require some extra return for investing in risky assets. This is the time preference of money as the basic financial theory, which depends on the following:

- If companies and individuals think logically and rationally, they usually prefer money today rather than the promise of returns in the future. Money today is more certain than the promise of funds in the future. Companies and individuals can be said to be risk averse and require some sort of monetary gain to give up the certainty of funds today.

- Inflation affects the decision as it can quickly erode gains when translated into current purchasing power. This may not be significant in Europe at present; however, there have been recent periods where inflation was much higher. For example, UK inflation was around 25 per cent in the mid 1970s.

- Some forms of lending are riskier than others. Loans to certain governments can sometimes be considered 'risk free' and perhaps attract a lower risk premium than corporate lending. In theory, the risk premium should reflect the timescale and relative risk such that the decision to delay provides a greater gain. Ratings agencies specialise in grading institutions and countries according to the perceived risk they represent.

These three factors underpin the concepts of time value of money and discounted cash flows, which drive the financial concepts in this book.

SIMPLE INTEREST

The easiest interest rate to compute is a simple rate. Simple or flat rate interest charges a price for the principal and does not take account of the time value of money, and it is therefore a simplification of compounding covered later in this chapter. Interest is calculated only on the principal and does not take into account the payback of the principal during the period. Similarly it does not take account of skipped periods or structured paybacks. Nevertheless, simple interest is usually used for periods of less than a year, and there is an array of conventions for bills, deposits, bonds, etc., within the financial markets.

The simple interest INT on an investment (or loan) of a present value (initial) amount at an annual interest rate of r for a period of t years is:

$$INT = PV * r * t$$
$$INT = interest$$
$$PV = present\ value$$

The future value (*FV* or maturity value) of a simple interest investment of *PV* dollars at an annual interest rate of *r* for a period of *t* years is:

$$FV = PV + INT = PV(1 + rt)$$

This is the amount that you would have at the end of the period. You can also solve for the present value *PV* to obtain:

$$PV = FV/(1 + rt)$$
$$PV = present\ value$$
$$FV = future\ value$$

These calculations can easily be translated into Excel as on the Simple Interest sheet.

Figure 2.1

Example 1

⊿	A	B	C	D	E	F
4						
5		Amount (PV)	1,000,000.00			
6		Simple Interest Rate {r}	10.00%			
7		Start Date	28-Feb-20			
8		Finish Date	28-Feb-21			
9		360 Day Year	360.0 days			
10						
11			Act/360	30/360	Act/Act	
12		Days	366	360	366	
13		Year	360	360	366	
14						
15		Result	1.0167	1.0000	1.0000	
16						
17		Interest Payable	101,666.67	100,000.00	100,000.00	
18						
19		FV = PV + INT = PV(1 + rt)	1,101,666.67	1,100,000.00	1,100,000.00	
20						
21		PV = FV/(1 + rt).	1,000,000.00	1,000,000.00	1,000,000.00	

Figure 2.1 shows the simple interest on 1,000,000 from 28 February to the next year in a leap year. Three conventions show the number of days and the standardised number of days in the year. The interest, future value and present value are calculated using the formulas above.

Cell D12 uses the function DAYS360 to calculate the days between the dates on a 360-day basis. Cell D12 in Figure 2.1 uses the US (NASD) method and the rules the function adopts are:

■ US (NASD) method: if the start date is the 31st of a month, it becomes equal to the 30th of the same month. If the end date is the 31st of a month and the start date is earlier than the 30th of a month, the end date becomes equal to the 1st of the next month, otherwise the end date becomes equal to the 30th of the same month.

- European method: start dates and end dates that occur on the 31st of a month become equal to the 30th of the same month.

Cell E13 contains the formula for calculating the actual number of days in the year:

```
=DATE(YEAR(C7)+1,MONTH(C7),DAY(C7))-DATE(YEAR(C7),
MONTH(C7),DAY(C7))
```

This calculates one year from the start date with the DATE function and then subtracts the start date in the same format.

Example 2

Figure 2.2

⊿ A	B	C	D	E	F
4					
5	Amount (PV)	1,000,000.00			
6	Simple Interest Rate {r}	10.00%			
7	Start Date	28-Feb-20			
8	Finish Date	01-Mar-20			
9	360 Day Year	360.0 days			
10					
11		Act/360	30/360	Act/Act	
12	Days	2	3	2	
13	Year	360	360	366	
14					
15	Result	0.0056	0.0083	0.0055	
16					
17	Interest Payable	555.56	833.33	546.45	
18					
19	FV = PV + INT = PV(1 + rt)	1,000,555.56	1,000,833.33	1,000,546.45	
20					
21	PV = FV/(1 + rt).	1,000,000.00	1,000,000.00	1,000,000.00	

Figure 2.2 shows the effect across a shorter period of three days, where the interest payable is different under all three methods. Here the gap between the two dates is two days, but it is calculated as three on a 30/360-day basis. The addition of the standard number of days in the year results in three different levels of interest based on the simple rate of 10 per cent.

Simple interest could be used for calculating loan payments and is frequently used for hire purchase (US – dollar out) or lease purchase contracts. These are often structured as transactions with deposits and the balance of payments over a period. Figure 2.3 shows a 1,000,000 loan with a 10 per cent deposit repayable monthly over five years at a simple interest rate of 10 per cent.

The net advance is 900,000 after the 10 per cent deposit. The annual interest is 90,000 at 10 per cent, so the total interest payable is 450,000. The total payable is 1,350,000 after the deposit, which can be divided by 60 monthly payments. The monthly rental is 22,500 and the total payable

Figure 2.3

Simple loan interest

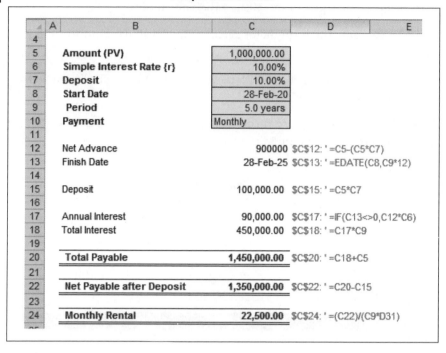

	A	B	C	D	E
4					
5		Amount (PV)	1,000,000.00		
6		Simple Interest Rate {r}	10.00%		
7		Deposit	10.00%		
8		Start Date	28-Feb-20		
9		Period	5.0 years		
10		Payment	Monthly		
11					
12		Net Advance	900000	$C$12: ' =C5-(C5*C7)	
13		Finish Date	28-Feb-25	$C$13: ' =EDATE(C8,C9*12)	
14					
15		Deposit	100,000.00	$C$15: ' =C5*C7	
16					
17		Annual Interest	90,000.00	$C$17: ' =IF(C13<>0,C12*C6)	
18		Total Interest	450,000.00	$C$18: ' =C17*C9	
19					
20		Total Payable	1,450,000.00	$C$20: ' =C18+C5	
21					
22		Net Payable after Deposit	1,350,000.00	$C$22: ' =C20-C15	
23					
24		Monthly Rental	22,500.00	$C$24: ' =(C22)/(C9*D31)	

with the deposit 1,450,000. Notice that the total payable does not vary as you select monthly, quarterly, semi-annual or annual payments. This is because the method does not recognise the effect of the different time periods.

Cell C10 is validated using a data list in the range B29:B32 (see Figure 2.4).

Figure 2.4

Lookup functions

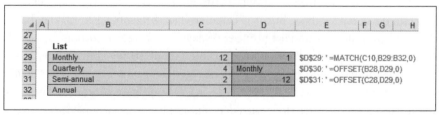

	A	B	C	D	E	F	G	H
27								
28		List						
29		Monthly	12		1	$D$29: ' =MATCH(C10,B29:B32,0)		
30		Quarterly	4	Monthly		$D$30: ' =OFFSET(B28,D29,0)		
31		Semi-annual	2		12	$D$31: ' =OFFSET(C28,D29,0)		
32		Annual	1					

The MATCH function in cell D29 finds the index position on the period selection in the inputs. The OFFSET function turns the index number back into the selected periodicity and number of payments per annum.

COMPOUND INTEREST

Compound interest takes into account the capital outstanding and the time value of money of investments. Compounding means that interest is calculated not only on the initial investment but also on the interest of previous periods. Time value of money calculations underpin many applications in finance, such as investment analysis, bonds, options, etc., and can be:

- single cash flow time value of money, such as an annuity;
- multiple cash flows or discounted cash flows, such as project cash flows.

The interest rate is made up of three components:

- Risk-free rate – this is a rate that investors could invest funds at no or little risk. Typically this is a 10-year government bond as a proxy to a risk-free rate.
- Risk premium – this is a rate above the risk-free rate that investors demand as compensation for losing the use of the money today and potentially investing in riskier assets than government bonds at the risk-free rate.
- Inflation premium – inflation eats away at real returns and again investors need compensation for the loss of purchasing power.

In the previous section, the amount payable was the same irrespective of the payment period; however, compounding would lead to different results due to the intervals between payments. The terminology often used in these calculations is:

N – number of periodic payments

I – periodic interest

PV – present value or capital value

PMT – periodic payment

FV – future value

It is often useful to draw time lines of problems to understand the timing of cash flow or alternatively to draw a grid of the known and unknown parameters. Figure 2.5 shows a present value of 1,000. The annual nominal interest rate is 14 per cent, and with quarterly payments the periodic rate is 3.5 per cent per period. As with all financial modelling, the cash flow notation is used: cash out is negative and cash in is positive.

Figure 2.5
Time line

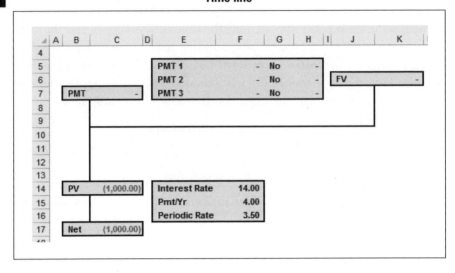

This is a specimen grid showing the known and unknown parameters as an alternative to a time line:

Item	Inputs	Notes
N	12	
Payment Interval	3	Quarterly rentals
I	14%	
PV	−1,000	
PMT	?	
No. of Rents at Start	1	
FV	0	
Advance/Arrears	1	1 = Advance, 0 = Arrears

Future value

The future value is the amount to which a deposit will grow over time with compound interest. The formula is:

$$Future\ value = FV = PV(1 + I/Y)^N$$
$$I/Y = periodic\ interest\ rate$$
$$N = number\ of\ compounding\ periods$$

Figure 2.6 uses the formula and the FV function. A negative present value produces a positive future value:

$$FV = 1000 * (1 + 0.833\%)^{\wedge}12 = 1,511.07$$

Future value

Figure 2.6

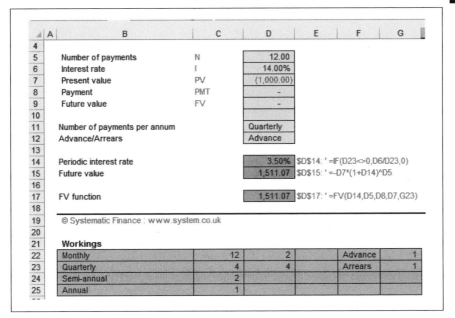

	A	B		C	D	E	F	G
4								
5		Number of payments	N		12.00			
6		Interest rate	I		14.00%			
7		Present value	PV		(1,000.00)			
8		Payment	PMT		-			
9		Future value	FV		-			
10								
11		Number of payments per annum			Quarterly			
12		Advance/Arrears			Advance			
13								
14		Periodic interest rate			3.50%	$D$14: ' =IF(D23<>0,D6/D23,0)		
15		Future value			1,511.07	$D$15: ' =-D7*(1+D14)^D5		
16								
17		FV function			1,511.07	$D$17: ' =FV(D14,D5,D8,D7,G23)		
18								
19		© Systematic Finance : www.system.co.uk						
20								
21		Workings						
22		Monthly		12	2		Advance	1
23		Quarterly		4	4		Arrears	1
24		Semi-annual		2				
25		Annual		1				

Present value

The future value formula can be restated to calculate the present value of a single future value (see Figure 2.7). This is discounting the future cash flow back to today's value:

$$Present\ value = PV = FV/(1 + I/Y)^N$$

The example shows present values 1,511.07 back over 12 periods at a rate of 3.5 per cent per period. The answer is, of course, 1,000. The example spreadsheet uses both the formula and the PV function to derive the answer (see Figure 2.8 below).

Other variables

The full formula for solving other variables is:

$$0 = PV + (1 + iS)\ PMT \left[\frac{1 - (1 + i)^{-n}}{i} \right] + FV(1 + i)^{-n}$$

where S is a payment toggle denoting whether payments are made at the beginning or the end of each period. It makes a difference whether you receive the payments at the beginning or the end of a period. For example,

payments at the beginning reduce the net advance and the amount outstanding in every period.

I = *periodic interest rate*

Since the result of the formula must equal zero, it follows that a change in,
for example, present value must lead to a change in another of the five key
variables if the result is to be zero.

Figure 2.7

Present value

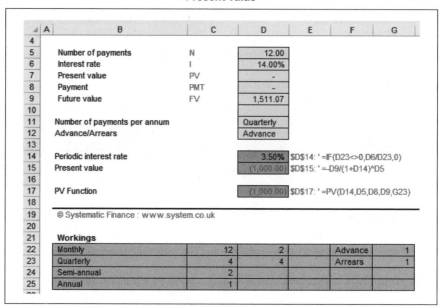

Figure 2.8

PV Function

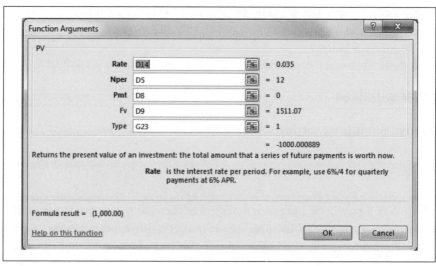

While the number of payments, payment or interest rate can be calculated manually, it is simpler to use the built-in functions in Excel. The functions assume that each of the periods is the same length and that the payments are all the same. These are:

- NPER – number of payments
- RATE – periodic interest rate
- PV – present value
- PMT – periodic payment
- FV – future value

Time value of money (TVM) calculator

Figure 2.9

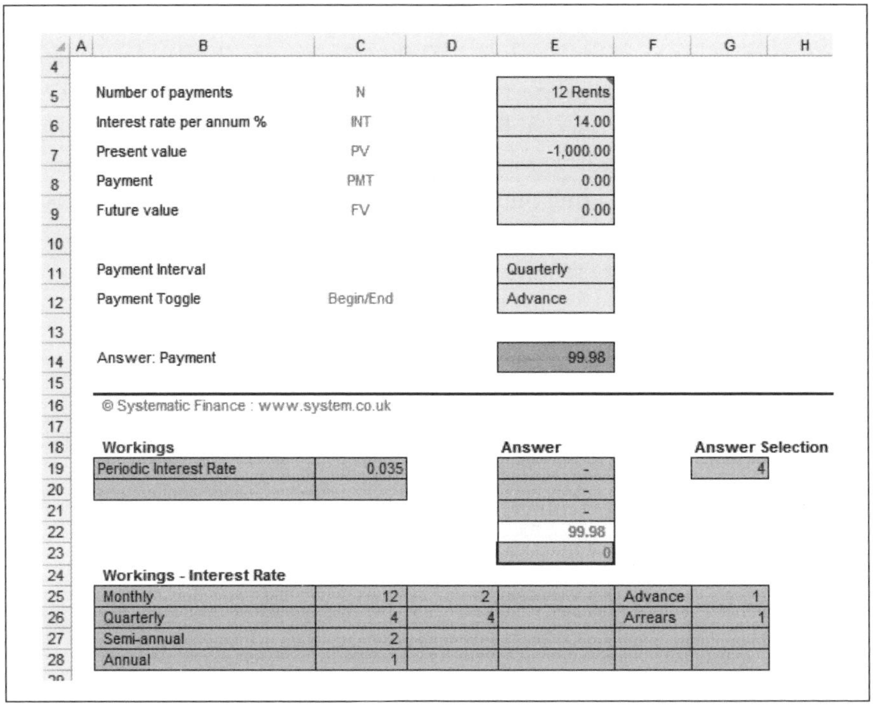

The cells E5:E12 in Figure 2.9 indicate the inputs at the top as a loan of 1,000 over 12 periods quarterly in advance with no future value. The model works out the periodic interest and the answer section uses conditional IF statements to show an answer solely for the zero variable in the inputs section. The five formulas are:

```
=NPER(PERIODICINTRATE,PAYMENT,PRESENT_
VALUE,FUTURE_VALUE,PAYMENT_TOGGLE)
```

```
=RATE(NUMBER_OF_PAYMENTS,PAYMENT,PRESENT_VALUE,
FUTURE_VALUE,PAYMENT_TOGGLE)*100*(12/PAYMENT_
FREQUENCY) – the rate has to be multiplied back to an annual rate
```

```
=PV(PERIODICINTRATE,NUMBER_OF_PAYMENTS,PAYMENT,
FUTURE_VALUE,PAYMENT_TOGGLE)

=PMT(PERIODICINTRATE,NUMBER_OF_PAYMENTS,PRESENT_
VALUE,FUTURE_VALUE,PAYMENT_TOGGLE)

=FV(PERIODICINTRATE,NUMBER_OF_PAYMENTS,PAYMENT,
PRESENT_VALUE,PAYMENT_TOGGLE)
```

The answer is shown as 99.98. The model is set up to calculate any fifth variable when four are input. For example, the payment is only 90, so what is the future value left unamortised over the period? Twelve payments of 90.00 are not enough to write off the loan at an interest rate of 3.5 per cent per quarterly period (14 per cent per annum).

Since there are answers above, no answers are calculated in cells B19:B22. The future value is calculated as 150.90 (see Figure 2.10). As a further example, you could calculate the number of periods needed to write off 1,000 at 90.00 per period (see Figure 2.11). This is not an integer number of payments, with the answer as 13.70. Therefore the calculator is flexible since the initial formula must hold. If you change the payment and all other variables remain the same, solving for the number of payments will produce the number of payments required to write off the loan.

Figure 2.10	Future value calculation

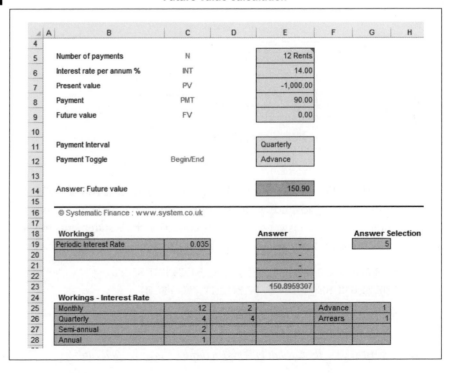

Basic monthly calculation

Figure 2.11

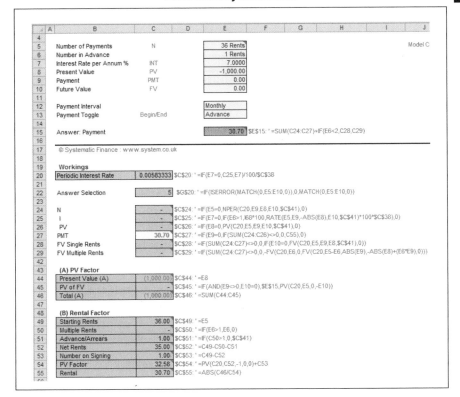

MULTIPLE PAYMENTS

The above examples work well if the rentals are the same and there are one or zero rentals on signing. Often rentals are quoted as 3 + 33 or 6 + 30 monthly in order to gain a higher deposit to compensate for increased credit risk. This means that the deposit consists of three or six equal monthly rentals followed by the first periodic rental starting in the next month. Where there is a residual or final payment, this is due on expiry rather than following directly after the periodic rentals. Thus 6 + 30 will give rise to five zero periods before any final payment is due.

The next two examples have three monthly rentals on signing and this presents problems for the simple calculator. There is nowhere to put the multiple rentals. The capital value is effectively the amounts less the three rentals due on signing, but you do not know the rental. This is a circular argument which you could solve with Goal Seek or Solver; however, there is a mathematical method using rental factors that will solve the payment directly.

The method is known as the step or $1 method and comprises four stages (Figure 2.11):

- Calculate the net outflow of everything you know about at the inception of the lease. This includes costs, tax depreciation and any other known cash flows.
- Calculate the final residual value or final payment (if applicable).
- Compute the present value of the net residual value at the required rate.
- Present value any other cash flows you know about, for example, costs.
- Add all the present values together to form the PV Factor (A).
- Compute the PV of the unknown periodic lease payments, letting $1 equal each payment.
- With multiple rentals on signing and in advance, add the number in advance to the PV factor. This is the Rental Factor (B).

You calculate the payment (PMT) by dividing the PV Factor (A) by the Rental Factor (B). When you have done this, you need to check the periodic cash flows to ensure that you have the correct rental. The example in Figure 2.12 comprises a 3 + 33 monthly rentals structure at a rate of 10 per cent. You can use this grid to find the lease payment required.

Figure 2.12

The 3+33 structure with a zero final value

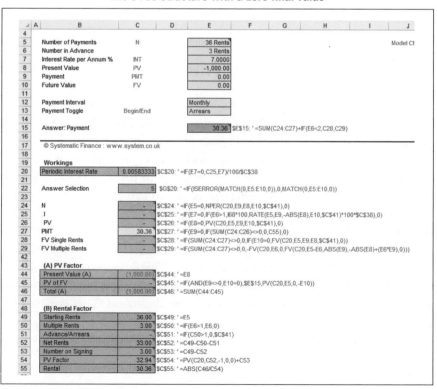

The 3+33 structure with a final payment

Figure 2.13

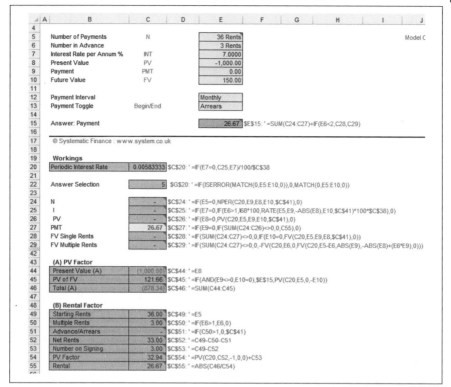

Since there are three rentals on signing, the factor is based on the 33 outstanding payments and adds the three received on signing. Where there is a final payment, this is a known value and has to be discounted back to inception. Cell C45 in Figure 2.13 displays the present value of the future value (150) and this is subtracted from the 1,000 starting capital. The PV Factor remains the same but the division results in a lower periodic rental.

Figure 2.14 plots the cash flows with three rentals on signing followed by 33 regular rentals and the final value on the three-year anniversary. The rate works back to 7 per cent.

DIFFERING INTEREST RATES

Where the rate changes in each period due to changing interest rates, the normal PMT formulas do not work and you have to calculate each rental in turn. There are various methods of dealing with this complication:

- Formula
- IPMT and PPMT functions
- PMT function
- Factors

Figure 2.14

Cash flows

	A	B	C	D	E	F	G	H	I	J
56										
57		Formulas	$C$70: ' =C5 $D$70: ' =IF(B70=E5+1,1,0)							
58			$C$71: ' =IF(B71<=E5-$C$53+1,1,0)							
59			$D$71: ' =IF(B71=E5+1,1,0)							
60			$E$70: ' =-IF(C26<>0,ABS(C26),ABS(E8))							
61			$F$71: ' =IF(E9<>0,E9,$C$55)*C71							
62			$G$71: ' =IF(AND($E$9<>0,$E$10=0,$C$26=0),IF($C$25<>0,0,$E$15),ABS($E$10)*D71)*D71							
63			$H$71: ' =SUM(E71:G71)							
64			$I$68: ' =IF(ISERROR(IRR(H70:H130)*$C$38),0,IRR(H70:H130)*$C$38)							
65			$I$70: ' =H70						Model Check: No Errors	
66			$I$71: ' =H71-FV($C$20,1,0,I70)						IRR 7.0000%	
67			$J$70: ' =PV($C$20,1,0,-J71)+H70							
68								Check	7.000%	
69		Period	Rents	FV	Capital	Rents	FV	Total	FV	PV
70		1	3	0	(1,000.00)	80.00	-	(920.00)	(920.00)	(0.00)
71		2	1	0		26.67	-	26.67	(898.70)	925.37
72		3	1	0		26.67	-	26.67	(877.28)	903.95
73		4	1	0		26.67	-	26.67	(855.73)	882.40
74		5	1	0		26.67	-	26.67	(834.06)	860.72
75		6	1	0		26.67	-	26.67	(812.26)	838.92
76		7	1	0		26.67	-	26.67	(790.33)	817.00
77		8	1	0		26.67	-	26.67	(768.28)	794.94
78		9	1	0		26.67	-	26.67	(746.09)	772.76
79		10	1	0		26.67	-	26.67	(723.78)	750.44
80		11	1	0		26.67	-	26.67	(701.34)	728.00
81		12	1	0		26.67	-	26.67	(678.76)	705.43
82		13	1	0		26.67	-	26.67	(656.05)	682.72
83		14	1	0		26.67	-	26.67	(633.22)	659.88
84		15	1	0		26.67	-	26.67	(610.24)	636.91
85		16	1	0		26.67	-	26.67	(587.14)	613.80
86		17	1	0		26.67	-	26.67	(563.90)	590.56
87		18	1	0		26.67	-	26.67	(540.52)	567.19
88		19	1	0		26.67	-	26.67	(517.01)	543.67
89		20	1	0		26.67	-	26.67	(493.36)	520.02
90		21	1	0		26.67	-	26.67	(469.57)	496.24
91		22	1	0		26.67	-	26.67	(445.65)	472.31
92		23	1	0		26.67	-	26.67	(421.58)	448.24
93		24	1	0		26.67	-	26.67	(397.37)	424.04
94		25	1	0		26.67	-	26.67	(373.03)	399.69
95		26	1	0		26.67	-	26.67	(348.54)	375.20
96		27	1	0		26.67	-	26.67	(323.90)	350.57
97		28	1	0		26.67	-	26.67	(299.13)	325.79
98		29	1	0		26.67	-	26.67	(274.21)	300.87
99		30	1	0		26.67	-	26.67	(249.14)	275.81
00		31	1	0		26.67	-	26.67	(223.93)	250.59
01		32	1	0		26.67	-	26.67	(198.57)	225.23
02		33	1	0		26.67	-	26.67	(173.06)	199.73
03		34	1	0		26.67	-	26.67	(147.41)	174.07
04		35	0	0		-	-	-	(148.27)	148.27
05		36	0	0		-	-	-	(149.13)	149.13
06		37	0	1		-	150.00	150.00	(0.00)	150.00
31		Total	36	1	(1,000.00)	959.96	150.00	109.96		

In this example (Figure 2.15) you bring forward the starting capital and calculate the periodic interest. This is a quarterly example, so the interest rate is divided by four. The annuity is calculated as:

Capital brought forward/[1 − (1 + *Periodic Interest Rate*) ^ − *Number of Rents Outstanding*].

The capital paid is simply the annuity less the interest. The reduced capital is carried forward to the next period and the process repeats itself. The check on the model is that the capital reduces to zero whatever rates are entered.

Alternatively, you can use the IPMT and PPMT functions to find the interest and principal payable based on reducing capital and the number of payments outstanding (Figure 2.16). The PMT function achieves the same result by finding the total rental. You can use the interest calculation in the first section to extract the interest and principal.

Formula

Figure 2.15

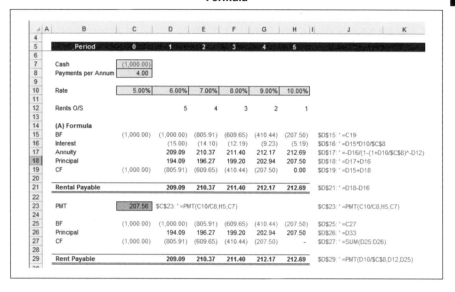

Functions and factors

Figure 2.16

	B	C	D	E	F	G	H	I	J
4									
5	Period	0	1	2	3	4	5		
30									
31	(B) IPMT and PPMT								
32	Int			15.00	14.10	12.19	9.23	5.19	$D$32: ' =IPMT(D10/$C$8,1,D12,D25)
33	Prin			194.09	196.27	199.20	202.94	207.50	$D$33: ' =PPMT(D10/$C$8,1,D12,D25)
34	FV			(805.91)	(609.65)	(410.44)	(207.50)	-	$D$34: ' =D25+D33
35	Rental			209.09	210.37	211.40	212.17	212.69	$D$35: ' =SUM(D32:D33)
36									
37	(C) PMT Function								
38	BF		(1,000.00)	(1,000.00)	(805.91)	(609.65)	(410.44)	(207.50)	$D$38: ' =C40
39	Principal			194.09	196.27	199.20	202.94	207.50	$D$39: ' =D42+D43
40	CF		(1,000.00)		(805.91)	(609.65)	(410.44)	(207.50)	(0.00)	$D$40: ' =SUM(D38:D39)
41									
42	Interest			(15.00)	(14.10)	(12.19)	(9.23)	(5.19)	$D$42: ' =D38*D10/$C$8
43	Rental			209.09	210.37	211.40	212.17	212.69	$D$43: ' =PMT(D10/$C$8,D12,D15)
44									
45	(D) Factors								
46	BF		(1,000.00)	(1,000.00)	(805.91)	(609.65)	(410.44)	(207.50)	$D$46: ' =C48
47	Principal			194.09	196.27	199.20	202.94	207.50	$D$47: ' =D50+D52
48	CF		(1,000.00)		(805.91)	(609.65)	(410.44)	(207.50)	0.00	$D$48: ' =SUM(D46:D47)
49									
50	Interest			(15.00)	(14.10)	(12.19)	(9.23)	(5.19)	$D$50: ' =D46*D10/$C$8
51	PV Factor			(4.78)	(3.83)	(2.88)	(1.93)	(0.98)	$D$51: ' =PV(D10/$C$8,D12,1,0)
52	Payment			209.09	210.37	211.40	212.17	212.69	$D$52: ' =D46/D51

Part D uses the factors method from earlier in the chapter to find a rental factor which can be divided into the capital outstanding. In the first period you discount five 'ones' at the periodic rate to form the rental factor and then divide into the initial capital of 1,000. The process is repeated to find the other rentals.

Each method generates the same answers, so you can either use a non-functions approach with the first method or use a mixture of functions and interest calculations with the other three procedures.

NOMINAL AND EFFECTIVE RATES

The interest rates above are nominal or stated annual interest rates. This means that a rate of 3.5 per cent with quarterly payments is quoted as 14 per cent, that is 3.5 per cent multiplied by four payments per annum. The rate of return that is actually paid or charged depends on the number of compounding periods in the year, and this is the effective or effective annual rate (EAR). Adjustments have to be made for the number of compounding periods, so the rate will vary between monthly, quarterly, semi-annual and annual payments. Note that in Figure 2.17 the text mixes up nominal and effective rates as 14 per cent payable quarterly cannot have the same nominal and effective rates.

Figure 2.17   **Number of periods calculation**

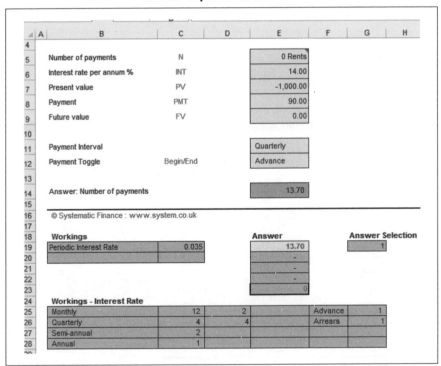

The formula to migrate from a nominal to an effective rate is:

$$[(1 + Nominal/C) \wedge C] - 1$$

where C is the number of compounding periods.

The formula to determine a nominal rate from an effective rate is:

$$[1 + (Effective) \wedge (1/C) - 1] * C$$

Nominal and effective

Figure 2.18

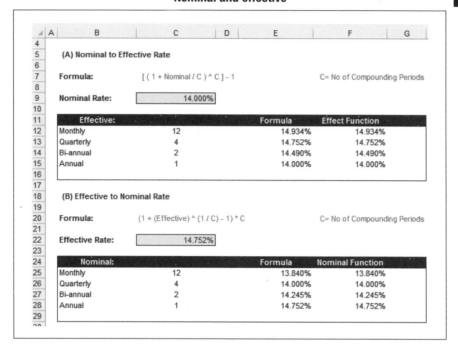

The example in Figure 2.18 uses 14 per cent as a nominal rate and calculates the effective rates and back again. This example of 14 per cent with quarterly periods is:

Formula $= [(1 + 14\%/4) \wedge 4] - 1 = 14.752\%$

Excel has built-in functions for interest rate conversions such as EFFECT and NOMINAL and these are shown on the sheet (see Figure 2.19). Note that the Analysis ToolPak has to be installed for these functions to be available. The inputs are the rate and the number of periods and the function calculates the result without the need for a formula. You can test the model by working backwards and forwards. Annual effective and nominal rates will always be the same since there is only one period in the year.

CONTINUOUS DISCOUNTING

You can apply interest over smaller and smaller periods until it becomes continuous rather than discrete (see Figure 2.20). The mathematical relationship is:

Formula: $(1 + effective\ rate) = e \wedge nominal\ rate$

where *e* is Euler's constant of 2.718281828, the base of natural logarithms, and gained by using the function EXP in Excel with the argument 1. This constant is the inverse of LN, the natural logarithm of a number.

Figure 2.19

Effect function

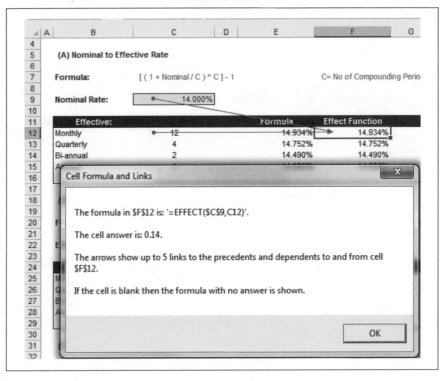

Figure 2.20

Continuous discounting

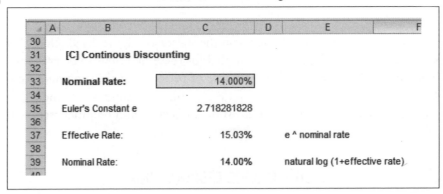

The continuous effective rate for 14 per cent is 15.03 per cent, which compares with the monthly rate of 14.9 per cent using the EFFECT function. This method of compounding arises in option pricing and is included on most financial calculators.

CONVERSIONS AND COMPARISONS

It is important to understand the cash flows since it can be misleading to look at cash flows over different time periods. The example in Figure 2.21 compares a quarterly transaction with payments at the beginning of the period against a monthly transaction with payments at the end of the respective periods. In each case, the nominal rate is 14 per cent and the PMT function is used to calculate the regular payment from N, I, PV, FV, together with the periods per annum and the advance/arrears switch.

Comparison

Figure 2.21

	B	Quarterly		Monthly		Variance
N		12		36		
I		14.00%		14.00%		
PV		(1,000.00)		(1,000.00)		
FV		0		0		
Periods per Annum		4		12		
Begin		1		0		
Periodic Interest Rate		3.50%		1.17%		
PMT		99.98		34.18		
Total Payable		1,199.81		1,230.39		(30.58)
Net Advance		900.02		965.82		(65.81)
Effective Period		2.75		3.00		(0.25)
Charges		199.81		230.39		(30.58)
Simple Interest Rate		8.07%		7.95%		0.12%
Nominal Rate		14.00%		14.00%		-
Effective Rate		14.75%		14.93%		(0.18%)

The simple interest rate is calculated based on the charges and the true period. This is 11 quarters in the first case and 36 months in the second case (rentals are in arrears). The simple interest rate is higher for the quarterly transaction since the periodicity is not taken into account. The effective rate is higher for the monthly option since there are 12 compounding periods as against four.

EXERCISE

■ A loan of 100,000 is payable over five years with monthly payments of 60,000 commencing one month after the inception date. The loan repayment is 2,000 per month and the nominal rate 10 per cent. How much capital remains at the end of five years?

■ If the future value is 5,000 what does the loan payment need to be?

Build a spreadsheet using the functions demonstrated in this chapter.

SUMMARY

This chapter reviews basic building blocks of simple, nominal and effective rates with regular and more complex annuity cash flows and shows how these can be calculated directly in Excel using basic functions such as FV, PMT, PV, RATE and NPER. Interest rates can easily be converted using functions such as EFFECT and NOMINAL.

Cash flows

File: MFMaths3e_03.xls

The previous chapter dealt with single cash flows and this chapter shows how to model more complex cash flows and calculate the present value or the internal rate of return. Where you have a forecast of future cash flows, you need to know the value today to compare the potential gain against the possible risks. This is based on the key assumptions that $1 today is worth more than $1 at some future period and that each project should earn more than the inherent cost. The models in this chapter use a simple grid for calculating either the value or the yield to show the timing and effect of individual cash flows.

NET PRESENT VALUE

The model generates a grid of cash flows from an initial investment of 1,000 growing at a constant rate of 10 per cent. The number of periods is five and on expiry the salvage value is 100. The grid uses a simple IF statement to grow the cash flows up until the expiry period:

```
=IF(E12<=$C$9,SUM(D14:D15)*(1+$C$7/100),0)
```

The net cash flow sums the cash flows above. The discount factor is calculated as:

Cash flow$/(1 +$ *periodic interest rate*$) \wedge N$
$N =$ *number of compounding periods*

Therefore period 3 is:

$1/(1 + 10\%) \wedge 3 = 0.7513$

The cash flow can then be multiplied by the factor and the net cash flows added to form the net present value (see Figure 3.1). The cash flow today is not discounted and therefore multiplied by one.

The simpler method is to use the NPV function to reduce the amount of code and therefore the possibility of error (see Figure 3.2). You select the interest rate and the outstanding cash flows. The answer here is 1,198 and then you add the cash flow today. If you include all the cash flows, Excel assumes that the first cash flow is also to be discounted and will assume that the subsequent cash flows occur one period later.

The net present value is greater than the initial investment, so the internal rate of return must be higher than the discount rate of 10 per cent. The internal rate is simply the rate at which net present value is equal to zero. The net present value will vary depending on the discount rate: as the discount rate increases, the net present value falls.

Figure 3.1

Net present value

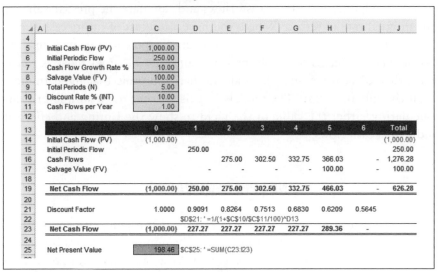

	B	C	D	E	F	G	H	I	J
4									
5	Initial Cash Flow (PV)	1,000.00							
6	Initial Periodic Flow	250.00							
7	Cash Flow Growth Rate %	10.00							
8	Salvage Value (FV)	100.00							
9	Total Periods (N)	5.00							
10	Discount Rate % (INT)	10.00							
11	Cash Flows per Year	1.00							
12									
13		0	1	2	3	4	5	6	Total
14	Initial Cash Flow (PV)	(1,000.00)							(1,000.00)
15	Initial Periodic Flow		250.00						250.00
16	Cash Flows			275.00	302.50	332.75	366.03	-	1,276.28
17	Salvage Value (FV)		-	-	-	-	100.00	-	100.00
18									
19	Net Cash Flow	(1,000.00)	250.00	275.00	302.50	332.75	466.03	-	626.28
20									
21	Discount Factor	1.0000	0.9091	0.8264	0.7513	0.6830	0.6209	0.5645	
22			$D$21: ' =1/(1+$C$10/$C$11/100)^D13						
23	Net Cash Flow	(1,000.00)	227.27	227.27	227.27	227.27	289.36	-	
24									
25	Net Present Value	198.46	$C$25: ' =SUM(C23:I23)						

Figure 3.2

NPV function

Function Arguments

NPV

Rate	C10/$C$11/100	= 0.1
Value1	D19:I19	= {250,275,302.5,332.75,466.025,0}
Value2		= number

= 1198.455769

Returns the net present value of an investment based on a discount rate and a series of future payments (negative values) and income (positive values).

Rate: is the rate of discount over the length of one period.

Formula result = 198.46

Help on this function   OK   Cancel

The schedule contains a simple data table to show the effect of interest rate changes (see Figure 3.3).

The data table is a built-in sensitivity function accessed through `Data`, `Data Tools`, `What-If Analysis` on the menus (see Figure 3.4). The single variable grid has to be set out with variables across and the answer in the next row down on the left. You highlight the whole grid ($B$33:$I$34) and then enter the variable $C$10, the interest rate, in a `Data Table` dialogue box. Excel completes the results in cells $C$34:$I$34 showing the net present value at varying discount rates.

Data table

Figure 3.3

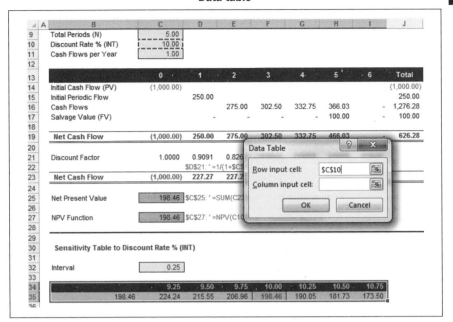

Sensitivity chart

Figure 3.4

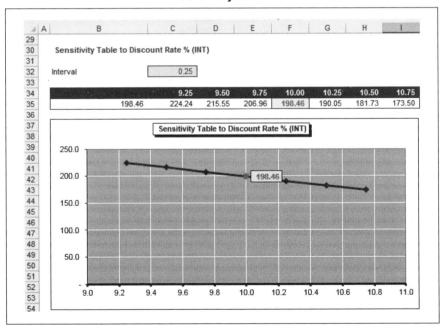

VARYING INTEREST RATES

The NPV2 sheet provides more complex examples to show how to calculate net present values when the discount rate varies in each period. Part A in Figure 3.5 demonstrates the error of including the first cash flow where period 0 is generally assumed to be today. The correct net present value is 198.46.

Figure 3.5

Varying interest rates

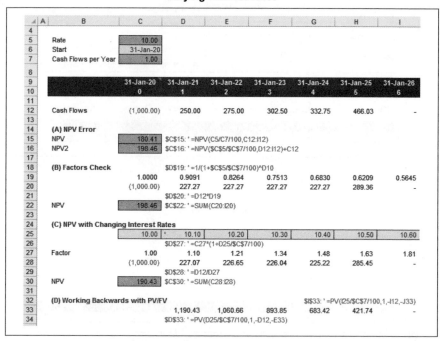

Where the discount rate changes you have to calculate an accumulating factor. Line 19 starts with one and compounds this in the next period by multiplying it by one plus the periodic rate. The next period takes this factor and multiplies it by one plus the next rate and so on. The discounted cash flow is therefore the cash divided by the factor in each period and the net present value is the sum of the discounted cash flows. This example results in a lower net present value of 190.43 since the rates are rising in each period.

Alternatively you could work backwards from the last cash flow as shown in part (D) below. In the last period you find the present value of the final cash flow and this becomes the future value of the next to last cash flow. Working backwards this builds up to the net present value

Present value cash flows

Figure 3.6

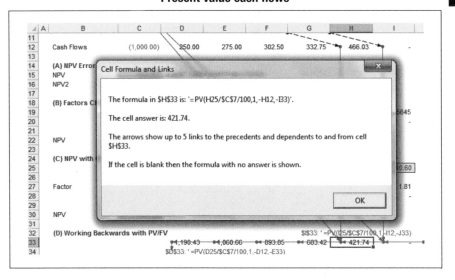

(Figure 3.6). Note that you have to be careful with the signs: both the cash flow and the future value are negative in order to arrive at a positive net present value.

INTERNAL RATE OF RETURN

The alternative calculation is internal rate of return or yield when you know the net present value. This is the maximum percentage that could be afforded before the net present value becomes negative. Alternatively this is the break-even rate at which the net present value is zero.

It is possible to compute an internal rate by calculating two net present values at assumed rates and then working towards the solution using the formula:

$$IRR = Positive\ rate + \left(\frac{Positive\ NPV}{Positive\ NPV + Negative\ NPV} \times Range\ of\ rates \right)$$

The model in Figure 3.7 calculates a net present values at 10 and 20 per cent of 198.46 and −77.88, respectively. The adjustment using the formula is 7.18 per cent and the adjustment is added to the lower rate. The workings for the adjustment are:

```
=($E$19/(ABS($E$19)+ABS($E$20)))*(($D$20-$D$19))
```

Again, Excel has a built-in function for the internal rate of return, IRR, which is simpler than computing rates (see Figure 3.8). In this case, the interest rate guess is left blank since the default is 10 per cent. This is simple cash flow

Figure 3.7

IRR

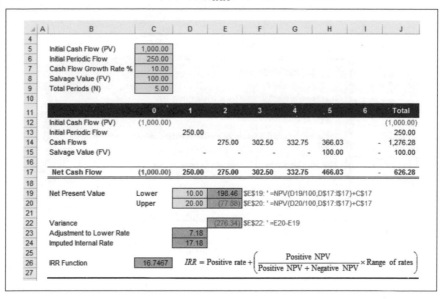

Figure 3.8

IRR function

with only one crossing from positive to negative cash flows and therefore there can be only one solution. Where there are multiple sets of positive and negative cash flows, there can be more than one potential result.

An alternative method uses a chart to plot the interest rates and the net present values (see Figure 3.9). The net present value is zero at a rate of 16.75 per cent. The data table shows the results at rates above and below the correct answer.

The TREND function will also show the correct answer since there is an inverse linear relationship between the interest rate and the net present value (see Figure 3.10). As input with the chart series reversed, the known Y series is the interest rates and the known X series the net present values.

Sensitivity to IRR

Figure 3.9

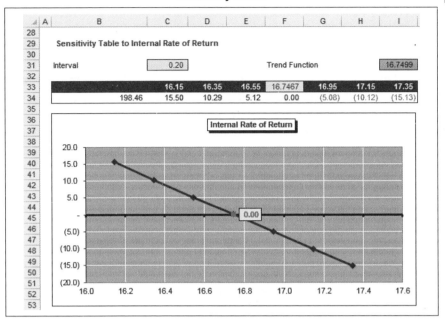

TREND function

Figure 3.10

You want the rate at which the net present value is zero. This is expressed as the new X value using the least squares simple regression formula:

$$Y = mx + b$$

$$m = slope$$
$$b = intercept$$
$$x = new\ x$$

The example in Figure 3.11 shows extreme cash flows which cross twice from positive to negative. This means that there are multiple solutions as shown by the sensitivity table. The trend line crosses twice, meaning that IRR results from these figures are unreliable with two possible answers. It would be better to use a known discount rate and discount the cash flows to a net present value. This would be advantageous if you wanted to rank or compare results from two sets of cash flows. Care should be taken when using IRR in isolation as it assumes that all the periods are the same length and that all cash is received on time and will be reinvested at the internal rate.

When interest rates are dropping there may be limited opportunities for maintaining the rate.

Figure 3.11

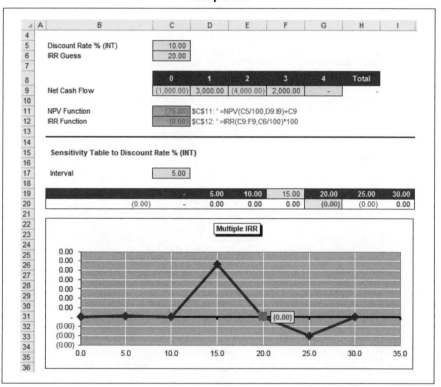

Multiple IRR

XNPV AND XIRR

Excel contains more advanced functions for net present value and internal rate of return, which allow you to select uneven or irregular periods. The standard functions assume that each period such as a month is the same length. Similarly, project models may mix monthly cash flows for construction and semi-annual or annual cash flows for operations. This means that the default is a

30-day month and a 360-day year. Annual payments have leap years whereas monthly periods are punctuated with months of 28, 29, 30 and 31 days. For example, a power station has 24 more hours of output to sell every four years.

The example in Figure 3.12 calculates the net present value and internal rate using the XNPV and XIRR functions. Note that these functions are in the Analysis ToolPak and you have to install this add-in as in the installation instructions. If you do not, then you will see errors on the schedule.

The answers on the standard functions are 16.75 per cent and 198.46. Answers using the day-to-day functions are normally slightly lower than the standard functions due to the effect of irregular days in a month and leap years.

XNPV and XIRR

Figure 3.12

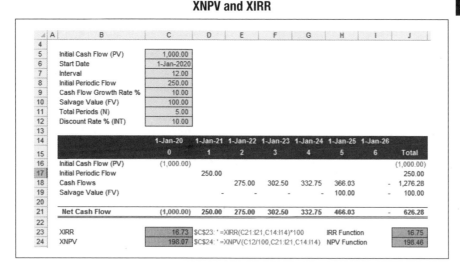

XNPV PERIODIC EXAMPLE

You have to be careful with XNPV and XIRR since they use annual effective rather than periodic nominal rates and this is not explained clearly in the Excel Help files. The example in Figure 3.13 generates a three-year cash flow at 14 per cent with quarterly payments based on a 1,000 present value. This is a loan or rental of 99.98.

The IRR function calculates a yield of 14 per cent, exactly the same as the input rate. The XIRR function yields 14.75 per cent, which is the effective rate. The NOMINAL function reduces the yield to 14 per cent. Similarly, the XNPV function using the effective rate produces a net present value close to the present value of 1,000. Note that you include all the cash flows as well as the opening cash flow on the XNPV function, in contrast to the NPV function where you only include the outstanding cash flows.

Figure 3.13	XNPV periodic example

	A	B	C	D	E	F	G	H	I
4									
5		Start Date	01-Jan-20						
6		Interval	3						
7		Capital	1,000.00						
8		Starting Rental	99.98						
9		Growth	0.00%						
10									
11			0	1	2	3	4	5	6
12			1-Jan-20	1-Apr-20	1-Jul-20	1-Oct-20	1-Jan-21	1-Apr-21	1-Jul-
13									
14		Rental	99.98	99.98	99.98	99.98	99.98	99.98	99
15									
16		Capital	(1,000.00)						
17									
18		Cash Flow	(900.02)	99.98	99.98	99.98	99.98	99.98	99
19									
20		Net Cash Flow	199.76		$C$20: ' =SUM(C18:N18)				
21									
22		IRR Rate	14.00		$C$22: ' =IRR(C18:N19,0.1)*(12/Interval)*100				
23		XIRR Rate	14.75		$C$23: ' =XIRR(C18:N18,C12:N12,0.1)*100				
24		Nominal Rate	14.00		$C$24: ' =NOMINAL(XIRR_Rate/100,12/Interval)*100				
25									
26		NPV Result	1,000.00		$C$26: ' =NPV(IRR_Rate/100/(12/Interval),D14:N14)+C14				
27		Effective Rate	14.75		$C$27: ' =EFFECT(IRR_Rate/100,(12/Interval))*100				
28		XNPV Result	999.99		$C$28: ' =XNPV(Effective_Rate/100,C14:N14,C12:N12)				

MODIFIED INTERNAL RATE OF RETURN

The modified internal rate of return attempts to overcome the disadvantages of using an internal rate. This uses a separate finance and reinvestment rate in order to deal with multiple positive and negative cash flows. Using the same data as the Multiple IRR sheet with a finance rate of 10 per cent and a reinvestment rate of 5 per cent, the answer is 4.02 per cent (see Figure 3.14). As with net present values, projects or loans can be ranked in order based on this measure. For example, leveraged tax leases need to be measured using this more advanced internal rate function, since you are not sure that rentals received can be reinvested at the same rate as the initial lease.

The full equation for the function is:

$$\left(\frac{-NPV\left(rrate, values\left[positive\right]\right) * \left(1 + rrate\right)^{n}}{NPV\left(frate, values\left[negative\right]\right) * \left(1 + frate\right)} \right)^{\frac{1}{n-1}} - 1$$

The table in Figure 3.15 shows how the MIRR function changes with increasing finance and reinvestment rates. The highest rate is at the bottom right of the table whereas the lowest rate is at the top left-hand corner.

MIRR function

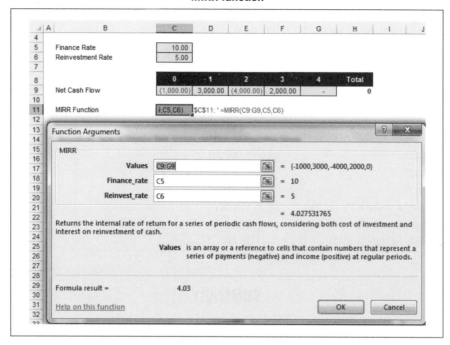

Figure 3.14

MIRR sensitivity to the finance and reinvestment rate

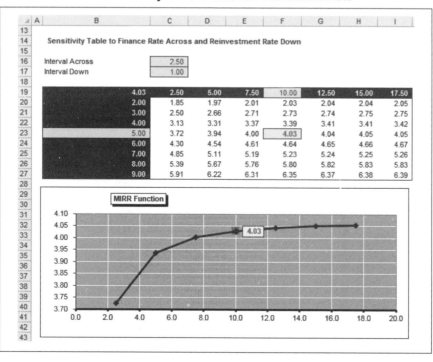

Figure 3.15

EXERCISE

A 100,000 loan agreement has payments and inputs as follows. Calculate the XNPV, XIRR, NPV and IRR of the resulting cash flows.

Item	Notes
Initial Cash Flow (PV)	10,000.00
Start Date	01-Jan-2020
Interval (Months)	6
Year 1	1,000.00
Year 2	1,500.00
Year 3	2,000.00
Salvage Value (FV)	100.00
Total Periods (N)	12.00
Discount Rate% (INT)	10.00

SUMMARY

Single cash flow problems can be solved using functions such as PV and PMT; however, multiple cash flows require further formulas or net present value, internal rate or modified internal rate functions. You can use the basic functions that assume equal periods or XNPV and XIRR functions which require dates together with cash flows. With these functions you can assess the present value or the internal return on series of cash flows.

4

Bonds calculations

File: MFMaths3e_04.xls

Bonds are a form of medium- and long-term securities issued by governments, supra-governmental bodies such as the World Bank or major companies for financing as an alternative to bank finance. They were invented several hundred years ago as a method of financing war and government expenditure, and, due to their attractiveness, the market has grown to vast proportions today. The individual amounts vary but the period of maturity is typically five to fifteen years and perhaps longer for governmental bodies. The upper limit is set by what investors will accept rather than any rules, since investing in bonds involves real risks such as default and final return of the principal. The mathematics for bonds concerns pricing, the yield and various measures of risk.

DESCRIPTION

There are many classes of bonds; however, the majority pay interest on the principal or coupons at regular intervals and the principal is repayable only on expiry or some earlier agreed date. The majority of bonds are issued on a fixed-rate basis but a floating rate is also possible. This is borrowing directly from the capital markets and dealing without the intervention of a bank. A bond is a form of security, which means that it is transferable to other investors during the term and the issuer needs to keep a register of the owners. The transferability means that bonds can be traded with prices set solely by supply and demand. The borrower pays interest in the form of coupons and the final principal on expiry to the registered holder. Therefore, the bond in its simplest form consists of a series of distinct cash flows, which can be valued using the building blocks from the previous two chapters.

Specific examples of bonds are:

- Domestic bonds issued in the domestic currency and sold locally.

- Eurobonds – where an issuer sells the bond outside the domestic country.

- UK government securities known as gilt-edged securities or 'gilts', which mostly pay coupons semi-annually. Interest is calculated on an actual (known as ACT/ACT) basis.

- US treasury bonds for varying periods with semi-annual coupons with maturities of two, five, ten and thirty years. Federal agencies also issue bonds, for example: Federal National Mortgage Association (FNMA or 'Fanny Mae'), Federal Home Mortgage Association (FHMC or 'Freddy Mac'), Student Loan Marketing Association (SLMA or 'Sally Mae') and the Government National Mortgage Association (GNMA or 'Ginny Mae'). Interest on these securities is usually calculated on a 30/360 basis (using a 30-day banking month and 360-day year).

Bond markets use specific vocabulary:

Issue date:	Original issue date of the bond
Settlement:	Pricing or yield date for calculation
Maturity:	Date when principal is repayable and final coupon is due
Redemption value:	Par value, usually 100
Coupon %:	Interest rate fixed for the period of the bond
Coupons per annum:	Usually paid once (annual) or twice (semi-annual) per year
Basis:	See below
Yield to maturity:	Inherent interest rate which may vary during the period based on current market interest rates
Price:	Price of bond based on yield to maturity as the present value of a series of cash flows

There are different bases for calculating periods and year. So far the price of the bond is the present value of all the cash flows (coupons and principal) calculated using normal discounted cash flow techniques at a rate which reflects the perceived risk. There is an inverse relationship between the price and discount rate since the present value goes down as the discount rises. It therefore follows that the price of the bond falls as interest rates rise. Bond pricing assumes:

- Round periods rather than actual days as used for other borrowing instruments. Money market instruments use the exact number of days for simple interest rate calculations.
- Individual periods are regular.
- Pricing is the compounded net present value of the cash flows.

If the pricing is required on the date a coupon is due, then there are no problems. The price is simply the present value of the coupons and principal. Between periods, a seller expects to receive the accrued coupon within the period, while the buyer will only pay the present value of the future payments. Prices are quoted as:

- clean price – the present value of the coupons and principal (dirty price – accrued coupon);
- dirty price – the clean price plus the accrued interest (net present value of all cash flows).

Interest on the coupon is payable using simple interest calculations. If there are 30 days from the start of the period and 360 days are assumed in the year, then the interest would be calculated as 30/360 multiplied by the coupon rate. The first period could be less than the coupon periods depending on the purchase date, but thereafter coupons are payable annually, semi-annually or sometimes quarterly. The dates are the same, for example, 17 January and 17 July for a semi-annual bond, and are not based on the exact number of days.

Day and year conventions vary and they are used in the various Excel functions. The methods are the number of days in the month and days in the year.

	Actual	Actual number of calendar days
Days	30 (European) 30 (US)	Day 31 is changed to 30 If the second day is 31 but the first date is not 31 or 30, then the day is not changed from 31 to 30
Year	365 360 Actual	Assumes 365 days in the year Assumes 360 Actual including leap years

The combinations used in Excel functions are as below:

0   *US (NASD) 30/360*
1   *Actual/actual*
2   *Actual/360*
3   *Actual/365*
4   *European 30/360*

There are a number of defined bond pricing and yield functions in Excel as shown below (contained in Excel and the Analysis ToolPak):

ACCRINT	Accrued interest for a security that pays periodic interest
ACCRINTM	Accrued interest for a security that pays interest at maturity
COUPDAYBS	Number of days from the beginning of the coupon period to the settlement date
COUPDAYS	Number of days in the coupon period that contains the settlement date
COUPDAYSNC	Number of days from the settlement date to the next coupon date
COUPNCD	Next coupon date after the settlement date
COUPNUM	Number of coupons payable between the settlement date and maturity date
COUPPCD	Previous coupon date before the settlement date
CUMIPMT	Cumulative interest paid between two periods
CUMPRINC	Cumulative principal paid on a loan between two periods
ODDFPRICE	Price per $100 face value of a security with an odd first period

▶

ODDFYIELD	Yield of a security with an odd first period
ODDLPRICE	Price per $100 face value of a security with an odd last period
ODDLYIELD	Yield of a security with an odd last period
PRICE	Price per $100 face value of a security that pays periodic interest
PRICEDISC	Price per $100 face value of a discounted security
PRICEMAT	Price per $100 face value of a security that pays interest at maturity
TBILLEQ	Bond-equivalent yield for a treasury bill
TBILLPRICE	Price per $100 face value for a treasury bill
TBILLYIELD	Yield for a treasury bill
YIELD	Yield on a security that pays periodic interest
YIELDDISC	Annual yield for a discounted security, for example, a treasury bill
YIELDMAT	Annual yield of a security that pays interest at maturity

CASH FLOWS

The file **MFMaths3e_04** contains bonds calculators. The sheet called Price sets out the flows for an example bond. The cash flow convention is:

Cash in = positive
Cash out = (negative)

Figure 4.1 shows a bond with a coupon rate of 10 per cent with 10 semi-annual coupons remaining. The price is calculated using a yield of 10 per cent and this is a simple net present value function. The interest rate is divided by the number of coupons per annum since the function requires a periodic interest rate.

```
Cell H6:  =NPV($H$7,Price!$H$14:$H$63)
```

Column D discounts the individual cash flows and adds them up to 1,000 as an alternative to the function. The cash flows are nine periods of 50 followed by one period of 50 plus the principal of 1,000. The periodic nominal rate is 10 per cent divided by two or five per cent per half year. The discounted value in period 2 in cell D15 is therefore:

($C18) * (1/((1 + $H$7)^B18))
50 / (1 + 5%)^2 = 45.35

The price is 100 since the coupon rate and discount rates are the same. Note that the principal of 100 is repayable with the last coupon and the interest payments occur at the end of each period. This can be proved with the TVM calculator (see Chapter 2) which confirms the value of the cash flows (Figure 4.2).

Simple bond

Figure 4.1

A	B	C	D	E	F	G	H
4							
5	Face/Par Amount Of Bond		1000		Summary		
6	Coupon Interest Rate Per Year		10.00%		Price / Value of Bond		1,000.00
7	Years To Maturity		5.0		Rate / Period		5.00%
8	Required Return / Discount Rate		10.00%		Net Present Value		1,000.00
9	Number of Coupons pa		2.0		IRR		10.00%
10					Total Periods		10.0
11							

	Period	Interest Cash Flows	Discounted Interest Cash Flows	Principal Cash Flows	Discounted Principal Cash Flows	Sum Of Discounted Cash Flows	Cash Flows For Calculation of IRR
13	0			(1,000.00)	(1,000.00)	(1,000.00)	(1,000.00)
14	1	50.00	47.62	-	-	47.62	50.00
15	2	50.00	45.35	-	-	45.35	50.00
16	3	50.00	43.19	-	-	43.19	50.00
17	4	50.00	41.14	-	-	41.14	50.00
18	5	50.00	39.18	-	-	39.18	50.00
19	6	50.00	37.31	-	-	37.31	50.00
20	7	50.00	35.53	-	-	35.53	50.00
21	8	50.00	33.84	-	-	33.84	50.00
22	9	50.00	32.23	-	-	32.23	50.00
23	10	50.00	30.70	1,000.00	613.91	644.61	1,050.00
64							
65	Total	500.00	386.09	-	(386.09)	(0.00)	500.00

TVM calculator

Figure 4.2

A	B	C	D	E
4				
5	Number of payments	N		5 Rents
6	Interest rate per annum %	INT		10.00
7	Present value	PV		0.00
8	Payment	PMT		50.00
9	Future value	FV		1,000.00
10				
11	Payment Interval			Semi-annual
12	Payment Toggle	Begin/End		Arrears
13				
14	Answer: Present value			- 1,000.00
15				

Where there is no credit risk, estimating the value of the cash flows is straightforward. Apart from credit risk there are three conditions where estimating cash flows can be difficult:

- Conversion or exchange privileges, where you are not sure when bonds could be converted into stocks and shares.

- Variable rather than fixed coupons, which reduce certainty. An example is a floating rate note (FRN) where coupons are re-fixed periodically at a rate such as margin over LIBOR.

- Embedded options, for example, call features and sinking fund provisions such that the length of the cash flows cannot be estimated with certainty. Such options often require a redemption amount that is greater than the amount at maturity as compensation. These options protect the issuer from paying too much if the option is exercised.

The discount rate in Figure 4.1 has been given as 10 per cent. In reality the rate should be the combination of a risk-free rate such as a 10-year government bond plus a premium for perceived risk borne by the investor. Non-governmental securities carry extra credit risk as a premium:

Yield on non-governmental bond = yield on a risk-free bond + perceived risk premium

ZERO COUPONS

Zero coupon bonds have no interest payments, so the only cash flows are the issue amount and the repayment of the principal. It follows, therefore, that the bond must be priced at a deep discount to compensate for the lack of coupons during the lending period. The zero coupon element reduces some uncertainty since there are no coupons to reinvest and the final principal is known. The example in Figure 4.3 shows a zero coupon at 10 per cent, where the calculation is effectively $1,000/(1 + 5\%)^{10}$ or 613.91.

Figure 4.3

Zero coupon bond

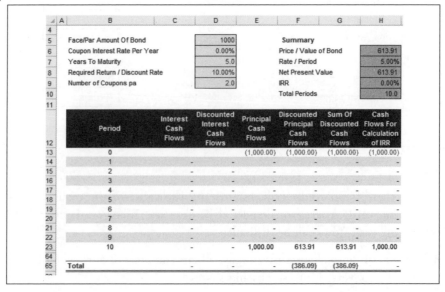

Period	Interest Cash Flows	Discounted Interest Cash Flows	Principal Cash Flows	Discounted Principal Cash Flows	Sum Of Discounted Cash Flows	Cash Flows For Calculation of IRR
0			(1,000.00)	(1,000.00)	(1,000.00)	(1,000.00)
1	-	-	-	-	-	-
2	-	-	-	-	-	-
3	-	-	-	-	-	-
4	-	-	-	-	-	-
5	-	-	-	-	-	-
6	-	-	-	-	-	-
7	-	-	-	-	-	-
8	-	-	-	-	-	-
9	-	-	-	-	-	-
10	-	-	1,000.00	613.91	613.91	1,000.00
Total	-	-	-	(386.09)	(386.09)	-

Summary fields:
- Face/Par Amount Of Bond: 1000
- Coupon Interest Rate Per Year: 0.00%
- Years To Maturity: 5.0
- Required Return / Discount Rate: 10.00%
- Number of Coupons pa: 2.0
- Price / Value of Bond: 613.91
- Rate / Period: 5.00%
- Net Present Value: 613.91
- IRR: 0.00%
- Total Periods: 10.0

YIELD

The previous section calculated the market price from a given yield. It follows that you can perform the same calculations the other way around and derive the yield from the price (see Figure 4.4). These measures are similar to the net present value and the internal rate of return in discounting. Since the cash flows for an option-free bond are fixed, it follows that any changes to yield will be reflected in the price of the bond.

The model finds the internal rate of return in the cash flows as 10 per cent. Notice that the effective rate is 10.25 per cent based on semi-annual cash flows.

Yield   Figure 4.4

	A	B	C	D	E	F	G	H
4								
5		Face/Par Amount Of Bond		1,000.00		Summary		
6		Coupon Interest Rate Per Year		10.00%		Yield to Maturity		10.00%
7		Years To Maturity		5.0		Rate / Period		5.00%
8		Coupons per Annum		2.0				
9		Required Return / Discount Rate		10.00%		Current Yield		10.00%
10		Price / Value of Bond		1,000.00		Capital Gains Yield		(0.00%)
11						Effective Annual Rate		10.25%
12		Total Number of Periods		10.00		Net Present Value		1,000.00
13						IRR		10.00%
14								

	Period	Interest Cash Flows	Discounted Interest Cash Flows	Principal Cash Flows	Discounted Principal Cash Flows	Sum Of Discounted Cash Flows	Cash Flows For Calculation of IRR
16	0			(1,000.00)	(1,000.00)	(1,000.00)	(1,000.00)
17	1	50.00	47.62	–	–	47.62	50.00
18	2	50.00	45.35	–	–	45.35	50.00
19	3	50.00	43.19	–	–	43.19	50.00
20	4	50.00	41.14	–	–	41.14	50.00
21	5	50.00	39.18	–	–	39.18	50.00
22	6	50.00	37.31	–	–	37.31	50.00
23	7	50.00	35.53	–	–	35.53	50.00
24	8	50.00	33.84	–	–	33.84	50.00
25	9	50.00	32.23	–	–	32.23	50.00
26	10	50.00	30.70	1,000.00	613.91	644.61	1,050.00
67							
68	Total	500.00	386.09	–	(386.09)	(0.00)	500.00

YIELD TO CALL

Figures 4.5 and 4.6 calculate the cash flows and yield as if the bond continued to maturity. This confirms a price of 1,000 and a yield of 10 per cent. The bond is callable after two and a half years or five coupons. The price offered is 1,016, which equates to an effective internal rate of 10.25 per cent. This is confirmed by the internal rate of return in cell H13.

Figure 4.5

Yield to call

Period	Interest Cash Flows	Discounted Interest Cash Flows	Principal Cash Flows	Discounted Principal Cash Flows	Sum Of Discounted Cash Flows	Cash Flows For Calculation of IRR

Summary block:

Par / Face Value Of Bond	1,000.00
Coupon Interest Rate pa	10.00%
Years To Maturity	10
Current Price Of Bond	1,000.00
Call Price Of Bond	1,016.00
Years To First Call	5
Coupons per Annum	2
Total Periods	20.00

Summary:
Yield To Call	10.25%
Current Yield	10.00%
Capital Gains Yield	0.25%
Yield To Maturity	10.00%
Current Yield	10.00%
Capital Gains Yield	(0.00%)
Rate / Period	5.00%
Effective Annual Rate	10.49%

Period	Interest Cash Flows	Discounted Interest Cash Flows	Principal Cash Flows	Discounted Principal Cash Flows	Sum Of Discounted Cash Flows	Cash Flows For Calculation of IRR
0			(1,000.00)	(1,000.00)	(1,000.00)	(1,000.00)
1	50.00	47.62	-	-	47.62	50.00
2	50.00	45.35	-	-	45.35	50.00
3	50.00	43.19	-	-	43.19	50.00
4	50.00	41.14	-	-	41.14	50.00
5	50.00	39.18	-	-	39.18	50.00
6	50.00	37.31	-	-	37.31	50.00
7	50.00	35.53	-	-	35.53	50.00
8	50.00	33.84	-	-	33.84	50.00
9	50.00	32.23	-	-	32.23	50.00
10	50.00	30.70	-	-	30.70	50.00
11	50.00	29.23	-	-	29.23	50.00
12	50.00	27.84	-	-	27.84	50.00
13	50.00	26.52	-	-	26.52	50.00
14	50.00	25.25	-	-	25.25	50.00
15	50.00	24.05	-	-	24.05	50.00
16	50.00	22.91	-	-	22.91	50.00
17	50.00	21.81	-	-	21.81	50.00
18	50.00	20.78	-	-	20.78	50.00
19	50.00	19.79	-	-	19.79	50.00
20	50.00	18.84	1,000.00	376.89	395.73	1,050.00

Figure 4.6

Yield to call cash flows

Period	Interest Cash Flows	Discounted Interest Cash Flows	Principal Cash Flows	Discounted Principal Cash Flows	Sum Of Discounted Cash Flows	Cash Flows For Calculation of IRR
0			(1,000.00)	(1,000.00)	(1,000.00)	(1,000.00)
1	50.00	47.62	-	-	47.62	50.00
2	50.00	45.35	-	-	45.35	50.00
3	50.00	43.19	-	-	43.19	50.00
4	50.00	41.14	-	-	41.14	50.00
5	50.00	39.18	-	-	39.18	50.00
6	50.00	37.31	-	-	37.31	50.00
7	50.00	35.53	-	-	35.53	50.00
8	50.00	33.84	-	-	33.84	50.00
9	50.00	32.23	-	-	32.23	50.00
10	50.00	30.70	1,016.00	623.74	654.43	1,066.00

PRICE AND YIELD RELATIONSHIP

The relationship between price and yield is not exactly linear. Rather it is slightly curved or convex. Higher prices are linked to lower yields. As the bond yield increases, prices fall at a decreasing rate. Alternatively, as bond yields fall, prices rise at a decreasing rate. This is positive convexity, which means that bond prices go up faster than they decrease.

The example in Figure 4.7 shows the trade-off between price and yield and the convexity of the relationship. The table in lines 22 to 25 demonstrates the yield–price matrix. Line 24 shows the difference to a yield of 10 per cent while line 25 provides the difference from one data point to the next on the right. The chart at the bottom plots line 23 against line 24 as a curve.

Price–yield relationship

Figure 4.7

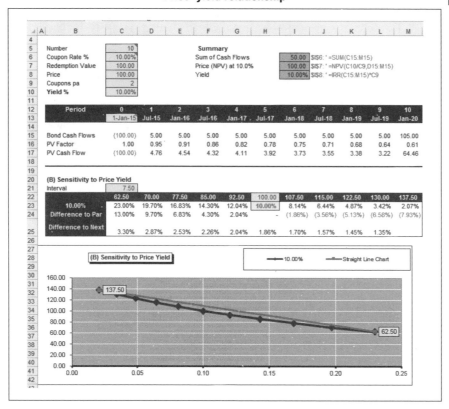

YIELD CURVE PRICING

This example in Figure 4.8 uses the yield curve to price the bond. The table in the range $B$11:$D$21 provides the rates and periods and column D uses a LOOKUP function to insert the correct rate for the semi-annual bond.

In practice, the yield curve represents the rates on a zero coupon bond plus a premium for the perceived credit risk on reinvestment. The first part of the formula checks that the period number is less than the total number of periods:

```
=IF(B25<=$D$7*$D$9,LOOKUP((B25+1)/$D$9,$B$12:$B$21,
$D$12:$D$21),0)
```

Figure 4.8

Yield curve

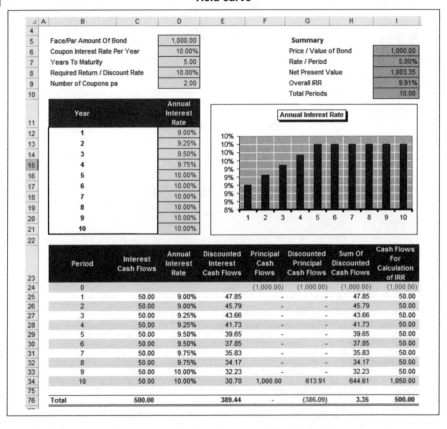

Each period is discounted at the applicable rate for the period using the formula:

Cash flow/(1 + interest rate) ^ period number
```
Cell E25: =($C25)*(1/((1+(D25/$D$9))^B25))
```

The example in Figure 4.9 compares the price against a bond priced at 10 per cent. The RATE function allows you to select a present value as the sum of the discounted cash flows as the investment and the par value as the future value. The answer here is 9.91 per cent against the input target rate of 10 per cent. Note that the RATE function produces the periodic interest rate and this has to be multiplied by two as a semi-annual bond:

```
Cell I9: =RATE(D7*D9,D5*D6/D9,-I8,D5,0)*D9
```

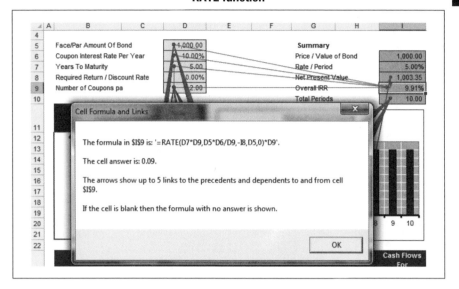

RATE function

Figure 4.9

OTHER YIELD MEASURES

There are several functions in Excel which will calculate price, yield, coupon days and accrued interest. The bond functions sheet demonstrates these functions. The example is brought forward from previous sections, but now the settlement and maturity dates do not fall into exact periods. Interest has to be accrued between periods and this is based on the formula:

(Number of days between settlement date and next coupon date)/number of days in coupon period

The complete price formula therefore consists of the present value of the coupons and principal plus the accrued interest. The total price paid is known as the 'dirty' price and this is made up of the 'clean' price plus the accrued interest.

$$
PRICE = \left[\frac{redemption}{\left(1 + \dfrac{yld}{frequency}\right)^{\left(N-1+\frac{DSC}{E}\right)}} \right] + \left[\sum_{k=1}^{N} \frac{100 \times \dfrac{rate}{frequency}}{\left(1 + \dfrac{yld}{frequency}\right)^{\left(k-1+\frac{DSC}{E}\right)}} \right]
$$
$$
- \left(100 \times \frac{rate}{frequency} \times \frac{A}{E}\right)
$$

DSC = number of days from settlement to next coupon date
E = number of days in coupon period in which the settlement date falls
N = number of coupons payable between settlement date and redemption date
A = number of days from beginning of coupon period to settlement date.

The example in Figure 4.10 represents a 10-year bond issued at the start of 2020 with maturity in 2033. The settlement date is 1 April 2025. The model calculates the clean price as 99.96 as the present value of the coupons and principal. There have been 91 coupon days based on a 360-day year since the last coupon date. Therefore, half of one coupon is accrued and added to form the dirty price of 102.47.

Figure 4.10

Bond functions

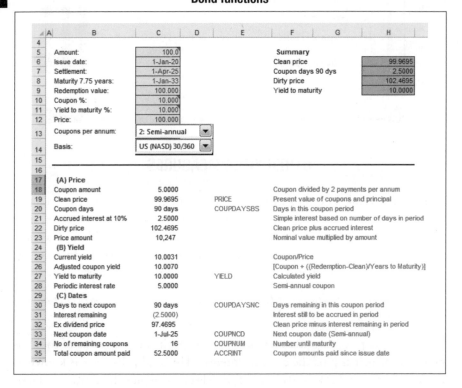

The clean price is produced using the PRICE function:

```
Cell C19: =PRICE($C$7,$C$8,$C$10/100,$C$11/100,$C$9,
$C$41,$F$46)
```

The day conventions are as noted earlier:

0   US (NASD) 30/360
1   Actual/actual
2   Actual/360
3   Actual/365
4   European 30/360

Provided that neither the settlement date nor the next coupon date falling due contain the 31st day of the month, the US and European 30/360 will yield the same results for accrued interest. With actual dates, the key date is 29 February where the actual/actual and the actual/365 conventions will produce the same result.

YIELD MEASURES

Bonds with more than one coupon remaining offer three sources of income:

- periodic interest payment;
- return of the principal together with any capital gain or loss on sale;
- reinvestment income on the coupons received since failure to reinvest will result in lower returns.

Yield measures therefore vary given the uncertainty in the reinvestment income. The yield section contains three common measures of bond yield:

- current yield;
- simple yield to maturity;
- yield.

Current yield

This is a simple measure and calculated as:

Current yield = Coupon rate/[clean price/100]

In this case, it is 10/[96.9595/100} = 10.0031 per cent. The method ignores the time value of money and therefore it cannot be used for comparing bonds with differing maturity dates and coupon periods. Also, it ignores any capital gain or loss arising from the difference between the amounts paid and the principal received on expiry.

Simple yield to maturity

The simple yield to maturity again does not consider the time value of money or capital gains and is also known as the adjusted coupon yield:

[Coupon + ((redemption − clean)/years to maturity)]/clean
YTM = (10% − ((99.9695 − 100)/((1-Jan-33 − 1-Apr-25)/365.25)))/99.9695
YTM = 10.0070%

Yield to maturity

The yield can be calculated using the YIELD function (see Figure 4.11), which includes the total cash flows over the life of the bond to maturity. There are further inputs for the 'days' convention and the number of coupons per annum below the visible entries. The limitations of this function are as follows:

- The bond will be held to maturity and not redeemed or varied during the period.
- All cash flows are discounted at the same rate, which assumes a flat yield curve which rarely exists in the real world.
- All cash flows are assumed to be received promptly with no delays and then promptly reinvested at the same rate.

The formula is:

$$YIELD = \frac{\left(\dfrac{redemption}{100} + \dfrac{rate}{frequency}\right) - \left(\dfrac{par}{100} + \left(\dfrac{A}{E} \times \dfrac{rate}{frequency}\right)\right)}{\dfrac{par}{100} + \left(\dfrac{A}{E} \times \dfrac{rate}{frequency}\right)} \times \frac{frequency \times E}{DSR}$$

A = *number of days from the beginning of the coupon period to the settlement date (accrued days);*

DSR = *number of days from the settlement date to the redemption date;*

E = *number of days in the coupon period.*

Figure 4.11

Yield function

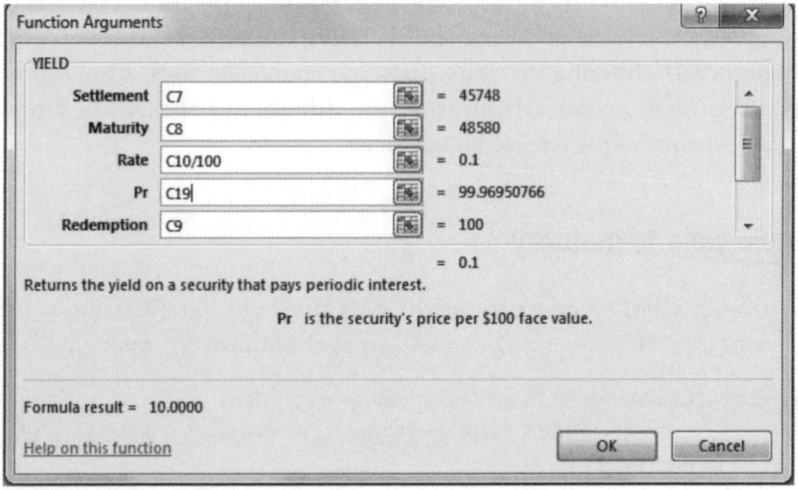

Function Arguments

YIELD

Settlement	C7	= 45748
Maturity	C8	= 48580
Rate	C10/100	= 0.1
Pr	C19	= 99.96950766
Redemption	C9	= 100

= 0.1

Returns the yield on a security that pays periodic interest.

Pr is the security's price per $100 face value.

Formula result = 10.0000

Help on this function

OK   Cancel

The chart and table in Figure 4.12 show the relationship between the bond yield measures. With prices below par, the order of values is current yield, yield to maturity and adjusted coupon yield. Above par, this order is reversed.

Yield and price

Figure 4.12

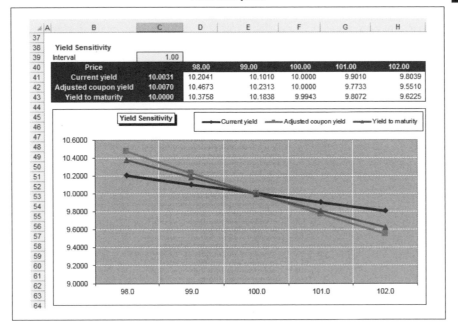

			98.00	99.00	100.00	101.00	102.00
Price							
Current yield	10.0031		10.2041	10.1010	10.0000	9.9010	9.8039
Adjusted coupon yield	10.0070		10.4673	10.2313	10.0000	9.7733	9.5510
Yield to maturity	10.0000		10.3758	10.1838	9.9943	9.8072	9.6225

EXERCISE

Two bonds bear the characteristics below. Calculate the prices and, using a data table in Excel, check the relevant prices if the yield falls or rises by 1 per cent. This should confirm the bond which is more responsive to changes in yield.

Period	6.0 years	10.0 years
Coupon Rate %	10.00	9.75
Redemption Value	100.00	100.00
Coupons per annum	1	1
Yield %	9.50	9.50

SUMMARY

Bond mathematics uses the simple interest methods for pricing accrued interest and compounding for coupons and principal. Using the basic building blocks, you can find the price or the yield by setting out and analysing the relevant cash flows. Excel also has a number of extra built-in functions in the Analysis ToolPak for simplifying the calculations. The next chapter reviews bond risks and sets out the main calculations for understanding the responsiveness of bonds to changes in interest rates.

Bond risks

File: MFMaths3e_05.xls

RISKS

Bonds can be analysed as a trade-off between risk and return. Since the value of investments can vary due to a number of factors and the values of the coupon payments are normally fixed, investors need to understand the potential risks before investment. Risk factors can also change during the investment period, so investors need to make decisions on whether to hold, reduce or increase the investment. There are several classes of risk, which include:

- changes in interest rates;
- reinvestment risk on the coupons and principal;
- yield curve risk;
- prepayment and call risk;
- credit risk defined as default and downgrading;
- liquidity;
- exchange rates;
- inflation;
- macro and exterior risk.

Interest rates

Since bonds consist of a series of cash flows, their value reduces as interest rates rise or inflation eats away at the real value of future cash flows. If market interest rates increase, coupons on existing bonds will be worth less. Since lower coupons will be less attractive to investors, then their value has to drop to a market value in a freely traded market. The opposite is true as interest rates fall because the relationship is the inverse.

When market yields fall below the coupon rate the bond price will increase above par value and therefore it will trade at premium prices. When the yield and coupon rate are the same the bond will trade at par value. It follows, therefore, that the bond will trade at a discount when market yields rise above coupon rates.

The direction of the change in yields and the size of the change have an effect on bond prices. There are two key factors:

- Maturity, where a bond with a longer maturity is more sensitive to changes in interest rates than a shorter-term bond.
- Coupon rates exert an influence as lower coupons present more interest risk because a small change has a larger effect.

Reinvestment risk

This was discussed earlier (see Chapter 4) as the yield calculations assumed that all coupons could be reinvested at the yield rate. In reality, reinvestment rates reduce when yields decline. This means that bonds with high coupon rates are risky since the investor cannot be sure of the reinvestment rate. The real value of the coupons can be eroded by inflation and uncertainty. Investors may, therefore, wish to balance reinvestment against price risk.

Yield curve risk

The relationship between the term to maturity and the yield to maturity is known as the yield curve. The term nature of interest rates means that the rate could change at each coupon date. Yield curves could be flat, rising or falling, and this affects the value of the fixed bond cash flows.

Prepayment and call risk

Embedded options affect pricing as the uncertainty makes the future cash flows harder to predict. Since callable bonds can be redeemed before maturity, the bond holder can lose potential gains with early redemption. There are effectively two elements: the value of the bond without any termination rights less the value of the embedded call option. Where yields fall the call option becomes more valuable to the issuer, and as the yield rises towards the coupon rate, callable bonds approach the call price and do not rise any further.

Credit risk defined as default and downgrading

This can be defined as default risk, credit spread or downgrade risk. Default risk means that the issuer becomes unable to meet its obligations, such as a failure to pay regular interest rates or a breach of other terms. In the event of default, there may be a recovery rate which from past history will vary with the credit rating of the issuer, but the assumption remains that the investor will lose the majority of the investment.

■ Credit spread means the premium above a perceived risk-free rate, such as a 10-year government bond. Since investors need to be rewarded for accepting increased risks, rational investors should receive an increased return.

■ Downgrade risk means that a bond is reclassified by a ratings agency as a riskier investment. This increases the required yield and therefore decreases the value of the bond. The ratings agency may of course assign an increased rating and therefore the opposite would be true.

Grading explanation

Figure 5.1

Explanation	S&P	Fitch	Moodys	Quality	Grade
Prime – highest safety	AAA	AAA	Aaa	High	Investment
High Quality	AA+	AA+	Aa1		
	AA	AA	Aa2		
	AA-	AA-	Aa3		
Upper medium credit	A+	A+	A1		
	A	A	A2		
	A-	A-	A3		
Lower medium credit	BBB+	BBB+	Baa1		
	BBB	BBB	Baa2		
	BBB-	BBB-	Baa3		
Speculative – low quality	BB+	BB+	Ba1	Lower	Speculative
	BB	BB	Ba2		
	BB-	BB-	Ba3		
Highly speculative		B+	B1		
	B	B	B2		
		B-	B3		
Very high risk – poor quality	CCC+	CCC+	Caa	Low	Highly Speculative
	CCC	CCC			or Default
May be in default soon	CC	CC	Ca		
	C	C	C		
No interest being paid	CI				
Default	D	DDD			
		DD			
		D			

Grading explanation

Figure 5.1 summarises the grading used by the principal US ratings agencies, which are indicators of probable default. If a bond is rated as AAA, there is a strong likelihood that it will remain an AAA in one year's time. At the lower end of the scale, there is a higher probability of default within a defined time period. The ratings agencies produce migration probabilities based on the starting grade: it is highly probable that an AAA-rated bond will remain AAA over the next 12 months but with a much lower percentage for a lower-rated bond.

Liquidity

Some bonds are more tradable than others with a ready market. Dealers in bonds post a bidding and asking price, and as liquidity falls the spread between the two prices increases. Liquidity can of course vary over the lifetime of a bond. This is in effect a transaction cost and must be considered part of the cost of holding the bond.

Exchange rates

If the coupon and principal payments are denominated in a foreign currency then the cash flows may be worth more or less when translated into the home currency. If the home currency appreciates against the foreign currency then the payments will be worth less and vice versa.

Inflation

Future inflation also affects the real value of future payments by eroding the purchasing power. If the coupon is 10 per cent and inflation is 4 per cent, then the real return is only 6 per cent. This loss of value has to be factored into the evaluation of returns.

Macro and exterior risk

There are a number of exterior events which cannot be controlled or perhaps foreseen at the time of investment. These include political risks affecting the issuer's ability or willingness to pay, changes in regulation, capital transfers or natural disasters. For corporate bonds, non-controllable risks can include corporate restructuring such as buyouts, mergers and disposals.

DURATION

Interest rate risk is the key bond risk, and the rest of this chapter concentrates on the risk measures of duration and convexity. The simple maturity of a bond is not a suitable indicator for a bond since the cash flows occur during the period to and at maturity. A bond with a longer maturity may be riskier since an investor is exposed to changes in yield rates for a longer period. Duration is the most widely used measure of a bond's volatility and attempts to provide a measure of how the bond will respond to changes in interest rates. Therefore this measure provides a measure of risk in the future cash flows, which can be used to compare different bonds. Alternative definitions are the weighted average maturity or the present value weighted number of years to maturity.

Yield, maturity date and the coupon rate affect duration. Duration decreases with an increasing yield as distant cash flows become worthless. Normally duration increases with a longer maturity date, whereas a low coupon bond will have a higher duration than a high coupon bond. In summary:

Long maturity, low coupon, low yield = high duration

Duration is given by the formula:

$$Duration = \frac{\sum PV \text{ of Cashflow} * \text{Period No}}{Price}$$

Figure 5.2 shows the example used.

Bond example

Figure 5.2

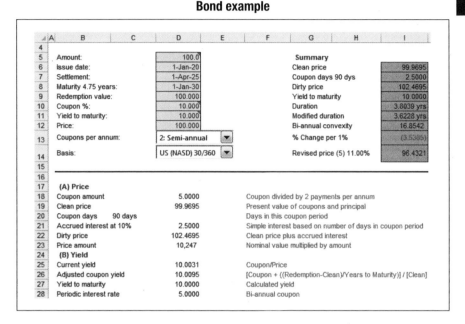

	A	B	C	D	E	F	G	H	I
4									
5		Amount:		100.0			Summary		
6		Issue date:		1-Jan-20			Clean price		99.9695
7		Settlement:		1-Apr-25			Coupon days 90 dys		2.5000
8		Maturity 4.75 years:		1-Jan-30			Dirty price		102.4695
9		Redemption value:		100.000			Yield to maturity		10.0000
10		Coupon %:		10.000			Duration		3.8039 yrs
11		Yield to maturity:		10.000			Modified duration		3.6228 yrs
12		Price:		100.000			Bi-annual convexity		16.8542
13		Coupons per annum:		2: Semi-annual ▼			% Change per 1%		(3.5385)
14		Basis:		US (NASD) 30/360 ▼			Revised price (5) 11.00%		96.4321
15									
16									
17		(A) Price							
18		Coupon amount		5.0000			Coupon divided by 2 payments per annum		
19		Clean price		99.9695			Present value of coupons and principal		
20		Coupon days	90 days				Days in this coupon period		
21		Accrued interest at 10%		2.5000			Simple interest based on number of days in coupon period		
22		Dirty price		102.4695			Clean price plus accrued interest		
23		Price amount		10,247			Nominal value multiplied by amount		
24		(B) Yield							
25		Current yield		10.0031			Coupon/Price		
26		Adjusted coupon yield		10.0095			[Coupon + ((Redemption-Clean)/Years to Maturity)] / [Clean]		
27		Yield to maturity		10.0000			Calculated yield		
28		Periodic interest rate		5.0000			Bi-annual coupon		

The Duration sheet calculates duration using the function DURATION by building up the cash flows (see Figure 5.3). The present value of the cash flow is multiplied by its period number and added. The sum of these cash flows is then divided by the price.

The results in cells G5 and G6 are the same. The formula is:

```
=DURATION(Settlement_Date,Maturity_Date,Coupon/
100,Yield_to_Maturity/100,Pmt_Year,Basis)
```

Basis is the days/years convention. The cell formula uses the function EDATE to find the maturity date since this is not an input variable, as in cell C11:

```
=IF(EDATE(C10,Interval)<=Model!$D$8,EDATE(C10,12/
Interval),"-")
```

If the bond carries no coupon as in a zero coupon bond, then the duration will always be its maturity. Duration can be applied to any groups of cash flows to find the average maturity. If you have cash flows received and paid out, you can cancel the risk or immunise the cash flows by obtaining cash flows with equal duration. At some point between the date and maturity, the loss

Figure 5.3	Duration calculation

	A	B	C	D	E	F	G
4							
5		**Duration Cash flows**			DURATION Function		3.8039
6					Sum/Price		3.8039
7							
8		Period	Date	Cashflow	PV	Weighting	Duration
9			1-Apr-25	–			
10		0.50	1-Jul-25	5.0000	4.8795	0.0476	0.0238
11		1.50	1-Jan-26	5.0000	4.6471	0.0454	0.0680
12		2.50	1-Jul-26	5.0000	4.4259	0.0432	0.1080
13		3.50	1-Jan-27	5.0000	4.2151	0.0411	0.1440
14		4.50	1-Jul-27	5.0000	4.0144	0.0392	0.1763
15		5.50	1-Jan-28	5.0000	3.8232	0.0373	0.2052
16		6.50	1-Jul-28	5.0000	3.6412	0.0355	0.2310
17		7.50	1-Jan-29	5.0000	3.4678	0.0338	0.2538
18		8.50	1-Jul-29	5.0000	3.3026	0.0322	0.2740
19		9.50	1-Jan-30	105.0000	66.0528	0.6446	6.1238
20		10.50	–	–	–	–	–
21		11.50	–	–	–	–	–
22		12.50	–	–	–	–	–
23		13.50	–	–	–	–	–
24		14.50	–	–	–	–	–
25		15.50	–	–	–	–	–
26		16.50	–	–	–	–	–
27		17.50	–	–	–	–	–
28		18.50	–	–	–	–	–
29		19.50	–	–	–	–	–
30		20.50	–	–	–	–	–
31		21.50	–	–	–	–	–
32		22.50	–	–	–	–	–
33		23.50	–	–	–	–	–
34		24.50	–	–	–	–	–
35				150.0000	102.4695	1.0000	7.6078

of interest returns and the capital gain from a higher bond price balance or cancel each other out if an investor devises an immunised portfolio where:

- the present value of assets equals the present value of liabilities;
- the duration of assets is equal to the duration of liabilities.

You might like to know how much a bond's price would change with a change in yield. There is a simple formula on the sheet, which calculates the price movement based on a 1 per cent yield change (see Figure 5.4). The coupon rate is the periodic rate rather than the annual rate:

$$Formula = -Duration * Price * [1/(1 + periodic\ coupon\ rate)] * 0.01$$

Change in price

Figure 5.4

	B	C	D	E	F	G	H	I
16								
17	(A) Price							
18	Coupon amount		5.0000		Coupon divided by 2 payments per annum			
19	Clean price		99.9695		Present value of coupons and principal			
20	Coupon days	90 days			Days in this coupon period			
21	Accrued interest at 10%		2.5000		Simple interest based on number of days in coupon period			
22	Dirty price		102.4695		Clean price plus accrued interest			
23	Price amount		10,247		Nominal value multiplied by amount			
24	(B) Yield							
25	Current yield		10.0031		Coupon/Price			
26	Adjusted coupon yield		10.0095		[Coupon + ((Redemption-Clean)/Years to Maturity)] / [Clean]			
27	Yield to maturity		10.0000		Calculated yield			
28	Periodic interest rate		5.0000		Bi-annual coupon			
29	(C) Duration							
30	Duration		3.8039 yrs		Maturity: 4.75 years			
31	Modified duration		3.6228 yrs		Duration / [1+(Yield / No of Coupons)] = Slope of series			
32	SLOPE		(3.7229)		Slope function			
33	Alternative duration formula		3.6243		(Upper price - lower price)/(2 * bond price*Δ Yield)			
34	(D) Dates							
35	Next coupon date		1-Jul-25		Next coupon date (Bi-annual)			
36	No of remaining coupons		10.00		Number until maturity			

This formula is an approximation since the actual changes for larger figures yield a curve rather than a straight line. The effect of convexity is discussed in the next section. The formula equates approximately to the slope of the change in yield against the price.

You can calculate the slope using the function SLOPE, as in line 33 on the Model sheet:

```
=-SLOPE(Model!C51:I51,Model!C47:I47)
```

There is a further variant of duration called the modified duration (also called volatility) on the Model sheet. The relevant Excel function is MDURATION which uses this formula:

$$Modified\ Duration = Duration/\left[1 + \left(Yield/No\ of\ coupons\ per\ annum\right)\right]$$

The modified duration is useful for calculating the price change per 1 per cent of yield:

$-Dirty\ price * change\ in\ yield * modified\ duration$
$Modified\ duration = 3.6228\ yrs$

The table in Figure 5.5 on the Sensitivity sheet shows the actual change in line 21 where it changes as the bond price changes with yield. The calculated change varies from the actual change due to the curvature or convexity of the relationship.

Figure 5.5

Convexity table

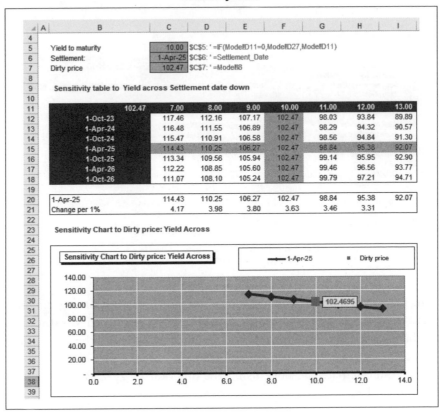

There is a further formula for duration on the Model sheet, which is the amount you would expect the price to change for each 1 per cent increase or decrease in yield:

$$Duration = [Upper\ price - lower\ price]/[2 * price * yield]$$
$$= [106.27 - 98.84]/[2 * 100 * 1\%]$$
$$= 3.715$$

CONVEXITY

Duration and modified duration do not fully explain the linkage between prices and yield, and convexity provides a solution to predicting prices. The actual change depends on the amount of curvature, and this is known as convexity. There are a number of different formulas for computing the convexity, and these are set out on the Model sheet.

The general formula for a change in price is:

$$\Delta Price = -Modified\ Duration * \Delta Yield + \frac{Convexity}{2} * \Delta Yield^2$$

Convexity

Figure 5.6

	A	B	C	D	E	F	G	H	I
4									
5		Change per 1%		(3.6217)		Duration * Price * [1/1+Int] * 1.00%			
6		% Change per 1%		(3.6228)		Change*(Par/Price)			
7		Revised price (1) 11.00%		96.3478		Price+Change			
8									
9		Change per 1%		(3.6206)		Percentage change			
10		% Change per 1%		(3.6217)		Price * Modified duration * Δ yield			
11		Revised price (2) 11.00%		96.3489		Price+Change			
12									
13		Convexity		8.4293		(UP – LP – 2 * Price) / (2 * Price*Δ Yield)^2			
14		Convexity effect		0.0008					
15		Duration effect		(3.6243)		As above			
16		Sum Combined Effect		(0.0354)		-D * Δ Yield + C * (Δ Yield) ^2			
17		Revised price (3) 11.00%		96.4306		Price+Change			
18									
19		Convexity formula (A)		17.2757		Formula: [(ΔP ₊₁ /P) + (ΔP ₋₁ /P)] * 10^8			
20		% Change per 1%		(3.5364)		Variance to simple formula: 0.0864			
21		Revised price (4) 11.00%		96.4342		Price+Change			
22									
23		Periodic convexity formula (B)		67.4169		PV convexity cash flow			
24		Bi-annual convexity		16.8542		Periodic = annual /(N periods ^ N periods)			
25		% Change per 1%		(3.5385)		Variance to simple formula: 0.0843			
26		Revised price (5) 11.00%		96.4321		Price+Change			
27									
28		Data table change per 1%		(3.5914)		Variance to simple formula: 0.0314			
29		Revised price (6) 11.00%		96.3792		Actual Price		96.3421	(0.0363)

The errors between the data table and the simpler approximate answers are given on the sheet (see Figure 5.6). With greater differences, the simpler formula (1) of becomes more inaccurate.

$$Duration * Price * [1 / (1 + INT)] * Change$$

Formula 1

The first formula is an approximation to be used for small changes since it still assumes a simple linear relationship. The formula calculates the price movement based on a 1 per cent yield change. The coupon rate is the periodic rate rather than the annual rate. This is the formula for a 1 per cent change:

$$Formula = -Duration * Price * [1/(1 + periodic\ coupon\ rate)] * 0.01$$

```
=-Model!$D$30*Model!$D$19*(1/(1+(Model!$D$27/
Model!$C$58)))*Model!C44
```

This is derived as −3.6217 or 3.62 per cent for an increase of 1 per cent yield. The answer is revised price (1), 96.34.

Formula 2

The modified duration can also be used for calculating the price change per 1 per cent of yield using the formula:

*−Dirty price * change in yield * modified duration*

This results in almost the same answer as the formula above. Again this assumes a linear relationship and will become progressively inaccurate with larger changes.

Formula 3

A further convexity formula using the duration formula in line 33 of the Model sheet is:

*Convexity = (UP − LP − 2 * Price) / (2 * Price * _Yield)^2*
*Change in price = −D * _Yield + C * (_Yield)^2*

UP = Price plus X basis points
LP = Price minus X basis points
_Yield = Change in yield by X basis points

Convexity is 8.4293, which can then be combined with the duration effect using the second formula to produce the slightly higher answer of 96.4306. The bond therefore is not expected to reduce as much as the simple linear formula. The convexity means nothing on its own but can be useful for comparison purposes since a higher figure means more price volatility than a lower figure.

Formula 4

This convexity formula uses an approximation:

$$C = 10^8 \left[\frac{P_{d+1}}{P_d} + \frac{P_{d-1}}{P_d} \right]$$

This involves calculating the price change for plus and minus 100 basis points. The workings are on a data table at the bottom of the Model sheet (see Figure 5.7). Convexity is calculated as:

```
Cell D19: =(((Model!C84/Model!D19)+(Model!E84/
Model!D19))*10^8)
```

Convexity workings from the Model sheet

Figure 5.7

A	B	C	D	E	F
80					
81	Convexity Workings - Formula 4				
82		9.99	10.00	10.01	11.00
83	99.9695	100.0066	99.9695	99.9324	96.34212484
84	Change	0.0371		(0.0371)	(3.5903)
85	%	0.0371		(0.0371)	(3.5914)
86	(4) Variances				
87	Data table to convexity			(0.0550)	
88	Data table to simple formula			0.0314	
89	Convexity to simple formula			0.0864	

The formula for a change in price in cell D20 is then:

$$\Delta Price = -Modified\ Duration * \Delta Yield + \frac{Convexity}{2} * \Delta Yield^2$$

```
=(-Model!$D$31*(Model!$C$44/100)+0.5*D19*
(Model!$C$44/100)^2)*100
```

The final result due to the curvature is 96.4342 rather than 96.34 by the simpler linear formula.

Formula 5

The model (see Figure 5.8) also includes the full convexity formulas in the cash flow on the Model sheet shown as a schedule using the formula below:

$$Convexity = \frac{1}{P} \cdot \frac{\Delta^2 P}{(\Delta y)^2} \cdot \sum_{t=1}^{y} t \cdot (t+1) \frac{C_t}{(1+y)^t} / P$$

The weightings column is the present value in column E divided by the sum of the cash flows at the bottom. The duration is the period number multiplied by the weighting. The convexity for the period is:

*Period + Next Period * Weighting * (1 / (1 + Periodic Yield))^2*

```
Cell I11: =B11+B12*F11*(1/(1+(Model!$D$27/Pmt_
Year/100))/^2)
```

At the bottom of the schedule the periodic convexity results (see Figure 5.9) are added according to the formula above:

```
Cell I35: =SUM(I10:I34)
```

Figure 5.8

Convexity workings on the Duration sheet

	Period	Date	Cashflow	PV	Weighting	Duration		Convexity
		1-Apr-25	-					
	0.50	1-Jul-25	5.0000	4.8795	0.0476	0.0238		0.0324
	1.50	1-Jan-26	5.0000	4.6471	0.0454	0.0680		0.1543
	2.50	1-Jul-26	5.0000	4.4259	0.0432	0.1080		0.3428
	3.50	1-Jan-27	5.0000	4.2151	0.0411	0.1440		0.5876
	4.50	1-Jul-27	5.0000	4.0144	0.0392	0.1763		0.8795
	5.50	1-Jan-28	5.0000	3.8232	0.0373	0.2052		1.2099
	6.50	1-Jul-28	5.0000	3.6412	0.0355	0.2310		1.5712
	7.50	1-Jan-29	5.0000	3.4678	0.0338	0.2538		1.9568
	8.50	1-Jul-29	5.0000	3.3026	0.0322	0.2740		2.3606
	9.50	1-Jan-30	105.0000	66.0528	0.6446	6.1238		58.3218
	10.50	-	-	-	-	-		-
	11.50	-	-	-	-	-		-
	12.50	-	-	-	-	-		-
	13.50	-	-	-	-	-		-
	14.50	-	-	-	-	-		-
	15.50	-	-	-	-	-		-
	16.50	-	-	-	-	-		-
	17.50	-	-	-	-	-		-
	18.50	-	-	-	-	-		-
	19.50	-	-	-	-	-		-
	20.50	-	-	-	-	-		-
	21.50	-	-	-	-	-		-
	22.50	-	-	-	-	-		-
	23.50	-	-	-	-	-		-
	24.50	-	-	-	-	-		-
			150.0000	102.4695	1.0000	7.6078		67.4169
				Price:				102.4695
				Annual Convexity				16.8542
				% Change per 1%				(3.5385)

Figure 5.9

Duration cash flows

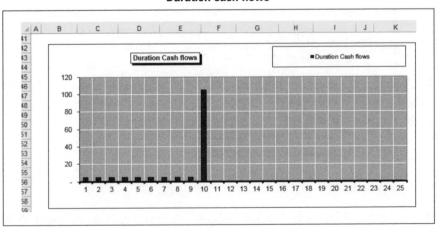

The annual rate is the sum divided by (Payments per year ^ Payments per year). The convexity is 16.8542 and with this factor the change in the bond price can be derived from:

$$\Delta Price = -Modified\ Duration * \Delta Yield + \frac{Convexity}{2} * Yield^2$$

This is (3.5385) and the revised value is 74.8675.

Formula 6

The schedule also includes data table workings for comparison with the calculated values and this is 74.8878.

COMPARISON

The Convexity sheet calculates the bond price at each of the yield to maturities on the left using a PRICE function:

```
Cell E37: =PRICE(Model!$D$7, Model!$D$8,
Model!$D$10,B37, Model!$D$9, Model!$C$58,
Model!$F$63)
=PRICE(Settlement,Maturity,Coupon,Yield,Redemption,
Frequency,Basis)
```

Column F repeats formula 2, namely (−Dirty price * change in yield * modified duration), as the duration multiplied by the change in yield to obtain the simple percentage change based on duration alone. This can then be multiplied out against the existing price. Column I uses formula 5 to obtain the percentages and these are added in column J. You can see that the differences are small close to the current yield to maturity, but, due to convexity, become more pronounced as you move further and further from the existing price (see Figure 5.10).

Two further charts illustrate the table. The first plots the actual and predicted changes in amounts from formulas 2 and 5 (see Figure 5.11). The convexity formula 5 rather than the duration-based formula is more accurate in tracking the actual price changes. The periodic convexity closely follows the actual change.

Figure 5.12 plots the percentage differences against the predicted actual prices. The duration-based formula becomes progressively less accurate away from the current yield of 10 per cent. By contrast, formula 4 based on the convexity cash flows remains more accurate further from the current yield.

Figure 5.10

Summary table

	Yield to maturity	Change in yield	Actual change %	Clean price	Price * Modified duration * Δ yield	Revised price (2) 11.00%	Difference (2)	Periodic convexity formula (B)	Revised price (5) 11.00%	Difference (5)
36	6.00	(4.0000)	16.3388	116.3033	14.4911	114.4562	1.8472	15.8394	115.8041	0.4992
37	6.50	(3.5000)	14.1236	114.0888	12.6797	112.6453	1.4435	13.7120	113.6774	0.4114
38	7.00	(3.0000)	11.9604	111.9263	10.8683	110.8345	1.0918	11.6268	111.5927	0.3336
39	7.50	(2.5000)	9.8479	109.8144	9.0569	109.0237	0.7908	9.5836	109.5502	0.2642
40	8.00	(2.0000)	7.7848	107.7519	7.2455	107.2128	0.5391	7.5826	107.5498	0.2021
41	8.50	(1.5000)	5.7697	105.7374	5.4342	105.4020	0.3354	5.6238	105.5916	0.1458
42	9.00	(1.0000)	3.8013	103.7696	3.6228	103.5912	0.1785	3.7070	103.6754	0.0942
43	9.50	(0.5000)	1.8785	101.8474	1.8114	101.7803	0.0671	1.8325	101.8014	0.0460
44	10.00	–	0.0000	99.9695	–	99.9695	0.0000	–	99.9695	0.0000
45	10.50	0.5000	(1.8353)	98.1348	(1.8114)	98.1587	(0.0239)	(1.7903)	98.1797	(0.0449)
46	11.00	1.0000	(3.6285)	96.3421	(3.6228)	96.3478	(0.0057)	(3.5385)	96.4321	(0.0900)
47	11.50	1.5000	(5.3807)	94.5904	(5.4342)	94.5370	0.0534	(5.2445)	94.7266	(0.1361)
48	12.00	2.0000	(7.0930)	92.8786	(7.2455)	92.7262	0.1525	(6.9085)	93.0632	(0.1845)
49	12.50	2.5000	(8.7665)	91.2057	(9.0569)	90.9153	0.2904	(8.5302)	91.4419	(0.2362)
50	13.00	3.0000	(10.4020)	89.5707	(10.8683)	89.1045	0.4661	(10.1099)	89.8627	(0.2921)
51	13.50	3.5000	(12.0007)	87.9725	(12.6797)	87.2937	0.6788	(11.6474)	88.3257	(0.3532)
52	14.00	4.0000	(13.5633)	86.4103	(14.4911)	85.4828	0.9275	(13.1428)	86.8308	(0.4205)

Figure 5.11

Convexity chart

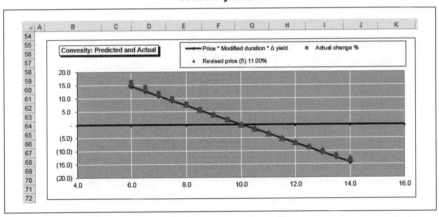

Figure 5.12

Percentage differences to actual prices

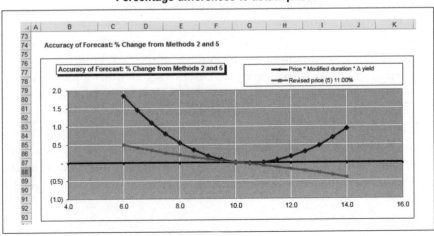

EXERCISE

An amount of 100,000 is required in 3.25 years' time. Interest rates are currently 8 per cent and a company wishes to invest an amount in bonds which will grow to 100,000 at the time of maturity. Two bonds are available (see Figure 5.13).

Exercise inputs

Figure 5.13

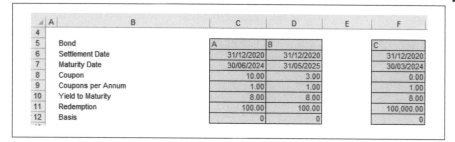

	A	B		C	D	E	F
4							
5	Bond			A	B		C
6	Settlement Date			31/12/2020	31/12/2020		31/12/2020
7	Maturity Date			30/06/2024	31/05/2025		30/03/2024
8	Coupon			10.00	3.00		0.00
9	Coupons per Annum			1.00	1.00		1.00
10	Yield to Maturity			8.00	8.00		8.00
11	Redemption			100.00	100.00		100,000.00
12	Basis			0	0		0

- Calculate the price, duration and modified duration, and estimate the change in value if interest rates rise by 1 per cent.
- Use Goal Seek to find out what proportion of each bond the company should invest in. The formula is:

$$\text{Portfolio duration} = (\text{Duration A} * \text{Percentage A}) + (\text{Duration B} * \text{Percentage B})$$

- Calculate the present value of 100,000 in 3.25 years at the input rate of 8 per cent as this is the amount to be invested now.
- Calculate the proportion of the present value to be invested in each bond.
- Divide the amount by the price to find out how many bonds are required.

SUMMARY

There are several classes of risk associated with investing in bonds apart from changes in interest rates. These include risks from reinvestment risk, changes in the yield curve, prepayment and call risk, credit, liquidity, exchange rates, inflation and external factors. Duration is the key measure for estimating changes in a bond's value due to interest rate changes; however, measures based solely on duration become increasingly inaccurate. Since the calculation needs to include the convexity of the price–yield relationship, further measures of convexity are needed to predict the changed price more accurately. Several measures of convexity are presented in this chapter along with simple and modified duration.

6

Floating rate securities

File: MFMaths3e_06.xls

FLOATING RATES

Floating rate securities are fixed income instruments which have a coupon rate or interest rate that varies based on a short-term rate index. Other terms are floating rate notes, floating rate certificates of deposit or variable rate notes. While this is more complex than fixed coupons, floating rates are generally advantageous for lenders when interest rates are rising, since they mitigate some of the risks.

Floating rate securities assume that the investor's return is a coupon linked to an index which will change during the life of the security. The index could be quarterly or semi-annual, such as three-month LIBOR (London Interbank Offer Rate). The British Bankers Association is the most widely used benchmark or reference rate for short-term interest rates and is the rate of interest at which banks borrow funds from other banks, in marketable size, in the London interbank market. Other interbank rates include Euro LIBOR, US Dollar LIBOR, GBP LIBOR and Japanese Yen LIBOR.

A floater is a fixed income instrument whose coupon fluctuates with some designated reference rate. A floating rate note (FRN) is a floater issued by a corporate or agency borrower. Typically, FRNs have maturities of about five years. The three-month and six-month LIBORs are two commonly used reference rates, as are treasury bill yields, the prime rate or the Federal funds rate. Collateralised mortgage obligations (CMOs) are also sometimes structured to have floating rate coupons.

For FRNs, the coupon rate is usually reset each time interest is paid. A typical arrangement might be to pay interest at the end of each quarter based on the value of three-month LIBOR at the start of the quarter. The coupon rate is calculated as the reference rate plus a fixed spread, which depends upon the issuer's credit quality and specifics of how the instrument is structured. One feature that can affect the spread is a provision that places a cap or floor on the floating coupon rate. For example, an FRN might be issued with a cap of 7.5 per cent and a floor of 1.5 per cent.

In assessing credit risk from a single counterparty, three issues need to be considered:

- Default probability: that is, the likelihood that the counterparty will default on its obligation either over the lifetime of the obligation or over some specified horizon, such as a year. Calculated for a one-year horizon, this may be termed the expected default frequency.

- Credit exposure: in the event of a default, how large will the outstanding obligation be when the default occurs?

- Recovery rate: in the event of a default, what fraction of the exposure may be recovered through bankruptcy proceedings or some other form of settlement?

The credit quality of an obligation refers generally to the counterparty's ability to perform on that obligation, which encompasses both the obligation's default probability and anticipated recovery rate. Note that every risk comprises two elements: exposure and uncertainty. For credit risk, credit exposure represents the former and credit quality represents the latter.

To investors, holding an FRN is similar to investing in money market instruments and continuously reinvesting as those instruments mature. The significant difference is the fact that the FRN entails long-term credit exposure to the issuer and this is typically reflected in the FRN's spread. FRNs tend to have stable market values. If the floating rate is reset with each coupon payment (as is typically done) the duration of an FRN is simply the time until the next interest payment.

CHARACTERISTICS OF INTEREST RATE SECURITIES

Issuer

An organisation which issues a bond is referred to as 'the issuer' or 'the borrower'. The most active issuers of bonds today are governments and government agencies (government bonds), banks and corporations (corporate bonds).

Face value

Face value is the amount that is to be paid to an investor at the maturity date of a bond. Bonds can be issued at different face values; however, floating rate securities typically have a unit face value of 100.

Interest coupon

The coupon represents an interest payment paid at regular intervals by the issuer to owners of interest rate securities. The coupon rate is the interest rate paid to investors during the life of the bond and is set when the issuer first sells the securities into the market. An FRN has a coupon that varies in line with a benchmark rate, usually at a margin above the bank-bill rate, and is different at each payment date. Since the amount of coupon interest is known in advance, its accumulation is spread over the relevant period. This is referred to as the daily accrued interest. This contrasts with a share dividend which is only known shortly before it is paid.

Coupon frequency

Coupon payments are made at regular intervals throughout the lifetime of the security and are usually quarterly or semi-annually. FRNs normally pay interest quarterly.

Yield

The yield is the return an investor receives on a security. The yield is based on the price paid by an investor for a security and the payments (coupons) received if the security is held to maturity. The most important types of yield are the nominal yield and the yield to maturity.

Maturity date

The final coupon and the face value of a bond are repaid to the investor on its maturity date. The time to maturity can vary greatly, although it is typically between two and twenty years.

Purchase price

The price is stated as a percentage of its face value. For example, a price of 100 means 100 per cent of face value; a price of 99.80 is 99.8 per cent of face value; a price of 102.5 is 102.5 per cent of face value.

The purchase price (also known as the gross price) is the total amount that an investor pays to the issuer. The total purchase price comprises the number of securities that an investor buys times the price paid for the security.

The purchase price includes two components:

- Capital price, which is the price as estimated by the market based on a number of variables, including interest rates, maturity date, ranking and credit quality.
- Accrued interest on the security, which is the amount of interest accumulated on a security since the last coupon payment. Because interest is paid at regular intervals the price increases daily by the amount of interest accruing. On a 6.50 per cent annual coupon, interest accrues at 1.78 per 100 per day. Immediately following the coupon payment the price should fall by the amount of that coupon payment.

YIELD EVALUATION

Two methods of evaluating the yield on floating securities are:

- effective margin, both simple and compound;
- current marginal income.

Since floating rate securities are linked to an index, an investor will be concerned with the margin above or below the index. A further position is the implied coupon date price, which is a price-based evaluation against the price in the market together with the cost of carrying the position. This is a way of marking the floating investment to market.

Effective margin

This is the total marginal return over the index to maturity and comprises a combination of margin (negative or positive) over the index plus capital growth or depreciation (see Figure 6.1). The formula is:

$$Simple\ effective\ margin\ =\ margin\ +\ (redemption\ value\ -\ price)/life$$

Life	10 years
Margin	25 basis points over six-month LIBOR
Clean price	99.0
Redemption	100

The second formula takes into account the price of the FRN as follows:

$$Modified\ simple\ effective\ margin\ =\ [margin\ +\ (redemption\ value\ -\ price)/life]/price$$

| Figure 6.1 | | Simple effective margin |

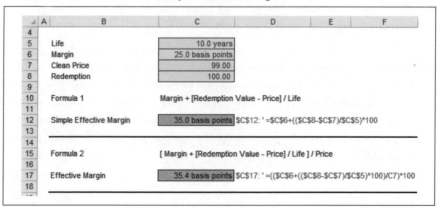

The simple effective margin is 35 basis points. This result can be compared with similar bonds as a basis for evaluation since the variables for the calculation are the life, margin over the index, price and par value. The effective margin is increased by a larger margin over LIBOR and conversely decreased by a smaller margin. The main factor is the price since the margin increases as the price falls (Figure 6.2).

Effect of a fall in price

Figure 6.2

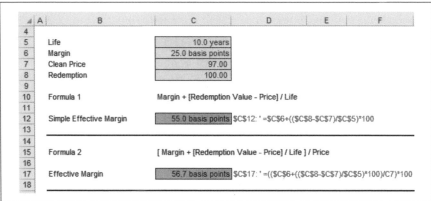

With the price reduced to 97.0 the margin rises to 55 basis points. This simple method does not take into account the present value of future cash flows in the same way as the simple yield on a fixed bond. Using standard bonds calculations you can calculate the bond as a fixed bond at par and then compare the yield on the variable bond.

Column C in Figure 6.3 shows an 8 per cent bond at par with the price and redemption value the same. Column D evaluates an 8.25 per cent semi-annual bond priced at 99. The coupon is therefore 4.125 payable every six months with 20 payments in total.

Compound effective margin

Figure 6.3

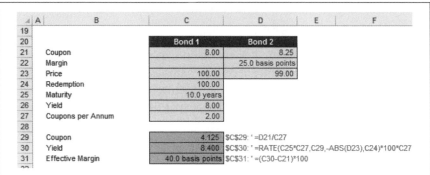

The RATE function (see Figure 6.4) derives the yield per period, and this is multiplied by two to form an annual nominal rate. The effective margin is therefore 8.4 per cent less the index value of 8 per cent. This figure can be used for evaluating a potential investment where the key factors are price, margin, period and index value. With dates in the calculation you could, of course, use the YIELD function in Excel.

Figure 6.4

RATE function

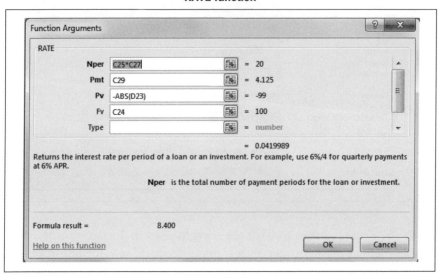

Current marginal income

The current marginal income (CMI) is a simple spread figure and represents the annual income from the floating rate security taking into account funding the investment at LIBOR. In other words, this is the difference between the cost of the investment and the benefit derived. The formula is:

$$Current\ marginal\ income = [LIBOR + FRN\ margin] - [price * LIBOR/100]$$
$$CMI = 8.25\% - (99 * 8\%) = 0.33\%$$

The price and LIBOR rate are key factors in generating the current marginal income. Figure 6.5 shows the effect: for example, the margin increases with an increase in LIBOR and a decrease in the price. The lowest margin in the table is found at the highest price and lowest LIBOR.

Current marginal income

Figure 6.5

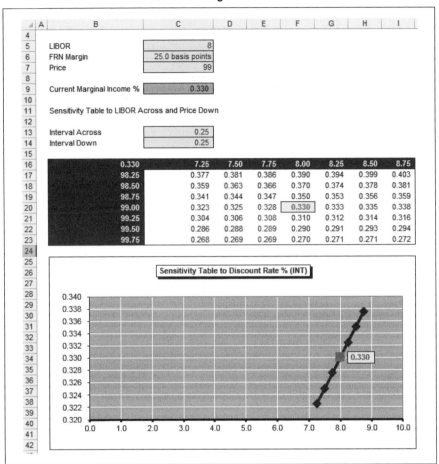

Implied coupon date price

The implied coupon date price is the level at which the security must be sold in order to break even on the investment (Figure 6.6). It is one method of marking the instrument to market the current holding in a specific security.

The formula is:

$Price + [(price * days\ A * cost/funds)/360 * 100] - (coupon * days\ B)/360$

$Days\ A = days\ from\ settlement\ to\ next\ coupon$

$Days\ B = days\ between\ coupons$

$360 = number\ of\ days\ in\ the\ reference\ year\ according\ to\ convention$

Figure 6.6

Implied coupon date price

	A	B	C	D	E	F	G
4							
5		Currency	USD				
6		Coupon	8.25				
7		LIBOR	8.00				
8		Purchase Settlement Date	25 May 2020				
9		Last Coupon	20 May 2020				
10		Next Coupon	20 Nov 2020				
11		Price	98.50				
12		Days in Year	360.0 days				
13							
14		Days	5.0 days				
15		(A) Gross Price	98.615		Clean Price + Accrued Interest		
16							
17		Cost of Carrying FRN to Next Coupon Date					
18		Days to Next Coupon Date	179.0 days				
19		(B) Cost	3.923		Price * Days * Cost / Basis Days		
20							
21		Days in Period	184.0 days				
22		[C] Coupon at Next Coupon Date	4.217		Coupon * Days / Basis Days		
23							
24		Implied Coupon Date Price	98.321		A + B - C		

The cost of holding the investment is [(price * days A * cost/funds)/360 * 100] and the reward is (coupon * days B)/360. The Excel sheet breaks the calculation down into three stages:

A. *Dirty price = clean price + accrued interest from 20 to 25 May*
$$= 98.50 + 5 * 8.25/360 = 98.615$$

B. *Cost of carrying FRN to the next coupon date*
$$Cost = (price * days\ A * cost/funds)/360 * 100$$
$$= (98.615 * 179\ days * 8.00)/36,000 = 3.923$$

C. *Less coupon to be received at the next coupon date*
$$Reward = (coupon * days\ B)/360$$
$$= (8.25 * 184\ days)/360 = 4.217$$

Therefore the total calculation is $98.615 + 3.923 - 4.217 = 98.321$.

The factors affecting the potential profit or loss on the investment against the market price are:

- purchase price of the security;
- cost of finding the purchase, current LIBOR or index;
- coupon as a combination of LIBOR and the margin. LIBOR could be different from the current rate depending on when the rate was set. This could arise if the floating rate security was purchased between coupons and LIBOR has moved since the last coupon was reset.

COUPON STRIPPING

Coupon stripping is a further use of discounting mathematics as a way of producing a profit from the difference in the coupon and market interest rates. A bond can be purchased at the market price and the coupons can be 'stripped off' and sold separately as zero coupon instruments. The bond without the coupons is a zero coupon bond.

The arbitrage possibility arises from the difference from reselling each of the cash flows separately and the bond itself. The individual profits will depend on the yield curve from selling an instrument over one, two, three, etc., years.

Figure 6.7 shows a 10-year bond with a 12 per cent coupon with a price of 101.00 based on a yield of 11.75 per cent. The first part of the spreadsheet confirms the present value of the cash flows at 11.75 per cent. The second part of the schedule shows the input yields and in line 25 the calculations for the individual discount factors. The formula is the cash flow/(1+interest rate)^period number. The stripped cash flows add up to 103.19 and this represents a potential profit of 1.77.

The difficulty of realising a profit depends primarily on the size of the coupon values to make it worthwhile in terms of time and effort. Nevertheless the difference in yields could give rise to a potential profit.

Coupon stripping

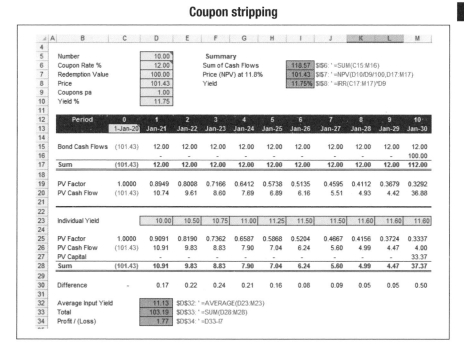

Figure 6.7

EXERCISE

Extend the coupon stripping model to allow for up to 20 periods and calculate the profit or loss on this scenario. The model (see Figure 6.8) requires the use of dates rather than a fixed number of periods, together with IF statements to cease the coupon payments after 31 December 2027 and trigger the principal repayment.

Figure 6.8

Exercise inputs

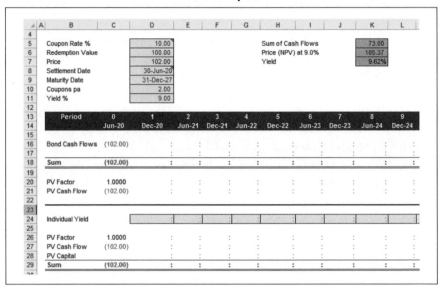

The rates to be applied to each of the periods are as follows:

Date	Rate
Dec-20	8.00
Jun-21	8.00
Dec-21	8.00
Jun-22	8.00
Dec-22	8.00
Jun-23	8.00
Dec-23	8.00
Jun-24	8.00
Dec-24	8.00
Jun-25	8.00
Dec-25	8.00
Jun-26	8.00
Dec-26	9.00
Jun-27	9.00
Dec-27	9.00

Figure 6.9 shows a portion of the answers with the individual coupons discounted at the individual rate and added together to form a profit.

Answer detail

Figure 6.9

	A	B	C	D	E	F	G	H	I	J	K
4											
5		Coupon Rate %		10.00				Sum of Cash Flows			73.00
6		Redemption Value		100.00				Price (NPV) at 9.0%			105.37
7		Price		102.00				Yield			9.62%
8		Settlement Date		30-Jun-20							
9		Maturity Date		31-Dec-27							
10		Coupons pa		2.00							
11		Yield %		9.00							
12											
13		Period	0	1	2	3	4	5	6	7	8
14			Jun-20	Dec-20	Jun-21	Dec-21	Jun-22	Dec-22	Jun-23	Dec-23	Jun-24
15											
16		Bond Cash Flows	(102.00)	5.00	5.00	5.00	5.00	5.00	5.00	5.00	5.00
17				-	-	-	-	-	-	-	-
18		Sum	(102.00)	5.00	5.00	5.00	5.00	5.00	5.00	5.00	5.00
19											
20		PV Factor	1.0000	0.9569	0.9157	0.8763	0.8386	0.8025	0.7679	0.7348	0.7032
21		PV Cash Flow	(102.00)	4.78	4.58	4.38	4.19	4.01	3.84	3.67	3.52
22											
23											
24		Individual Yield		8.00	8.00	8.00	8.00	8.00	8.00	8.00	8.00
25											
26		PV Factor	1.0000	0.9615	0.9246	0.8890	0.8548	0.8219	0.7903	0.7599	0.7307
27		PV Cash Flow	(102.00)	4.81	4.62	4.44	4.27	4.11	3.95	3.80	3.65
28		PV Capital		-	-	-	-	-	-	-	-
29		Sum	(102.00)	4.81	4.62	4.44	4.27	4.11	3.95	3.80	3.65
30											
31		Difference	-	0.02	0.04	0.06	0.08	0.10	0.11	0.13	0.14
32											
33		Average Input Yield		8.98							
34		Total		106.70							
35		Profit / (Loss)		1.33							

SUMMARY

This chapter reviews floating rate instruments where the coupon varies depending on the margin over an index rate. Relevant yield measures can be calculated such as the effective margin, current marginal income and the implied coupon date price. As a further example of discounting mathematics, coupon stripping shows a potential profit based on the difference in interest rates and the yield curve.

Amortisation and depreciation

File: MFMaths3e_07.xls

AMORTISATION

This chapter introduces methods of amortising loans or leases and compares the result with depreciation methods for writing off equipment.

Amortisation is the reduction of the value of an asset by prorating its initial cost over a number of periods. You can calculate the payment required under an annuity and then you need to split each payment into capital and interest. Due to the compounding nature of the time value of money, more capital is outstanding in the earlier periods and therefore more interest is payable on the outstanding balance. In effect, you pay for the capital outstanding. As the loan progresses, less interest is payable on the notional balance outstanding and more capital can be repaid in each period. Typical applications include house mortgages, bank loans or finance leases. To solve these problems, you need to construct a cash flow grid with the period number, rental payment, interest paid, capital repayment and balance outstanding.

The example below uses a capital value of 100,000 lent at a nominal rate of 8 per cent over three years with quarterly rentals. One rental payment is due on signing. Since there is no final rental, this results in a rental of 9,270.55 per quarter using the PMT function.

The amount lent is 100,000 less the first rental, which is 90,729.45. To calculate the interest for the first period, you multiply the capital outstanding by the periodic interest rate. This is 8 per cent/four rentals per annum. The first calculation is:

$$90,729.45 * 2 \text{ per cent} = 1,814.59$$

The capital repayment is then the difference between 9,270.55 and the interest payable. The capital of 7,455.96 is added to the capital to form the capital outstanding at the end of period 1. The process is then repeated with the period 2 interest calculated from the capital outstanding at the end of period 1, and so on. Progressing through the 12 periods means that the interest per period declines while the capital repayable grows. In the final period the capital outstanding reduces to zero.

The checks are that the total interest equals the total charges and the capital repayments add up to the original capital. As seen in Figure 7.1 the interest is 11,246.58 and the capital is 100,000.

There are also functions in Excel for calculating directly the interest or the capital for any period. IPMT will calculate the amortised interest and PPMT the capital. The functions take the same arguments as the PMT and PV procedures with the addition of the current period number. Figure 7.2 shows the inputs for the IPMT function in the first period.

Figure 7.1

Amortisation

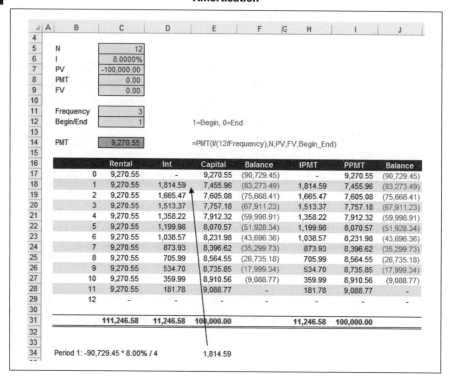

Figure 7.2

IPMT/PPMT function

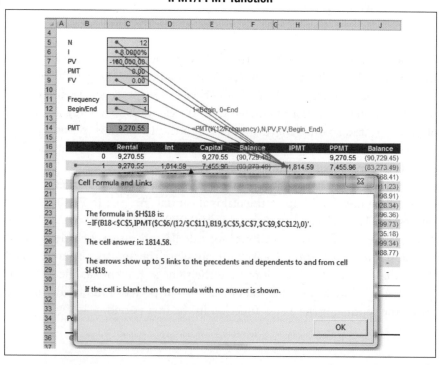

FULL AMORTISATION

It is possible to scale up the initial calculations. As an example, Figure 7.3 shows the amortisation of a 10-year loan with monthly rentals in advance at a nominal rate of 10 per cent. There is a final payment or residual value of 20,000. The same calculations are used to multiply out the outstanding capital by the periodic interest rate. Since there is a rental due on signing, the first capital value is the net advance of 98,786.24.

Ten-year amortisation

Figure 7.3

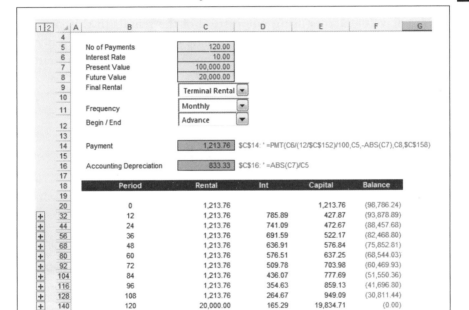

Again the check is the totals row where the total payable less the charges equals the capital value. The cash flow above contains 121 payments and is grouped in years in order to show the summary.

DELAYED PAYMENTS

The amortisation period of 120 payments can be structured to accept periods of lower rentals and can still be structured to split the subsequent rentals into interest and capital. If no rental is being paid then the capital outstanding rises due to the continuing cost of funding the balance outstanding.

Instead of the capital reducing, it rises due to the lack of repayments, since the outstanding balance has to be notionally financed.

The rental cannot be calculated directly and needs to be computed using the factors or $1 method. While you could use Solver or Goal Seek, this procedure will compute a rental or payment directly. The method is as follows:

- Derive the original capital value with cash out as negative and cash in as positive.

- Present value and payments during the period together with the final value.

- Add these two values to form the known present value (A).

- Present-value factors using one instead of the rental. In this case the model will need to present-value 11 cash flows of zero (since one is due on signing) followed by 108 payments of one at the period discount rate of 10 per cent/12. This is (B).

- The periodic rental is calculated by dividing (A) by (B).

Figure 7.4

Delayed rentals amortisation

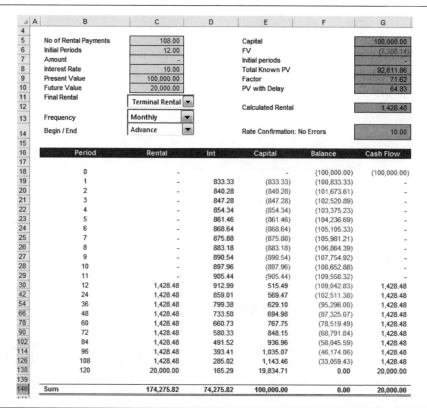

	B	C	D	E	F	G
5	No of Rental Payments	108.00		Capital		100,000.00
6	Initial Periods	12.00		FV		(7,388.14)
7	Amount	-		Initial periods		-
8	Interest Rate	10.00		Total Known PV		92,611.86
9	Present Value	100,000.00		Factor		71.62
10	Future Value	20,000.00		PV with Delay		64.83
11	Final Rental	Terminal Rental ▾				
12				Calculated Rental		1,428.48
13	Frequency	Monthly ▾				
14	Begin / End	Advance ▾		Rate Confirmation: No Errors		10.00
15						
16	Period	Rental	Int	Capital	Balance	Cash Flow
18	0	-		-	(100,000.00)	(100,000.00)
19	1	-	833.33	(833.33)	(100,833.33)	-
20	2	-	840.28	(840.28)	(101,673.61)	-
21	3	-	847.28	(847.28)	(102,520.89)	-
22	4	-	854.34	(854.34)	(103,375.23)	-
23	5	-	861.46	(861.46)	(104,236.69)	-
24	6	-	868.64	(868.64)	(105,105.33)	-
25	7	-	875.88	(875.88)	(105,981.21)	-
26	8	-	883.18	(883.18)	(106,864.39)	-
27	9	-	890.54	(890.54)	(107,754.92)	-
28	10	-	897.96	(897.96)	(108,652.88)	-
29	11	-	905.44	(905.44)	(109,558.32)	-
30	12	1,428.48	912.99	515.49	(109,042.83)	1,428.48
42	24	1,428.48	859.01	569.47	(102,511.38)	1,428.48
54	36	1,428.48	799.38	629.10	(95,296.00)	1,428.48
66	48	1,428.48	733.50	694.98	(87,325.07)	1,428.48
78	60	1,428.48	660.73	767.75	(78,519.49)	1,428.48
90	72	1,428.48	580.33	848.15	(68,791.84)	1,428.48
102	84	1,428.48	491.52	936.96	(58,045.59)	1,428.48
114	96	1,428.48	393.41	1,035.07	(46,174.06)	1,428.48
126	108	1,428.48	285.02	1,143.46	(33,059.43)	1,428.48
138	120	20,000.00	165.29	19,834.71	0.00	20,000.00
140	Sum	174,275.82	74,275.82	100,000.00	0.00	20,000.00

The capital value in Figure 7.4 is 100,000. The next stage is to present-value the final payment of 10,000 that is due in 120 months (see Figure 7.5). The TVM calculator (see Chapter 2) can be used to find the answer of 7,388.14. The formula for the calculation is:

$$Present\ value = 20,000/[1 + (10\%/12)]\wedge 20$$

The net present value labelled Total Known PV in Figure 7.4 is 92,611.86.

Present value of future value

Figure 7.5

⊿ A	B	C	D	E
4				
5	Number of payments	N		120 Rents
6	Interest rate per annum %	INT		10.00
7	Present value	PV		0.00
8	Payment	PMT		0.00
9	Future value	FV		20,000.00
10				
11	Payment Interval			Monthly
12	Payment Toggle	Begin/End		Arrears
13				
14	Answer: Present value			(7,388.14)
15				

There are 108 equal monthly payments to be calculated at the end of the 12-month payment holiday. Figure 7.6 present-values 108 payments of one and finds a factor of 71.62. This then needs to be reduced by a further 12 months. The present value of the cash flow is:

$$= PV((C8/100)/(12/C152), C6, 0, -G9, 0)$$
$$= PV(8\%/12, 12, 0, -71.62, 0)$$
$$= 64.83$$

This calculation could be rephrased as $= -71.62/[1 + (10\%/12)]\wedge12$.

The periodic rental is (A)/(B) $= 92,611.86/64.83 = 1,428.53$.

This is a complex calculation and so the model generates a cash flow of the deal in column G for check purposes. The basis is the 100,000 advance followed by the 11 payments of zero, followed by 120 payments of 1,428.53 and then followed by the final rental of 20,000.

Figure 7.6

Initial factor

	A	B	C	D	E
4					
5		Number of payments	N		108 Rents
6		Interest rate per annum %	INT		10.00
7		Present value	PV		0.00
8		Payment	PMT		-1.00
9		Future value	FV		0.00
10					
11		Payment Interval			Monthly
12		Payment Toggle	Begin/End		Advance
13					
14		Answer: Present value			71.62

The model uses a simple IRR formula in cell G14, which calculates the periodic yield and then multiplies it by 100 and the number of payments per annum. Since the IRR formula is an iterative calculation, a guess of the input yield is used in the formula:

```
=IRR(G18:G138,C8/100/(12/C152))*(12/C152)*100
="Rate Confirmation: "&IF(ROUND(C8,6)=ROUND(G14,6),
"No Errors","Check Cash Flows")
```

The yield is confirmed as 10 per cent and the model shows no errors. With a grid of the rentals and cash flow in place the amortisation is multiplied out. While the capital outstanding increases during the initial 12 months, it is paid off during the rental period such that the capital is completely recovered by the expiry rental.

SUM OF DIGITS

The Sum of Digits or the Rule of 78 method is an approximation to amortisation which is often used for hire purchase (lease purchase or $1 out) rental agreements with final purchase options (see Figure 7.7). The method allocates the interest, and for loans or leases with regular structures it will provide a charges amount which reduces based on the capital outstanding.

The name comes from the fact that $12 + 11 + 10 + ... + 1 = 78$. The example below shows a 12-quarter transaction with 11 quarters outstanding on commencement. The charges are the sum of the factors, which is 66, and

Sum of Digits/Rule of 78

Figure 7.7

	A	B	C	D	E	F	G	H	I
4									
5		N	12		Total Periods	66.00			
6		I	8.0000%		Total Charges	11,246.58			
7		PV	-100,000.00						
8		PMT	0.00						
9		FV	0.00						
10									
11		Frequency	3						
12		Begin/End	1		1=Begin, 0=End				
13									
14		PMT	9,270.55		=PMT(V(12/Frequency),N,PV,FV,Begin_End)				
15									
16			Rental	Int	Capital	Balance		O/S	SYD
17		0	9,270.55	-	9,270.55	(90,729.45)			
18		1	9,270.55	1,874.43	7,396.12	(83,333.33)		11	1,874.43
19		2	9,270.55	1,704.03	7,566.52	(75,766.81)		10	1,704.03
20		3	9,270.55	1,533.63	7,736.92	(68,029.89)		9	1,533.63
21		4	9,270.55	1,363.22	7,907.33	(60,122.56)		8	1,363.22
22		5	9,270.55	1,192.82	8,077.73	(52,044.83)		7	1,192.82
23		6	9,270.55	1,022.42	8,248.13	(43,796.70)		6	1,022.42
24		7	9,270.55	852.01	8,418.53	(35,378.17)		5	852.01
25		8	9,270.55	681.61	8,588.94	(26,789.23)		4	681.61
26		9	9,270.55	511.21	8,759.34	(18,029.89)		3	511.21
27		10	9,270.55	340.81	8,929.74	(9,100.15)		2	340.81
28		11	9,270.55	170.40	9,100.15	0.00		1	170.40
29		12	-	-	-	0.00		-	-
30									
31			111,246.58	11,246.58	100,000.00			66	11,246.58
32									
33		Sum of Digits: n * (n + 1) / 2		66					
34		Period 1: 11/66 * 11,247		16.67%	1,874.43				

the charges are 11,246.58. The first period is therefore $11/66 * 11,246.58$ and the next period $10/66 * 11,246.58$, etc.

There is a quick formula for calculating the factor. This is $N * (N + 1)/2$ where N is the number of payments. As in the amortisation table the capital drops out as the payment minus the interest payable. Again the check constitutes the totals at the bottom which must equate to the capital value, charges and total payable.

Excel has a function called SYD which saves having to calculate the factor. The inputs are cost, salvage value, total periods and current period, and you will obtain the same answers as the manual calculations. Cost is the amount you want to separate into periods such as the total interest payable to be spread over the outstanding periods.

STRAIGHT LINE AND DECLINING BALANCE DEPRECIATION

There are many methods of writing off equipment over successive periods rather than using an actuarial or Sum of Digits method. The simplest is straight line depreciation which divides the equipment less any salvage value by the number of periods and writes it off at an equal amount per period. While you can do this manually, Excel has a function called SL which includes a salvage value to perform this automatically.

The fixed declining balance method computes depreciation at a fixed rate. DB uses the following formulas to calculate depreciation for a period. This method results in a declining amount of depreciation per period that can be factored for the number of periods in the first tax year. The example in Figure 7.8 assumes an acquisition at the end of the sixth month. The formula is:

$$Factor = (cost - total\ accumulated\ depreciation) * rate$$

where:

$$Rate = 1 - ((salvage/cost) \wedge (1/life)),\ rounded\ to\ three\ decimal\ places$$

Depreciation for the first and last periods needs to be calculated separately. For the first period the method uses the formula:

$$Year\ one = Cost * rate * month/12$$

Figure 7.8

Declining balance

	A	B	C	D	E	F	G	H	I
4									
5		Initial cost		1,000,000.00					
6		Salvage value		2,000.00					
7		Rounding		3					
8		Lifetime in years		10					
9		Months in year one		6					
10									
11		Period	SL	Balance	DB	Balance	Factor	DB Depreciation	Balance
12		1	99,800.00	(900,200.00)	231,500.00	(768,500.00)	0.23	231,000.00	(769,000.00)
13		2	99,800.00	(800,400.00)	355,815.50	(412,684.50)	0.46	356,047.00	(412,953.00)
14		3	99,800.00	(700,600.00)	191,072.92	(221,611.58)	0.46	191,197.24	(221,755.76)
15		4	99,800.00	(600,800.00)	102,606.16	(119,005.42)	0.46	102,672.92	(119,082.84)
16		5	99,800.00	(501,000.00)	55,099.51	(63,905.91)	0.46	55,135.36	(63,947.49)
17		6	99,800.00	(401,200.00)	29,588.44	(34,317.47)	0.46	29,607.69	(34,339.80)
18		7	99,800.00	(301,400.00)	15,888.99	(18,428.48)	0.46	15,899.33	(18,440.47)
19		8	99,800.00	(201,600.00)	8,532.39	(9,896.10)	0.46	8,537.94	(9,902.53)
20		9	99,800.00	(101,800.00)	4,581.89	(5,314.20)	0.46	4,584.87	(5,317.66)
21		10	99,800.00	(2,000.00)	2,460.48	(2,853.73)	0.23	1,228.38	(4,089.28)
22		11	-	(2,000.00)	853.73	(2,000.00)	-	2,089.28	(2,000.00)
23		12	-	(2,000.00)	-	(2,000.00)	-	-	(2,000.00)
24		13	-	(2,000.00)	-	(2,000.00)	-	-	(2,000.00)
25		14	-	(2,000.00)	-	(2,000.00)	-	-	(2,000.00)
26		15	-	(2,000.00)	-	(2,000.00)	-	-	(2,000.00)
27									
28			998,000.00		998,000.00			998,000.00	

For the last period, DB uses the formula:

$$Last\ period = ((cost - total\ depreciation\ from\ prior\ periods) * rate * (12 - month))/12$$

The example above shows the formula using the DB function and the same example calculated manually. Both result in a final salvage value of 2,000.

UK DECLINING BALANCE METHOD

The UK tax authorities use a declining balance method based on a fixed percentage of the capital outstanding. For example, plant and machinery generally attract an allowance of 18 per cent per annum, while land and buildings attract 4 per cent per annum or less. Accounting depreciation is replaced with tax depreciation or capital allowances for the purposes of computing the tax payable.

The example in Figure 7.9 shows a 20 per cent reduction each year where the balance is simply multiplied by 20 per cent and added to the balance carried forward. The curve of the depreciation is asymptotic, in that it will mathematically never reach exactly zero. The method gives rise to a 'tail', and one method of writing off the end balance is to allow the full balance to be included after a set number of years. The UK tax authorities have rules for nominating assets as 'short life' and allowing the full allowances within a four-year period.

UK tax depreciation

Figure 7.9

	A	B	C	D	E	F	G
4							
5		Initial cost		1,000,000.00			
6		Rate		18.00%			
7		Life		10.00			
8							
9		Period	DB	Balance		Short Life	Balance
10		1	180,000.00	(820,000.00)		180,000.00	(820,000.00)
11		2	147,600.00	(672,400.00)		147,600.00	(672,400.00)
12		3	121,032.00	(551,368.00)		121,032.00	(551,368.00)
13		4	99,246.24	(452,121.76)		99,246.24	(452,121.76)
14		5	81,381.92	(370,739.84)		81,381.92	(370,739.84)
15		6	66,733.17	(304,006.67)		66,733.17	(304,006.67)
16		7	54,721.20	(249,285.47)		54,721.20	(249,285.47)
17		8	44,871.38	(204,414.09)		44,871.38	(204,414.09)
18		9	36,794.54	(167,619.55)		36,794.54	(167,619.55)
19		10	30,171.52	(137,448.03)		167,619.55	-
20		11	24,740.65	(112,707.39)		-	-
21		12	20,287.33	(92,420.06)		-	-
22		13	16,635.61	(75,784.45)		-	-
23		14	13,641.20	(62,143.25)		-	-
24		15	11,185.78	(50,957.46)		-	-
25		16	9,172.34	(41,785.12)		-	-
26		17	7,521.32	(34,263.80)		-	-
27		18	6,167.48	(28,096.31)		-	-
28		19	5,057.34	(23,038.98)		-	-
29		20	4,147.02	(18,891.96)		-	-
30							
31			981,108.04		-	1,000,000.00	

The short life column includes an `IF` statement to include the previous balance if the period number is equal to the total number of periods. Short life accelerates the depreciation by allowing the balance outstanding in the final period:

```
Cell F17: =IF(B19<$D$7,-G18*$D$6,-G18)
```

DOUBLE DECLINING BALANCE DEPRECIATION

Other tax regimes use double declining with or without the option to switch to straight line depreciation when it becomes advantageous to do so. The relevant function is DDB. Again the method needs a factor which is the rate at which the balance declines. If the factor is omitted, it is assumed to be two (the double declining balance method).

The double declining balance method derives depreciation at an accelerated rate. Depreciation is highest in the first period and decreases in successive periods. The formula used is:

Periodic depreciation = ((*cost* − *salvage*) − *total depreciation from prior periods*) ∗ (*factor*/*life*)

In the first period the calculation is $1,000,000 * 1.8/10 = 180,000$ or 18%. The balance of 820,000 is carried forward and multiplied by 1.8/10 and the result is 147,600.

Figure 7.10

DB and VDB

Period	DDB	Balance	VDB True	SL Comparison	Balance	VDB False	Balance
	Initial cost		1,000,000.00				
	Salvage value		2,000.00				
	Lifetime in years		10.00				
	Double declining factor		1.80				
	VDB declining factor		1.80				
1	180,000.00	(820,000.00)	180,000.00	(91,111.11)	(820,000.00)	180,000.00	(820,000.00)
2	147,600.00	(672,400.00)	147,600.00	(84,050.00)	(672,400.00)	147,600.00	(672,400.00)
3	121,032.00	(551,368.00)	121,032.00	(78,766.86)	(551,368.00)	121,032.00	(551,368.00)
4	99,246.24	(452,121.76)	99,246.24	(75,353.63)	(452,121.76)	99,246.24	(452,121.76)
5	81,381.92	(370,739.84)	81,381.92	(74,147.97)	(370,739.84)	81,381.92	(370,739.84)
6	66,733.17	(304,006.67)	73,747.97	(74,247.97)	(296,991.87)	66,733.17	(304,006.67)
7	54,721.20	(249,285.47)	73,747.97	(74,414.64)	(223,243.91)	54,721.20	(249,285.47)
8	44,871.38	(204,414.09)	73,747.97	(74,747.97)	(149,495.94)	44,871.38	(204,414.09)
9	36,794.54	(167,619.55)	73,747.97	(75,747.97)	(75,747.97)	36,794.54	(167,619.55)
10	30,171.52	(137,448.03)	73,747.97	-	(2,000.00)	30,171.52	(137,448.03)
11	-	(137,448.03)	-	-	(2,000.00)	-	(137,448.03)
12	-	(137,448.03)	-	-	(2,000.00)	-	(137,448.03)
13	-	(137,448.03)	-	-	(2,000.00)	-	(137,448.03)
14	-	(137,448.03)	-	-	(2,000.00)	-	(137,448.03)
15	-	(137,448.03)	-	-	(2,000.00)	-	(137,448.03)
	862,551.97		998,000.00			862,551.97	

You can change the factor if you do not want to use exactly the double declining balance method. The US tax system uses a method of double declining balance while allowing a switch to straight line when the straight line depreciation is higher than the double declining balance. The VDB function can also be used for the double declining balance and there is a switch (true or false) to allow you to choose whether to change to straight line depreciation or not. Figure 7.10 provides an example of both functions with the switches set to true and false. Column F calculates the straight line depreciation on the remaining balance to show why the function continues to choose the double declining balance. When the flag is set to true the function changes to straight line in period 6 and depreciates down to the salvage value of 2,000.

FRENCH DEPRECIATION

The French accounting system uses prorated depreciation when equipment is purchased partway through a period. The functions are in the Analysis ToolPak, so if you see an error ensure that the ToolPak is installed by checking in the Excel options under Add-Ins.

The specific functions are:

AMORDEGRC *AMORtissement DÉGRessif Comptabilité*
AMORLINC *AMORtissement LINeaire Comptabilité*

The syntax of the first function is:

AMORDEGRC(cost,date_purchased,first_period,salvage,period,rate,basis)

The date inputs must be real dates and not periods since the function uses dates as numbers and not text. The variables are as follows:

Date purchased is the date of the purchase of the asset.
First period is the date of the end of the first period such as the accounting year end.
Period is the current period.
Rate is the rate of depreciation.
Basis is the year basis to be used in the same way as bond functions (see Chapter 4) as below:
0 = 360 days (NASD method)
1 = Actual dates
3 = 365 days in a year (leap years ignored)
4 = 360 days in a year (European method)

The function prorates the first year and then uses a factor (25 per cent based on 10 years) to write off the equipment. The depreciation coefficients are based on a life of 1/depreciation percentage. In the example this is $1/10\% = 10$. The factors are:

Between 3 and 4 = 1.5
Between 5 and 6 = 2
More than 6 = 2.5

The first calculation is 1,000,000 * 25% * percentage remaining of year under the NASD convention. In the next year the balance is brought forward and multiplied by 25 per cent. In the last periods the balance is written off using the straight line method (see Figure 7.11).

The cash flow uses EDATE to progress the dates. The correct method is to fix the start dates and multiply out the number of periods from the start date:

```
=EDATE($E$7,B15*$E$11)
```

Figure 7.11

French depreciation

Cost			1,000,000.00				
Date purchased			30-Jun-20	AMORDEGRC AMORtissement DEGRessif Comptabilite			
Year end			31-Dec-20	AMORLINC AMORtissement LINeaire Comptabilite			
Salvage value			2,000.00				
Depreciation rate			10.00%				
Actual basis (see above)			1				
Interval			12				

Period	Date	AMORDEGRC	Balance	AMORLINC	Balance	Variance
0	31-Dec-20	125,683.00	(874,317.00)	50,273.22	(949,726.78)	75,409.78
1	31-Dec-21	218,579.00	(655,738.00)	100,000.00	(849,726.78)	118,579.00
2	31-Dec-22	163,934.00	(491,804.00)	100,000.00	(749,726.78)	63,934.00
3	31-Dec-23	122,951.00	(368,853.00)	100,000.00	(649,726.78)	22,951.00
4	31-Dec-24	92,213.00	(276,640.00)	100,000.00	(549,726.78)	(7,787.00)
5	31-Dec-25	69,160.00	(207,480.00)	100,000.00	(449,726.78)	(30,840.00)
6	31-Dec-26	51,870.00	(155,610.00)	100,000.00	(349,726.78)	(48,130.00)
7	31-Dec-27	38,902.00	(116,708.00)	100,000.00	(249,726.78)	(61,098.00)
8	31-Dec-28	58,354.00	(58,354.00)	100,000.00	(149,726.78)	(41,646.00)
9	31-Dec-29	58,354.00	-	100,000.00	(49,726.78)	(41,646.00)
10	31-Dec-30	-	-	47,726.78	(2,000.00)	(47,726.78)
11	31-Dec-31	-	-	-	(2,000.00)	-
12	31-Dec-32	-	-	-	(2,000.00)	-
13	31-Dec-33	-	-	-	(2,000.00)	-
14	31-Dec-34	-	-	-	(2,000.00)	-
15	31-Dec-35	-	-	-	(2,000.00)	-
		1,000,000.00		998,000.00		2,000.00

The AMORLINC function is a prorated straight line function which in this example takes approximately 50 per cent in the first year and then depreciates equally for the following periods. The last period contains the balance of the first year. Again the function has a switch for selecting the formalised days in the month and year:

AMORLINC(cost,date_purchased,first_period,salvage,period,rate,basis)
```
=AMORLINC($E$5,$E$6,$C$14,$E$8,B14,$E$9,$E$10)
```

This is a comparison of the different methods (see Figure 7.12). As you can see, the choice of method exerts a significant effect on the speed of write-off of the underlying asset.

Comparison

Figure 7.12

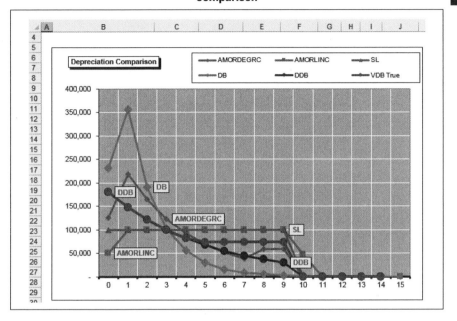

EXERCISE

Write a model to calculate and amortise a structured loan at a rate of 10 per cent. The cash flow is:

Six rentals of 1,000 on signing
Six further monthly rentals of 1,000
Sixty further rentals of X starting in the next month after the initial rentals
A final rental payable on expiry of 20,000.00

The model will need to use the factors method to find the subsequent rental X and a cash flow with an IRR could be used to check the final rental.

SUMMARY

The key to successful amortisation and depreciation calculations is setting out the model as a grid and using IF statements or flags to allow or disallow rentals and expiry rentals in particular periods. Amortisation methods and the Sum of Digits method can be used to split loan payments into interest and principal for accounting purposes. In addition, there are a number of depreciation methods for accounting or tax purposes which use a variety of declining balance methods to deal effectively with remaining balances.

8

Swaps

File: MfMaths3e_08.xls

117

Swaps

DEFINITIONS

Swaps can be used to manage financial risk and are essentially agreements between two parties to pay each other a series of cash flows over a specified time period based on a fixed sum of money. Somebody could borrow fixed but may prefer floating and another party may borrow floating but prefer fixed. This may seem an odd thing for each party to undertake, but this chapter will show that there can be advantages to both parties in entering into swap arrangements. To show the size of the market since their introduction in the early 1980s, swaps have expanded rapidly into a multi-trillion-dollar market. Total outstanding interest rate swaps currently exceed several hundred trillion dollars. Out of this total, transactions denominated in US dollars account for roughly 50 per cent of all interest rate swaps outstanding.

Swaps are typically divided into:

- single currency (interest rate or plain vanilla);
- cross currency (currency).

Interest rate swaps are contracts between two parties to exchange a variable interest rate payment for a fixed interest rate payment for a specific maturity on a notional amount of principal (see Figure 8.1). The underlying transaction remains in place and the cash flows are swapped for a specific period. The elements are as follows:

- Notional principal, which is a reference amount used only to calculate interest expense. No principal usually changes hands and the cash flows for interest are overlaid and netted.
- Maturities of swaps contracts usually range from two to fifteen years.
- Most frequently used variable interest rate is the London Interbank Offer Rate (LIBOR).

Interest rate swaps are generally priced at a specific fixed rate (swap rate) which counterbalances the implied forward interest of some floating rate index. It is also possible to price an interest rate swap 'off-market' and compensate for the discrepancy with an upfront cash payment from one party to the other. Like any commodity, a swap has a bid side and an offer side which are determined by market demand. The bid side is the fixed rate a market maker in a bank will pay to receive LIBOR. The offer side is the fixed rate a market maker will receive to pay LIBOR. The bid side swap rate is lower than the offer side swap rate in order to produce a margin. The difference between the two is called the bid–offer spread.

A swap spread is the margin above the underlying treasury where the swap rate is set. A 10-year swap, bid at 7.56 per cent when the 10-year treasury is yielding 7.22 per cent, has a swap spread of 34 basis points (7.56% − 7.22%).

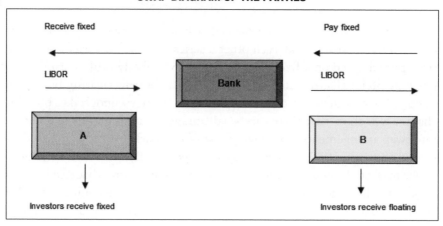

Figure 8.1 — SWAP DIAGRAM OF THE PARTIES

Swap rates in US dollars are often quoted simply as a spread to the comparable treasury (i.e. bid = +34, offer = +39).

The pricing conventions are similar to elsewhere in the money market:

Period	Convention	Description
Days	Actual	Actual number of calendar days
	30 (European)	Day 31 is changed to 30
	30 (US)	If the second day is 31 but the first date is not 31 or 30, then the day is not changed from 31 to 30
Year	365	Assumes 365 days in the year
	360	Assumes 360
	Actual	Actual including leap years

The usual combinations for transferring from one convention to another are:

- US (NASD) 30/360
- Actual/actual
- Actual/360
- Actual/365
- European 30/360

One obvious difficulty to be overcome in pricing a swap would appear to be the fact that the future stream of floating rate payments to be made by one counterparty is unknown at the time the swap is being priced. No one can predict with absolute certainty what the six-month sterling LIBOR rate will be in six months' time or twelve months' time. Nevertheless, the capital markets do possess a considerable body of information about the relationship between interest rates and future periods of time and can attempt to price accordingly.

In many countries, there is a large and liquid market in government interest-bearing securities issued. These securities pay coupon interest on a periodic basis and are issued with a wide range of maturities. Principal is re-paid only at maturity and at any given point in time the market values these securities based on current interest rates.

It is possible to plot a graph of the yields of such securities having regard to their varying maturities. This graph, discussed in the next chapter, is known generally as a yield curve as the relationship between future interest rates and time. A chart showing the yield of securities displaying the same characteristics as government securities is known as the par coupon yield curve. The classic example of a par coupon yield curve is the US treasury yield curve. A different kind of security from a government security or similar interest-bearing note is the zero coupon bond. The zero coupon bond does not pay interest at periodic intervals and is issued at a discount from its par or face value. When redeemed at par the accumulated discount which is then repaid represents compounded or 'rolled-up' interest. A graph of the internal rate of return (IRR) of zero cou-pon bonds over a range of maturities is known as the zero coupon yield curve and will be used in valuation later in the chapter.

Finally, at any time the market is prepared to quote an investor forward interest rates. The 12-month forward deposit rate is a mathematically de-rived rate which reflects an arbitrage relationship between current (or spot) interest rates and forward interest rates. Therefore, the 12-month forward interest rate will always be the precise rate of interest which eliminates any arbitrage profit. The forward interest rate will leave the investor indiffer-ent as to whether he invests for 12 months and then reinvests for a further 12 months at the 12-month forward interest rate, or whether he invests for a 24-month period at today's 24-month deposit rate.

The pricing picture is now complete. Since the floating rate payments due under the swap can be calculated as explained above, the fixed-rate payments will be of such an amount that when they are deducted from the floating rate payments and the net cash flow for each period is discounted at the appropri-ate rate given by the zero coupon yield curve, the net present value of the swap will be zero. It might also be noted that the actual fixed rate produced by the above calculation represents the par coupon rate payable for that maturity if the stream of fixed-rate payments due under the swap are viewed as being a hypothetical fixed-rate security. This could be proved by using the fixed-rate bond valuation techniques from previous chapters.

Any upfront payments are generally made two days after the trade date. Interest payments are made on the period end-date. On that date, rather than both parties making full payments, the party owing the largest amount will make a net payment. Floating rates are usually set two days in advance of the period begin date.

HOW SWAPS SAVE MONEY

Consider the following statements:

- A company with the highest credit rating, AA, will pay less to raise funds under identical terms and conditions than a less creditworthy company with a lower rating, say BB. The extra borrowing premium paid by a BB company ('credit quality spread') is greater in relation to fixed interest rate borrowings than it is for floating rate borrowings.
- The counterparty making fixed-rate payments in a swap is predominantly the less creditworthy participant.
- Companies have been able to lower their nominal funding costs by using swaps in conjunction with credit quality spreads.

The above statements are fully consistent and describe the mechanics of swap transactions based on comparative advantage and information. The essential reason is lowering the cost of borrowings, as will be shown in the worked examples later in the chapter.

- Names and credit quality where borrowers may be better known in some markets than in others.
- Differences in required spreads since investors in fixed-rate securities demand a higher credit spread as credit quality falls than investors in floating rate markets.
- Capital markets operate independently of each other and are governed by the economics of supply and demand. Some markets may be 'top heavy' with different types of debt.

Other theories provided from economics include the theory of comparative advantage and asymmetric or incomplete information.

Theory of comparative advantage

Swaps provide a 'comparative advantage' in a particular and different credit market, and an advantage in one market is used to obtain an equivalent advantage in a different market to which access was otherwise denied. The

AA company therefore raises funds in the floating rate market where it has an advantage, an advantage which is also possessed by company BB in the alternative fixed-rate market.

The mechanism of a swap allows each company to exploit its advantage in one market in order to produce interest rate savings in a different market to the benefit of both parties. The international capital markets are, however, fully mobile and companies can raise funds in different markets. In the absence of barriers to capital flows, theory suggests that arbitrage would eliminate any comparative advantage that exists within such markets, and therefore this theory cannot explain the continued existence of the markets.

Asymmetric information

While capital markets are thought to be efficient, there may also exist certain information asymmetries. A company will and should choose to issue short-term floating rate debt and swap this debt into fixed-rate funding as compared with its other financing options if:

■ it had non-public information, which would suggest that its own credit quality spread (the difference between the cost of fixed and floating rate debt) would be lower in the future than the market expectation;

■ it anticipates higher risk-free interest rates in the future than does the market and is more sensitive (i.e. risk averse) to such changes than the market generally;

■ in this situation the company is able to exploit its information asymmetry by issuing short-term floating rate debt and to protect itself against future interest rate risk by swapping such floating rate debt into fixed-rate debt.

ADVANTAGES OF SWAPS

The general benefits for companies can be summarised as:

■ Obtain lower cost funding.
■ Hedge interest rate exposure and manage risk.
■ Obtain higher yielding investment assets.
■ Create types of investment assets not otherwise obtainable.
■ Implement overall asset or liability management strategies.
■ Take speculative positions in relation to future movements in interest rates.

The advantages of interest rate swaps include the following:

- A floating-to-fixed swap increases the certainty of an issuer's future obligations.

- Swapping from fixed to floating rate may save the issuer money if interest rates decline.

- Swapping allows issuers to revise their debt profile to take advantage of current or expected future market conditions.

- Interest rate swaps are a financial tool that potentially can help issuers lower the amount of debt service.

TERMINATING INTEREST RATE SWAPS

At inception, the net present value of the aggregate cash flows that comprise an interest rate swap will be zero. As time passes, however, this will cease to be the case, since the shape of the yield curves used to price the swap initially will change over time. Assume, for example, that shortly after an interest rate swap has been completed there is an increase in forward interest rates: the forward yield curve rises. Since the fixed-rate payments due under the swap are, by definition, fixed, this change in the prevailing interest rate environment will affect future floating rate payments only since the market expects that the future floating rate payments due under the swap will be higher than those originally expected on inception. This benefit will accrue to the fixed-rate payer under the swap and will represent a cost to the floating rate payer. If the new net cash flows due under the swap are computed and if these are discounted at the appropriate new zero coupon rate for each future period (i.e. reflecting the current zero coupon yield curve and not the original zero coupon yield curve), the positive net present value result reflects how the value of the swap to the fixed-rate payer has risen from zero at inception. This demonstrates how the value of the swap to the floating rate payer has declined from zero to a negative amount.

The above example marks the interest rate swap to market. If, having done this, the floating rate payer wishes to terminate the swap with the fixed-rate payer's agreement, then the derived positive net present value figure represents the termination payment that will have to be paid to the fixed-rate payer. Alternatively, if the floating rate payer wishes to cancel the swap by entering into a reverse swap with a new counterparty for the remaining term of the original swap, the net present value figure represents the payment that the floating rate payer will have to make to the new counterparty in order to enter into a swap which precisely mirrors the terms and conditions of the original swap.

IMPLICIT CREDIT RISK

Since any interest rate swap involves joint obligations to exchange cash flows, there is a degree of credit risk implicit in the swap. A swap is a notional principal contract and therefore no credit risk arises in respect of the principal, unlike a loan. The cash flows to be exchanged under an interest rate swap on each settlement date are typically 'netted' (or offset) as simply the difference between fixed and floating rates of interest, and again the credit risk to the bank is reduced. The periodic cash flows under a swap will, by definition, be smaller than the periodic cash flows due under a comparable loan.

WORKED SINGLE CURRENCY SWAP

The amount is 100 million. Company A can borrow fixed at 8 per cent floating at LIBOR plus 20 basis points. On the other hand, company B can borrow fixed at 8 per cent floating at LIBOR plus 40 basis points. A would prefer a floating rate and B would prefer fixed.

The relative advantage is $(8.0\% - 7.0\%) - (0.40\% - 0.20\%) = 0.80\%$ which can be split between the parties by swapping the interest payments. The model builds up the cash flows to show the position of the parties at each stage (see Figure 8.2).

Initial inputs

Figure 8.2

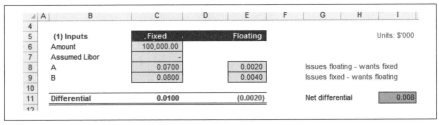

	B	C		E		G	H	I
(1) Inputs		.Fixed .		Floating			Units: $'000	
Amount		100,000.00						
Assumed Libor		-						
A		0.0700		0.0020		Issues floating - wants fixed		
B		0.0800		0.0040		Issues fixed - wants floating		
Differential		0.0100		(0.0020)		Net differential	0.008	

Company B negotiates to pay the bank 7.30 per cent and the bank agrees to pay company A 7.15 per cent and takes 0.15 per cent as a margin. A pays fixed 7 per cent and receives 7.15 per cent, making a benefit of 0.15 per cent. Given that the alternative floating rate is LIBOR plus 0.20 per cent, this makes a total benefit on floating rate of 0.35 per cent (see Figure 8.3).

On the other hand, company B pays LIBOR plus 0.40 per cent to investors and 7.30 per cent fixed to the bank. In return it receives LIBOR and the net position is a fixed rate of 7.70 per cent against the alternative fixed rate of 8 per cent.

Figure 8.3

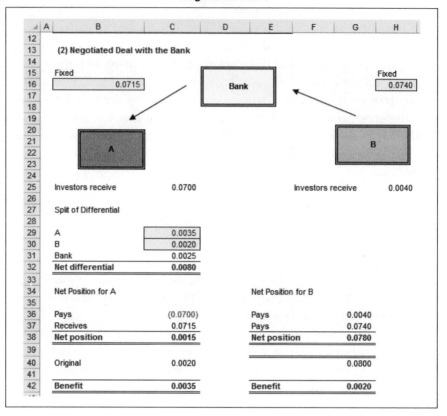

Negotiated deal

The full set of cash flows in Figure 8.4 shows the netting off of LIBOR and the result that company A pays a fixed and company B pays a floating rate. The benefit is split 0.35 per cent to company A and 0.30 per cent to company B, and the balance of 0.15 per cent is retained by the bank.

As the differential in the rates changes, the net benefit reduces or increases. As company A fixed rate and company B floating rate increase, the potential savings decline based on the bank offered rate (see Figure 8.5).

VALUATION

Valuation of an interest rate swap requires the calculation of the net present value. The correct rates to use for each of the cash flows are the zero coupon rates. The problem is that the future floating rate cash flows are not yet known. The solution is to calculate the forward-to-forward interest rates for each cash flow interval and then to discount each cash flow at this rate.

Full cash flows

Figure 8.4

	A	B	C	D	E	F	G
44							
45		(3) Cash Flows					
46							
47			A		Balance		B
48							
49		Investors receive	(0.0700)				(0.0040)
50							
51		Bank pays A	0.0715		(0.0715)		
52							
53		B pays Bank			0.0740		(0.0740)
54							
55		A pays Bank LIBOR	-		-		
56							
57		Bank pays B LIBOR			-		-
58							
59		Net position	0.0015		0.0025		(0.0780)
60							
61		Cost without Swap	(0.0020)				(0.0800)
62							
63		Benefit	0.0035		0.0025		0.0020
64							
65		Total saving	0.0080				
66							
67		Cost Saving (pa)	350.0000		250.0000		200.0000

Sensitivity

Figure 8.5

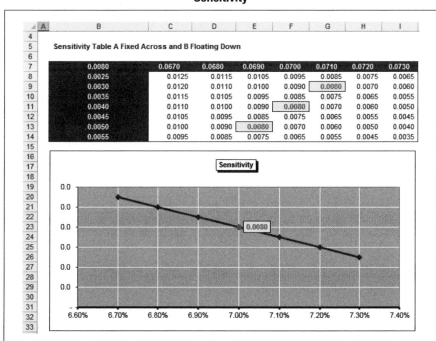

	A	B	C	D	E	F	G	H	I
4									
5		Sensitivity Table A Fixed Across and B Floating Down							
6									
7		0.0080		0.0670	0.0680	0.0690	0.0700	0.0710	0.0720	0.0730
8		0.0025		0.0125	0.0115	0.0105	0.0095	0.0085	0.0075	0.0065
9		0.0030		0.0120	0.0110	0.0100	0.0090	0.0080	0.0070	0.0060
10		0.0035		0.0115	0.0105	0.0095	0.0085	0.0075	0.0065	0.0055
11		0.0040		0.0110	0.0100	0.0090	0.0080	0.0070	0.0060	0.0050
12		0.0045		0.0105	0.0095	0.0085	0.0075	0.0065	0.0055	0.0045
13		0.0050		0.0100	0.0090	0.0080	0.0070	0.0060	0.0050	0.0040
14		0.0055		0.0095	0.0085	0.0075	0.0065	0.0055	0.0045	0.0035

Figure 8.6

Valuation

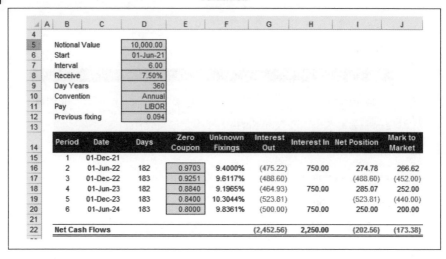

	A	B	C	D	E	F	G	H	I	J
4										
5		Notional Value		10,000.00						
6		Start		01-Jun-21						
7		Interval		6.00						
8		Receive		7.50%						
9		Day Years		360						
10		Convention		Annual						
11		Pay		LIBOR						
12		Previous fixing		0.094						
13										
14		Period	Date	Days	Zero Coupon	Unknown Fixings	Interest Out	Interest In	Net Position	Mark to Market
15		1	01-Dec-21							
16		2	01-Jun-22	182	0.9703	9.4000%	(475.22)	750.00	274.78	266.62
17		3	01-Dec-22	183	0.9251	9.6117%	(488.60)		(488.60)	(452.00)
18		4	01-Jun-23	182	0.8840	9.1965%	(464.93)	750.00	285.07	252.00
19		5	01-Dec-23	183	0.8400	10.3044%	(523.81)		(523.81)	(440.00)
20		6	01-Jun-24	183	0.8000	9.8361%	(500.00)	750.00	250.00	200.00
21										
22		Net Cash Flows					(2,452.56)	2,250.00	(202.56)	(173.38)

The objective here is to value the swap during period 2. The model in Figure 8.6 uses EDATE to derive the number of days between dates. The unknowns in period 2 are calculated as

```
Cell F17: = (E16 / E17-1)*($D$9 / D17)
         = (0.9703 / 0.9251)*(360/183)
         = 9.6117%
Cell G17: = -$D$5*F17*D17 / $D$9
         = -10,000*9.6117%*183/360 = 488.60
```

The interest in is the principal multiplied by an annual interest rate of 7.50 per cent. The net position is the sum of the interest out and in for each period. The overall position is therefore 173.38 negative.

CROSS CURRENCY SWAP

A cross currency swap is an agreement between two parties to exchange principal amounts in two different currencies, to pay interest based on those amounts during some period of time, and to re-exchange the principal amounts at maturity. The principal amounts in each currency remain constant throughout the transaction, and interest payments are a function of the fixed or floating rates in each currency.

The customer is able to lock in a specific exchange rate for the life of an asset or liability. The issuer is able to obtain lower-rate funding in currencies where it perhaps has weaker market recognition. The swap provides access to funds in currencies where an end-user has already saturated the primary debt markets.

The currency swap market has evolved as an extension of forward currency exchange contracts. US dollars account for more than 30 per cent of all currency swap notional amounts, up from one-third in the 1990s. Japanese yen notional amounts to one-fifth of all transactions. No other currency constitutes more than 10 per cent of the market.

Cross currency swaps are generally priced at a specific rate or at some spread to a major index in both currencies. It is also possible to price a currency swap 'off-market' and compensate for the discrepancy with an upfront cash payment from one party to the other. Any upfront payments are generally made two days after the trade date. The exchange rate is set as part of the trade. Interest payments are made on the period end-date and floating rates are usually set two days in advance of the period date.

The main difference between a single currency and multi-currency swap is that the principal amounts may be exchanged on inception and must then be re-exchanged on termination. Where the principal is involved, the risks are greater since there are an interest rate risk, currency position and default risk. This means that credit quality needs to be considered in more detail.

WORKED EXAMPLE

This example is a fixed multi-currency swap but deals could be negotiated fixed to floating or floating to fixed (see Figure 8.7).

Inputs

Figure 8.7

	A	B	C	D	E	F	G	H	I
4									
5		(1) Inputs	Domestic		Overseas				
6		Currency	GBP		EUR				
7		Amount	80,000.00		120,000.00				
8		Assumed Libor	-						
9		A	0.0600		0.0450		Issues domestic - wants overseas		
10		B	0.0700		0.0475		Issues overseas - wants domestic		
11									
12		Differential	0.0100		(0.0025)		Net differential		0.0075

Company A can borrow in sterling at 6 per cent or 4.5 per cent in euros, whereas company B has the reverse position of 7 per cent and 4.75 per cent. The net difference is 0.75 per cent which provides the impetus for the swap. Company A has a relative advantage in sterling and company B can borrow at not much more than company A in the overseas currency. They agree through the bank to enter into the swap for a fixed period.

The bank pays company A 6 per cent of the 80 million sterling and receives 4.35 per cent on euros. The bank pays company B the 4.35 per cent on euros and receives 6.25 per cent on sterling. The overall benefit is split evenly between the parties as above with each party receiving 0.25 per cent (see Figure 8.8).

| Figure 8.8 | Multi-currency swap structure |

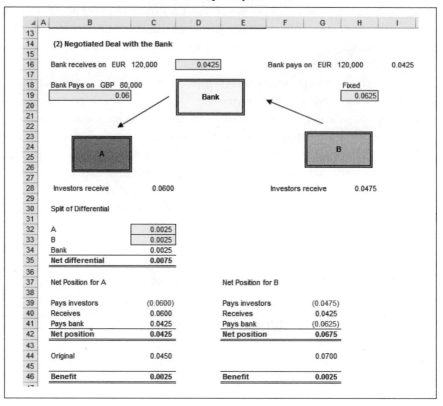

Company A achieves a rate of 4.25 per cent in euros against a cost without the swap of 4.50 per cent. On the other side, company B achieves a sterling rate of 6.75 per cent against a quoted rate of 7 per cent (see Figure 8.9).

SWAPTIONS

A swaption is an option to enter into an interest rate swap with other parties at some future date. Generally one party sells and the other party buys the right to pay or to receive at a specific fixed rate in a standard fixed/floating swap:

- A call swaption is the right but not the obligation to receive a fixed rate.
- A put swaption is the right but not the obligation to pay a fixed rate.

A swaption can be exercised only once, but the conditions under which the buyer can invoke the swap vary depending on the type of put or call swaption:

- European swaption is exercisable on a single date at some point in the future. On that date the owner has the right to enter a swap for a pre-specified term.

Summary of cash flows

Figure 8.9

	A	B	C	D	E	F	G
48							
49		(3) Cash Flows					
50							
51			A		Balance		B
52							
53		Investors receive	(0.0600)				(0.0475)
54							
55		Bank pays A	0.0600		(0.0600)		
56							
57		B pays Bank			0.0625		(0.0625)
58							
59		A pays Bank	(0.0425)		0.0425		
60							
61		Bank pays B LIBOR			(0.0425)		0.0425
62							
63		Net position	(0.0425)		0.0025		(0.0675)
64							
65		Cost without Swap	(0.0450)				-0.07
66							
67		Benefit	0.0025		0.0025		0.0025
68							
69		Total saving	0.0075				
70							
71		Cost Saving (pa)	200.00		200.00		200.00

- Fixed term American swaption is exercisable on any date during an exercise period. At any time during that period, the owner can invoke a swap for a pre-specified term.

- Contingent American swaption is exercisable on any date during an exercise period. At any time during that period, the owner can invoke a swap that begins on the exercise date and ends at a pre-specified maturity date. Thus, the term of the swap is contingent upon the date on which the swaption is exercised.

- Bermudan swaption, like an American swaption, can have either a fixed or a contingent term, but is not exercisable at any time. Instead, the owner of a Bermudan swaption can only invoke the swap periodically (e.g. every six months on a bond's coupon payment dates).

A customer is able to lock in the right to pay and to receive future interest rates for an upfront payment. Market swaptions began to be traded actively in 1987. Since that time, the market has grown quickly and has more than doubled in size nearly every two years.

EXERCISE

Value the cash flows for the floating side of this swap. The client has provided this information for the annual matched cash flows and wants to know whether the swap provides positive benefits.

Item	Input
Notional value	10,000.00
Start	01–Sept-20
Maturity	01–Sept-28 (8 years)
Interval	12 months
Receive	8.50%
Day years	360.00
Convention	Annual
Pay	LIBOR
Previous fixing	7.90%

In addition, the yields for zero coupon bonds are:

Period	Date	Zero Rate
1	01–Sep-21	8.0000%
2	01–Sep-22	8.1000%
3	01–Sep-23	8.2000%
4	01–Sep-24	8.3000%
5	01–Sep-25	8.4000%
6	01–Sep-26	8.5000%
7	01–Sep-27	8.6000%
8	01–Sep-28	8.7000%

SUMMARY

Swaps are one method of managing interest rate risk by exchanging cash flows with counterparties for mutual gain. Single currency and multi-currency swaps deal with interest rates and cross currencies, respectively, and the examples in this chapter build up the various cash flows and demonstrate the benefits to either party. Valuations are based on the future cash flows compared against zero coupons as an alternative instrument.

9

Forward interest rates

File: MFMaths3e_09.xls

DEFINITIONS

This chapter deals with interest instruments and models of future interest rates and pricing. Swaps are one way of controlling risk on interest rates; interest rate agreements provide another method of reducing future uncertainty by controlling funding costs.

For example, if a treasurer needed to borrow money in six months' time and fix the rate of interest now, he would have the choice of:

- borrowing now and investing the funds until needed;
- investing now and funding by borrowing.

This may not be the best use of company funds since it could use up limited company credit lines and will show as a liability on the balance sheet. The alternative is for a bank or a third party to initiate the transaction and carry the risk using its credit lines. This means that there must be a break-even or zero-gain position from borrowing or investing first. If there were a gain from either element first, this would create an arbitrage or trading position where a profit could be made from following one strategy over another. Arbitrage can be defined as the simultaneous buying and selling of the same commodity or foreign exchange in two or more markets to take advantage of price differentials.

EXAMPLE FORWARD RATES

A bank borrows 1,000,000 at a fixed rate of 5 per cent from the market over six months. The interest payable is 25,000. It invests the funds at 4.75 per cent over three months and receives 11,875 in interest. The cost so far is therefore 25,000 minus 11,875 and a net value of 13,125 (25,000 − 11,875). So that the bank does not lose money, it has to place the deposit plus interest at a rate which will pay the 25,000 interest on the loan due at the end of the six-month period. The example figures use a 30/360-day year (see Figure 9.1).

The break-even point formula is:

$$Net\ costs/(Principal\ +\ Earnings) * (360/Days\ in\ Period) * 100$$
$$= 13,125/(1,011,875) * (360/90) * 100 = 5.19\ per\ cent$$

Figure 9.1

Forward rate mathematics

	A	B	C	D	E	F
4						
5		Date Today		1-January-2020		
6		Amount		1,000,000.00		
7		Short rate – buy	3.00	5.00		
8		Short rate – sell		4.75		
9		Long rate – buy	6.00	5.00		
10		Long rate – sell		5.75		
11		Annual day convention		360.00		
12						
13		Short date		1-April-2020		
14		Days 360		90.00		
15		Long date		1-July-2020		
16		Days 360		180.00		
17						
18		Interest cost		(25,000.00)		
19		Reinvest		11,875.00		
20		Difference		(13,125.00)		
21						
22		Breakeven		5.19		
23		Extra		13,125.00		
24						

	Period	Date	Cashflow	Extra	Cumulative
25					
26	1	01-Jan-20	1,000,000.00	-	1,000,000.00
27	2	01-Feb-20	-	-	1,000,000.00
28	3	01-Mar-20	11,875.00	-	1,011,875.00
29	4	01-Apr-20	-	-	1,011,875.00
30	5	01-May-20	-	-	1,011,875.00
31	6	01-Jun-20	(25,000.00)	13,125.00	1,000,000.00
32	7	01-Jul-20	-	-	1,000,000.00
33	Total		986,875.00	13,125.00	1,000,000.00

This formula calculates the loan rate and the same methodology works equally well for deposits. Here you deposit long and borrow short and it should provide the same result of a zero-sum game. There is a formula for working out the figure required directly:

$$Forward = \frac{1}{(Time2 - Time1)} * \frac{(Time2 * Rate2) - (Time1 * Rate1)}{1 + \frac{(Time1 * Rate1)}{36,000}}$$

$Time1$ = short period in days

$Time2$ = long period in days

$Rate1$ = short-period interest rate

$Rate2$ = long-period interest rate

The tricky part is choosing the correct bid/offer rates. In the case of a forward-to-forward deposit:

- Rate1 = market offered rate (5 per cent)
- Rate2 = market bid rate (4.75 per cent)

In the case of the original example of a forward-to-forward loan (see Figure 9.2), the positions are reversed:

- Rate1 = market bid rate (4.75 per cent)
- Rate2 = market offered rate (5 per cent)

Forward rate formula

Figure 9.2

	A	B	C	D	E	F	G	H	I
4									
5		Date Today				01-Jan-20			
6		Amount				1,000,000.00			
7		Short rate - buy (offer)		3.00		5.00			
8		Short rate - sell (bid)				4.75			
9		Long rate - buy (offer)		6.00		5.00			
10		Long rate - sell (bid)				4.75			
11		Annual day convention				360.00			
12									
13		Short date				1-April-2020			
14		Short days 360				90			
15		Long date				1-July-2020			
16		Long days 360				180			
17									
18		Forward forward deposit				4.44			
19		Forward forward loan				5.19			
20									
21		Period	Date	Cashflow	Extra	Cumulative	Cashflow	Extra	Cumulative
22		1	01-Jan-20	1,000,000.00	-	1,000,000.00	(1,000,000.00)	-	(1,000,000.00)
23		2	01-Feb-20	-	-	1,000,000.00	-	-	(1,000,000.00)
24		3	01-Mar-20	11,875.00	-	1,011,875.00	(12,500.00)	-	(1,012,500.00)
25		4	01-Apr-20	-	-	1,011,875.00	-	-	(1,012,500.00)
26		5	01-May-20	-	-	1,011,875.00	-	-	(1,012,500.00)
27		6	01-Jun-20	(25,000.00)	13,125.00	1,000,000.00	23,750.00	(11,250.00)	(1,000,000.00)
28		7	01-Jul-20	-	-	1,000,000.00	-	-	(1,000,000.00)
29		Total		986,875.00	13,125.00	1,000,000.00	(988,750.00)	(11,250.00)	(1,000,000.00)

The left-hand side of the schedule shows the original example of a loan and the right-hand side a deposit forward. The forward-to-forward loan is calculated as:

$$Forward\_Loan = \frac{1}{(180-90)} * \frac{(180*5.0)-(90*4.75)}{1+\dfrac{(90*4.75)}{36,000}} = 5.19\%$$

In the case of the deposit:

$$Forward\_Deposit = \frac{1}{(180-90)} * \frac{(180*4.75)-(90*5.0)}{1+\dfrac{(90*5.0)}{36,000}} = 4.44\%$$

The cash flow confirms that the rates are correct. The 13,125 is calculated as the loan plus the deposit interest at the forward rate of 5.19 per cent. The deposit interest includes the loan plus the loan payment at 4.44 per cent. The figures prove that, whichever route is taken, the final figure is 1,000,000.

HEDGING PRINCIPLES

The previous section shows the basic forward calculations which can be combined to provide basic hedging. Suppose a treasurer wanted to borrow 3,000,000 in six months and to fix the rate today. The current spot rate is 5 per cent and the six-month rate is being quoted at 5.25 per cent. If no action is taken and rates go down, then the company is better off and the opposite is true if rates rise. In order to remove the uncertainty, a hedge can be constructed so that as rates increase and the interest charge is greater, the hedge will produce a profit. If rates fall, the hedge will lose money resulting in an overall zero-gain position.

The example in Figure 9.3 sets out the inputs to the model with the dates, prices and the amounts for variation. The chosen hedge is a future as described in more detail in the next chapter. With futures you need to purchase predetermined contract amounts, and here they are notional units of 1,000,000. The formula for calculating the number of required contracts is:

Cell D16:   =INT((Amount * No. of days)/
(Contract size * Contract time period))
$$= Integer[(3,000,000 * 182)/(1,000,000 * 90)] = 6$$

Figure 9.3   **Hedging method**

	Months	Date	Spot	Interest	Buy/Sell	Price	Cash flow

Loan amount: 3,000,000.00
Notional contract size: 1,000,000.00
Contract time period: 90.00
Year days basis: 360.00
Initial contract margin: 1,000.00
Variation (per tick): 25.00
Start date: 01-Jan-20
No of days: 182.00
Current rate: 5.00
Increased June spot: 6.00

Result
Net interest payment: (76,000.00)
Interest rate %: 5.01
Gain/(loss): (0.01)

6 month forward: 5.25
Inc 6 month forward: 6.25

No of contracts: 6.00
Initial margin payment: 6,000.00
Contract price: 94.75
June contract price: 93.75

Quote: 100 – annualised forward yield

Months	Date	Spot	Interest	Buy/Sell	Price	Cash flow
0	01-Jan-20	5.00		Sell	94.75	(6,000.00)
1	31-Jan-20	5.00		Sell		
2	29-Feb-20	5.00		Sell		
3	31-Mar-20	5.00		Sell		
4	30-Apr-20	5.00		Sell		
5	31-May-20	5.00		Sell		
6	30-Jun-20	6.00		Buy	93.75	6,000.00
12	31-Dec-20	6.00	(91,000.00)	Buy		15,000.00
Total			(91,000.00)			15,000.00

There is a margin to be paid up front of 6,000 calculated as six multiplied by 1,000 per contract. During the intervening six months interest rises to 6 per cent, and therefore the interest payable between June and December is higher at 91,000 as opposed to 75,833 (3,000,000 * 5 per cent * (182/360)). Since the spot rate is higher you need a mechanism that moves in an opposite direction, and therefore six futures are sold. Since you are selling you receive 6,000 in margin.

At the end of the period, the margin on the future is calculated as follows:

```
Cell H29:      = (Increased June spot - Current
Rate) * 100 * Variation per tick * No. of contracts
          = (6 - 5) * 100 * 25 * 6 = 15,000
```

Overall the hedge result is a cash flow of minus 6,000 plus 6,000 plus 15,000, which equals 15,000. The net interest payable over the six months results in a rate around the initial rate of 5 per cent:

$$Rate = ((91,000 - 15,000)/3,000,000) * (360/182) = 5.01 \text{ per cent}$$

The rate is not exact since the precise number of contracts required was 6.07. Nevertheless the use of the two instruments allows the rate to be fixed effectively for the period at the initial rate.

FORWARD RATE AGREEMENT

Forward agreements are designed to 'lock in' future interest rates and are 'over the counter' (OTC) or private transactions rather than contracts available exclusively at exchanges such as the London International Financial Futures Exchange (LIFFE). This is defined as a contract between two parties that sets out the interest rate that will apply to a future loan or deposit. There is no loan between the parties but merely an agreement to compensate the other in the event of movements in the underlying prices of the forward rate agreement and the relevant interest rate. Unlike a formal futures agreement, there are no margin calls during the lifetime of the agreement.

The forward rate agreement (FRA) covers a notional loan or deposit period known as the contract period in a contract amount of the contract currency. The contract period starts on the settlement day when the cash compensation is paid. The end of the contract period is the maturity date. In order to calculate the amount of compensation to pay, an agreed, guaranteed or future rate is referenced to the FRA, and this is the rate to be applied to the notional contract. The rate is compared with an agreed reference rate in the market and the difference between the agreed future rate and the reference rate is paid up front. The compensation formula is:

$$Compensation = [(L - F) * n/365 * Contract\ amount]/[1 + L * (n/365)]$$

$L = LIBOR\ reference\ rate\ on\ fixing\ date;$
$F = Future\ rate\ quoted\ as\ the\ price\ of\ the\ FRA;$
$n/365 = Number\ of\ days\ expressed\ as\ a\ decimal.$

In Figure 9.4, current LIBOR is 5 per cent and the company wants to borrow 1,000 in one or two months' time for a period of three months. The fixed rate for the notional loan is 5.25 per cent. On the fixing date, LIBOR has risen to 5.5 per cent and therefore the bank needs to compensate the client so that the fixed borrowing rate is 5.25 per cent. The amount is derived from the compensation formula below:

```
Cell G9: =((Settlement rate - Contract rate) *
(Days/Days in current year) * Contract amount)/
(1 + (Settlement rate * (Days/Days in current
year)))
```

The pricing formula above is:

```
Cell G15: =(((Days in current year * 12-month
rate) - (Days * Month rate))/(1 + (Days/Simple
rate days) * 3-month rate)) * (1/(Days in current
year - Days))
```

Figure 9.4

Forward compensation

	A	B	C	D	E	F	G
4							
5		Inputs			Management Summary		
6		Settlement date	30-Sep-21		Days		92 days
7		Maturity date	31-Dec-21		Days in current year		365 days
8		Current LIBOR	5.00%		Simple rate days		360 days
9		Contract rate	5.25%		Settlement		621.52
10		Settlement rate	5.50%		Payable		Paid by Bank
11		Contract amount	1,000,000		Percentage		0.0622%
12					Difference in rates		0.2500%
13							
14		3 month rate	5.25%		Pricing		5.5103%
15		12 month rate	5.50%		Implied Future		9,448

Therefore the bank needs to pay the client 621.52 in compensation for the higher rate. The sensitivity table in Figure 9.5 shows how the level of compensation changes based on the LIBOR rate.

Sensitivity

Figure 9.5

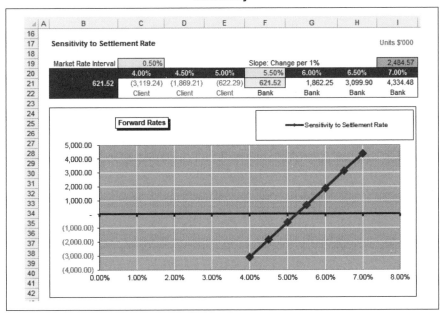

	A	B	C	D	E	F	G	H	I
16									
17		Sensitivity to Settlement Rate							Units $'000
18									
19		Market Rate Interval	0.50%			Slope: Change per 1%			2,484.57
20			4.00%	4.50%	5.00%	5.50%	6.00%	6.50%	7.00%
21		621.52	(3,119.24)	(1,869.21)	(622.29)	621.52	1,862.25	3,099.90	4,334.48
22			Client	Client	Client	Bank	Bank	Bank	Bank

In Figure 9.6, interest rate protection is needed for a six-month period starting in six months. The proposed amount is 5,000,000 and rates are forecast to rise. Therefore the company seeks to fix the loan interest payable.

Example 2

Figure 9.6

	A	B	C	D	E	F	G
4							
5		Inputs			Management Summary		
6		Settlement date	30-Sep-21		Days		92 days
7		Maturity date	31-Dec-21		Days in current year		365 days
8		Current LIBOR	6.00%		Simple rate days		360 days
9		Contract rate	6.25%		Settlement		6,195.95
10		Settlement rate	6.75%		Payable		Paid by Bank
11		Contract amount	5,000,000		Percentage		0.1239%
12					Difference in rates		0.5000%
13							
14		3 month rate	6.25%		Pricing		6.4807%
15		12 month rate	6.50%		Implied Future		9,351
16							

The contract rate is 6.25 per cent; however, on the settlement date the reference rate has risen to 6.75 per cent. Compensation is therefore due in line with the compensation formula. The advantages to the company are:

■ Future rates can be fixed without margin calls or other commitments.

- Transactions can be annulled by taking out an equal and opposite position to the original agreement.
- Agreements can be tailored to fix exact requirements of amount and period, unlike exchange-traded products such as futures and options.

YIELD CURVES

The term structure of interest rates is the mathematical relationship between the interest earned by investing money and the length of time that investors are prepared to invest funds. The relationship takes into account the investor's views on the likely direction and pricing of interest rates. Arbitrage also plays a part since you could invest today on a 12-month rate and roll the amount over for a further 12 months or borrow today on the two-year rate. In a perfect market without taxes and other costs, there should be no difference between the two routes, otherwise an arbitrage possibility would exist.

The yield curve is a representation of the levels of return for a range of maturities, as in the example of GBP rates (see Figure 9.7). Yield curves are

Figure 9.7

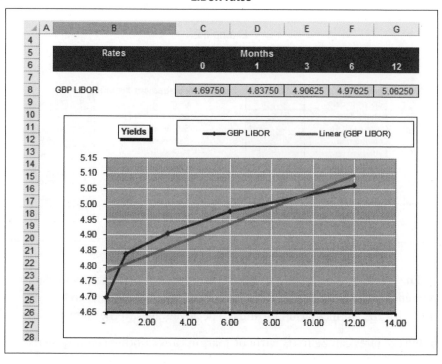

LIBOR rates

a dynamic representation of the past and expectation of the future. There are many reasons for different shapes of yield curve. Curve shapes are:

- Positive – normal sloping up.
- Negative – sloping down.
- Flat – no slope in either direction.
- Humped – higher rates in the middle.

There are a number of theories which purport to explain interest rate yield curves (see Figure 9.8). The terminology is:

- Steepening – the furthest maturities are rising and the earliest maturities are falling, or both.
- Flattening – the furthest maturities are falling and the nearer maturities rising.
- Parallel shift – the curve is moving upwards or downwards in a uniform manner.

The Expectations Hypothesis suggests that the shape of the yield curve results from the interest rate expectations of the market participants. More specifically, it holds that any long-term interest rate simply represents the geometric mean of current and future one-year interest rates expected to prevail over the term until maturity. Under such conditions, the equilibrium long-term rate is the rate that the long-term investor would expect to earn through successive

Figure 9.8

Yield curve shapes

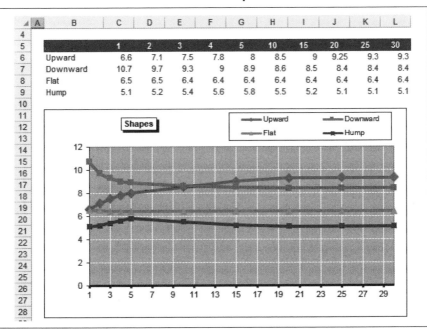

A	B	C	D	E	F	G	H	I	J	K	L
4											
5		1	2	3	4	5	10	15	20	25	30
6	Upward	6.6	7.1	7.5	7.8	8	8.5	9	9.25	9.3	9.3
7	Downward	10.7	9.7	9.3	9	8.9	8.6	8.5	8.4	8.4	8.4
8	Flat	6.5	6.5	6.4	6.4	6.4	6.4	6.4	6.4	6.4	6.4
9	Hump	5.1	5.2	5.4	5.6	5.8	5.5	5.2	5.1	5.1	5.1

investments in short-term instruments over the term to maturity. Therefore there is a choice between a longer-dated instrument and the successive short-term instruments, and the result should be the same.

The future interest rates expected are known as implied forward rates. An upward-sloping curve is produced when borrowers seek to delay increased interest costs and borrow in longer maturities. Investors who do not wish to be locked into a rising market invest in shorter-dated instruments and reinvest later at higher rates. The increase in liquidity on shorter maturities and decrease on longer maturities produce a positive swing in the yield curve.

Negative yield curves point towards interest falls and therefore borrowers and investors follow the reverse of the strategy above. Borrowers seek shorter dates and investors seek to maintain higher rates for as long as possible.

Figure 9.9 provides a worked example. The formula for the forward rate is:

$$Forward\ rate = 1 / \left[\left[(1 + {_t}R_{n+j})^{n+j} / (1 + {_t}R_n)^n \right] - 1 \right]^{(1/j)}$$

Spot rate (annual) of shortest maturity: R_n
Spot rate (annual) of longest maturity: R_{n+j}
No. of years from now when forward rate is calculated: n
Period covered by rate to be calculated: j

Figure 9.9

Expectation Hypothesis

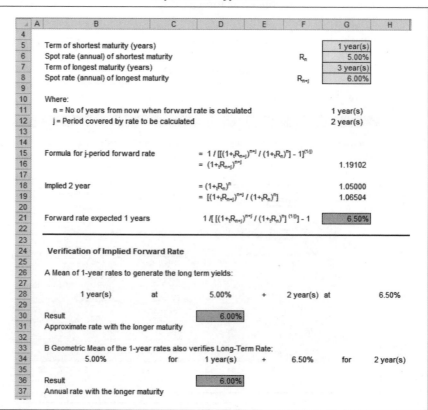

The answer is 6.5 per cent, which can be verified by substituting in the calculation of the mean over the period of one year and then two years. This results in the figure of 6 per cent which is the longer-dated rate.

Geometric mean: $= (((1 + Short\ Spot) \wedge Short\ Term) * ((1 + Forward\ Rate)\wedge(Long\ Term - Short\ Term)))\wedge(1/((Long\ Term - Short\ Term) + Short\ Term)) - 1$

Other theories on interest rates include the liquidity preference theory where investors demand a higher rate for longer-term deposits. There are risks other than liquidity, such as inflation and credit risk, and therefore a greater compensation is demanded. Central banks also have a part to play in managing interest rates by buying and selling treasury bills, thereby restricting the supply and demand for funds.

When you have a yield curve as in the example below, you can derive the implied rates. Here the yield curve is sloping upwards. The two-year rate is 4.25 per cent against a one-year rate of 4 per cent. The two-year rate compounded is:

Compound: $(1 + 4.25\%) \wedge 2 = 1.0868$
Subtract one $= 0.0868$
Divide by two $= 0.0434 = 4.34\%$

Figure 9.10 shows both series with the term rates and the implied forwards with the calculations over two, three, four and five years.

Implied forward rates

Figure 9.10

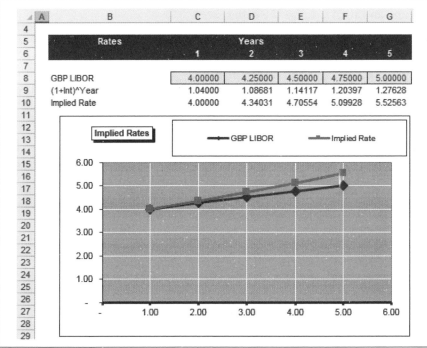

EXERCISE

Use the methodology in the chapter to price for dates that do not fall exactly on the quarter or period dates (see Figure 9.11). The current date is in November and no six-month figure has been quoted for the period December to June but the prices shown are available with a sloping yield curve.

Figure 9.11

Exercise data

◢	A	B	C	D	E	F
4						
5	Prices					
6		1	December	9400	6.0000	
7		2	March	9390	6.1000	
8		3	June	9380	6.2000	
9		4	September	9370	6.3000	
10						
11			Period	4.00		
12						

The due date is halfway through the period March to June, so it is necessary to work out a rate for December to June and another for March to June and then prorate the difference.

SUMMARY

The mechanics of forward rates, hedging and yield curves are discussed in this chapter to show the basic relationships between spot and forward rates and the compounding calculations. While sentiment and other factors may drive expectations of investors and borrowers, the basic relationships must hold, otherwise there must be an advantage as an arbitrage relationship exists.

10

Futures

File: MFMaths3e_10.xls

147

FUTURES MARKET

The futures market differs from forwards or swaps in that forward contracts are highly standardised in terms of quantity, quality, delivery date and maturity. A future is simply a legally binding agreement between a buyer and seller to buy or sell a particular asset (e.g. a commodity or shares) or an index (e.g. FTSE 100) at some time in the future, at a price agreed today. Trading takes place in a futures exchange using contracts with known standard quantities and maturity dates. Without known items it would be impossible to assess value and liquidity would fall since the number of standardised bargains would fall. Liquidity in a market provides the mechanism whereby values can be assessed accurately by buyers and sellers and deals concluded. The types of categories for futures contracts include:

- physical goods such as agricultural goods, oil, livestock, timber, foodstuffs and minerals;
- assets earning interest with a variety of maturities along the length of the yield curve;
- foreign exchange both for speculation and trading;
- indexes such as the FT Index; these contracts do not allow for actual delivery since this is impossible, and the liability is met by reversing the original trade.

You can 'open' a futures position by either buying or selling a future and can 'close' the futures position by doing the opposite, either selling or buying the same future. In practice, most futures contract positions are 'closed out' before they expire. The open interest is the number of contracts in existence and the trading volume represents the number of contracts being traded on the market.

If you believe that the underlying asset will rise, you could buy futures. This is known as a long futures position whereby the buyer is committed to take delivery of the underlying asset or equivalent cash value at a prearranged price and by a certain date. Conversely, if you believe that the price of the underlying asset will fall, you could sell a future, which is known as a short futures position. This commits the seller to deliver the underlying shares, or equivalent cash value, at a prearranged price and by a certain date.

If you do nothing then you are fully exposed to the rise and fall of the market if a commodity or asset is required at some time in the future. While market sentiment might believe that a market will rise, there could always be unwelcome shocks or unforeseen occurrences such as earthquakes, catastrophic storms or disease. Futures may be one method of reducing uncertainty, but futures also carry a risk that market prices may go in the opposite direction to the general market view.

Futures prices are calculated in a structured way since there is a link between the spot price and the futures price in the same way as a forward. No link would create arbitrage opportunities. Prices are quoted in two ways:

- Bid is the price at which a trader is prepared to buy a futures contract.
- Offer is the price at which a trader is prepared to sell a futures contract.

The futures price should be equal to the cost of financing the purchase of the underlying asset and the cost of holding (or, with a commodity, storing) it until the expiry date. In the case of shares, the price should reflect any interest income lost by holding shares rather than cash and any dividends paid to the holder of the shares before the contract expiry date. The formula is:

$$Fair\ equity\ futures\ price\ =\ today's\ share\ price\ +\ interest\ costs\ -\ dividends\ received$$

TERMINOLOGY

There is distinct terminology in the market:

- Unit of trading is a precise definition of the quantity and quality of the instrument to be bought or sold.
- Delivery months and delivery days since a futures contract consists of monthly cycles when delivery will occur. Contractual obligations of the contract must be met on the given day; in practice, most futures contracts are 'closed out' before delivery day.
- Last trading day is the day when trading in a particular contract will cease.
- Quotation specifies how a price is calculated and is affected by interest rates.
- Tick size represents the smallest amount a price can change.
- Exchange delivery settlement price (EDSP) is calculated to confirm the final value at a fixed time on the last trading day.
- Initial margin are funds or collateral that must be lodged with your broker in order to meet any obligations under the terms of the contract.
- Trading hours since all futures contracts have fixed times when futures can be traded.

Here is a specimen set of contract specifications for wheat:

- Unit of trading: 100 tonnes.
- Origins: EU.
- Quality: sound and sweet and in good condition and to contain no more than 3 per cent heat damage. Natural weight to be not less than 72.5 kg

per hectolitre. Moisture content not to exceed 15 per cent (all the above tests to be applied on weight basis).

- Delivery months: January, March, May, July, September, November, such that 10 delivery months are available for trading.

- Tender period: any business day from the seventh calendar day (if not a business day, then the next business day following) preceding the first business day of the delivery month, up to the last trading day of the delivery month inclusive.

- Price basis: pounds sterling and pence per tonne, free delivered to buyer's lorry in bulk, from a registered store in mainland Britain.

- Minimum price movement: (tick size and value) 5 pence per tonne (£5).

- Last trading day: 23rd calendar day of delivery month.

- Trading hours: 10:00–16:45.

BENEFITS

There are two key benefits of futures over forwards:

- Traders can profit when the market is falling and rising. When buying shares, you normally want to buy low and sell high in order to profit. In the futures market, you have the opportunity to sell futures (going short). If you think the market will fall you can consider selling futures. If the view is correct and the futures price falls in line with the underlying asset price, the position can be closed by buying back the future at a reduced price in order to make a profit.

- Cost efficiency – typically futures attract a lower commission structure when compared with trading shares and do not carry stamp duty.

General benefits are:

- Safeguarding or 'hedging' existing underlying assets if you believe the underlying price will fall. This is the prime reason to remove some of the market uncertainty since you could open a futures position to protect your existing asset (e.g. your share portfolio) in the event of a downturn in prices. As a holder of the asset, you could buy futures against your equities to avoid making losses and without having to incur the costs associated with selling the underlying asset. To 'close' the futures position you would buy the equivalent amount of futures in the market. Losses in the underlying asset can therefore be compensated by profit made on the futures position. Modelled examples are set out in the following sections.

■ Since there is a relationship between spot and futures prices such as interest rates, you can build up a picture of future prices as in interest yield curves.

■ Futures allow you to profit from volatile market conditions. By selling (short) or buying (long) futures, risk can be reduced and, if the view materialises, a profit gained by closing the position with undertaking an equal and opposite position in the same market to take advantage of the price difference.

CLEARING HOUSE OPERATION

At the centre of the exchange is the clearing house. Its function is to ensure that buyers and sellers uphold their obligations to each other. Essentially it divides each trade and acts for the opposing side by standing in the middle. The clearinghouse therefore allows every player to reverse positions without involving the other side. The risk of default is also reduced since the counterparty is the exchange.

To safeguard the clearing house, the exchange requires each trader to post margin and settle their accounts at the end of each trading day. Before being allowed to trade, traders must deposit funds with their broker who in turn deposits funds with the clearing house. Margin can be in cash, bank letter of credit, treasury bills or equivalent. There are three types of margin:

■ Initial margin, which is posted before any trading and is equal to about one day's price fluctuation.

■ Daily settlement by marking to market losses and gains on the day.

■ Maintenance margin, where the balance in the account falls below a critical level and the trader must bring the account up to the initial margin level.

For example, a trader buys one contract for a commodity at 2.00. The initial margin is 1,000. The next day the price falls by 0.05 which means a loss of 250. In the settlement process, marking to market means that 250 is removed from the account leaving a balance of 750. If you assume that the maintenance margin is 75 per cent and further price reductions will trigger a variation margin, then the trader will have to deposit more funds to bring the account back into line. Variation margin must be paid in cash or near cash as above. If the trader is unable to deposit more cash, the broker has no option but to close the position and deduct fees and losses before returning the account balance. The actions of the broker and the clearing house therefore protect the opposing parties from the losses they would suffer if dealing direct without the intermediary effect of the exchange.

BOND FUTURES

Bond futures are also available to hedge interest rate risk further out along the yield curve. The contracts are usually linked to bonds such as:

- US treasury bonds.
- Long gilt.
- Two-year German government treasury note (Schatz).
- Ten-year German government bond (Bund).
- Japanese government bond (JGB).

Trading in the future allows for speculation on future prices since only the margin rather than the full value is required. Small changes in price therefore have a more leveraged effect on the overall position. On expiry there is a contractual obligation to deliver the bond. Here are typical contract conditions for a 10-year German government bond (Bund) future:

- Unit of trading: 100,000 nominal value notional German government bond with 6 per cent coupon.
- Delivery months: March, June, September, December, such that the nearest three delivery months are available for trading.
- Quotation: per 100 nominal.
- Minimum price movement: 0.01 (10) (tick size and value).
- Last trading day: 12:30 Frankfurt time, two Frankfurt business days prior to the delivery day.
- Delivery day: 10th calendar day of delivery month. If such a day is not a business day in Frankfurt then the delivery day will be the following Frankfurt business day.
- Trading hours: 07:00–18:00.

HEDGING MECHANISMS

As per the time line in Figure 10.1, buying a future means that you have an agreement to buy an asset in the future at a price agreed today. Selling a future means that you have an agreement to sell an asset at a future date at a price agreed today.

If you do nothing and wait for asset prices to rise or fall then the profit or loss is a linear chart (see Figure 10.2). You gain when the price rises and lose as it falls towards the date of delivery.

Buying a future implies that you participate in the contract price increases whereas selling a future implies that you lose as the future price rises. To

Figure 10.1   **Time lines**

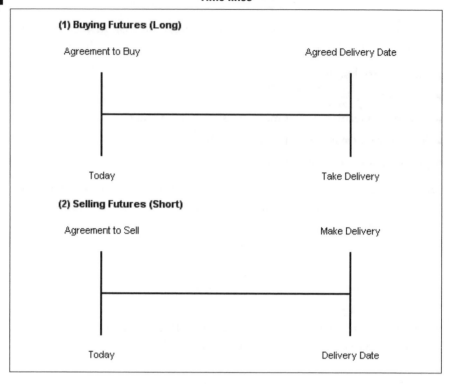

Figure 10.2   **Asset price**

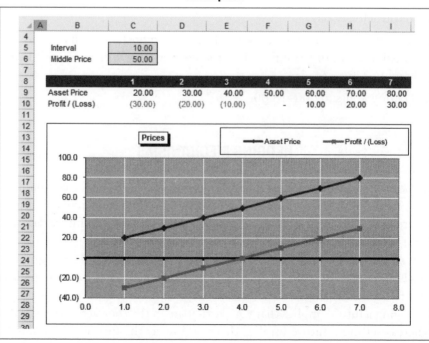

hedge, you need to buy an instrument which will rise or fall in an opposite direction to the underlying asset. It is not always obvious that you need to hedge since the exposure could be low or the hedge could cost too much relative to the perceived risk. If you think interest rates will rise, you want something that will make money as they rise. There is an inverse relationship between asset prices and futures: as interest rates rise, futures prices fall. To make money you sell futures contracts at the outset and close out the position at a lower price. Figure 10.3 shows the effect of buying and selling futures: as the futures price rises, you make money from buying and lose by selling. This margin must then be placed against the profit or loss on the underlying asset.

Short and long positions

Figure 10.3

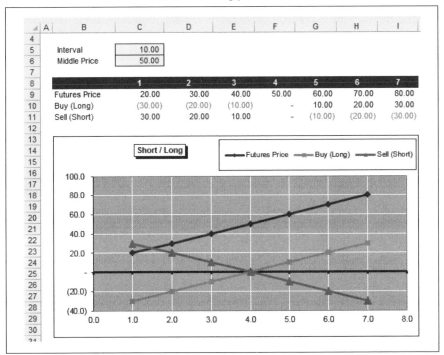

	1	2	3	4	5	6	7
Futures Price	20.00	30.00	40.00	50.00	60.00	70.00	80.00
Buy (Long)	(30.00)	(20.00)	(10.00)	-	10.00	20.00	30.00
Sell (Short)	30.00	20.00	10.00	-	(10.00)	(20.00)	(30.00)

Interval 10.00
Middle Price 50.00

HEDGING EXAMPLE 1

In Figure 10.4, the current spot price is 4,500 and futures are priced at 4,400, implying a fall in the market. Given that the market is expected to fall, you buy futures which make money with price increases. On expiry in December, the spot price has gone the other way and risen to 4,600.

Figure 10.4

Example – buying

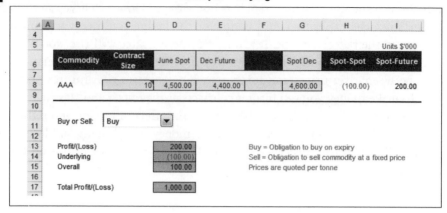

On the future you make 200 (4,600 − 4,400); however, there is a loss on the underlying commodity of 100 (4,600 − 4,500). The overall payoff is plus 100 and with 10 contracts the total margin is 1,000. If you sell contracts, the positions are reversed, as in Figure 10.5.

Figure 10.5

Example – selling

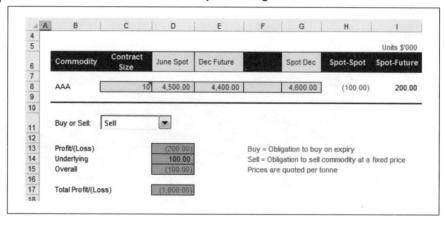

The negative margin on the futures contract is 200 (4,400 − 4,600) since you have to sell at 4,400; however, the underlying commodity has risen in price so the net effect is a loss of 100. Figure 10.6 builds up the figures using simple IF function logic statements to show the effect. It is easier to understand as a chart of the changes to the sell position based on the future price and the expiry spot price (see Figure 10.7). The profit or loss on the future can then be calculated and set against the position on the underlying asset.

Table

Figure 10.6

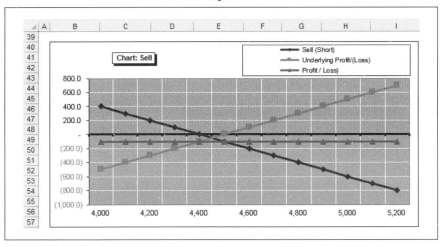

	Difference	Spot Dec	Buy (Long)	Underlying Profit/(Loss)	Profit / (Loss)	Sell (Short)	Underlying Profit/(Loss)	Profit / Loss)
25	500.00	4,000.00	(400.00)	500.00	100.00	400.00	(500.00)	(100.00)
26	400.00	4,100.00	(300.00)	400.00	100.00	300.00	(400.00)	(100.00)
27	300.00	4,200.00	(200.00)	300.00	100.00	200.00	(300.00)	(100.00)
28	200.00	4,300.00	(100.00)	200.00	100.00	100.00	(200.00)	(100.00)
29	100.00	4,400.00	-	100.00	100.00	-	(100.00)	(100.00)
30	-	4,500.00	100.00	-	100.00	(100.00)	-	(100.00)
31	(100.00)	4,600.00	200.00	(100.00)	100.00	(200.00)	100.00	(100.00)
32	(200.00)	4,700.00	300.00	(200.00)	100.00	(300.00)	200.00	(100.00)
33	(300.00)	4,800.00	400.00	(300.00)	100.00	(400.00)	300.00	(100.00)
34	(400.00)	4,900.00	500.00	(400.00)	100.00	(500.00)	400.00	(100.00)
35	(500.00)	5,000.00	600.00	(500.00)	100.00	(600.00)	500.00	(100.00)
36	(600.00)	5,100.00	700.00	(600.00)	100.00	(700.00)	600.00	(100.00)
37	(700.00)	5,200.00	800.00	(700.00)	100.00	(800.00)	700.00	(100.00)

Interval Across 100.00 / Interval Down 100.00

Payoff

Figure 10.7

HEDGING EXAMPLE 2

This example concerns trying to hedge a small portfolio of shares by buying or selling FT Index futures to cover potential shortfalls (see Figure 10.8). The target is to beat the index and remove the downside from sharp adverse movements. The first part of the table gives the number of shares, current price and beta (measure of volatility).

The MV (market value) column is calculated as the number of shares multiplied by the price. The MV multiplied by beta is derived from:

(*No. of shares * Price * Beta*)/*selected futures index value*

Figure 10.8   **Index example**

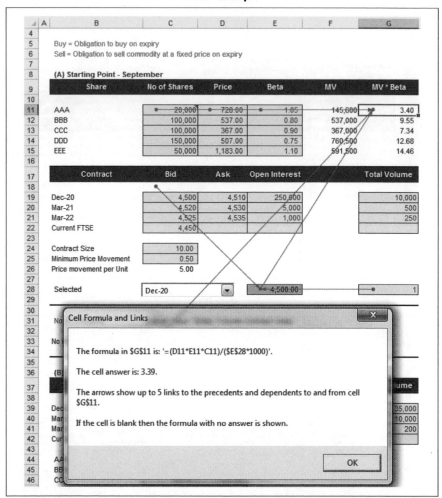

The nominal date is June and so September is chosen as the date with the most open interest and volume. The tick size is the smallest denomination for which a price can be quoted. This is 0.5 × GBP 10 = GBP 5.

Since you want something that makes money as the index goes down, you have to sell futures. If the index rises you would make money on the shares and lose on the future. The number of contracts required can be calculated using this equation:

$$No.\ of\ contracts = \frac{Market\ value\ of\ share * Beta\ of\ share}{Futures\ contract\ value}$$

A specimen FTSE 100 is being used as a proxy to the portfolio and as such it must represent a potentially imperfect hedge since the constituents of the portfolio do not match the index perfectly in terms of risk. The model calculates the number of required contracts as 47 (see Figure 10.9).

Futures

Figure 10.9

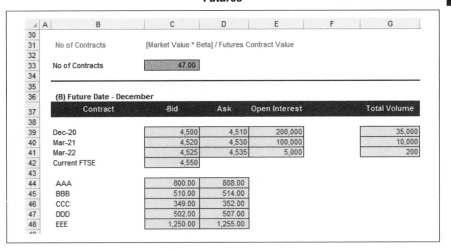

	B	C	D	E	F	G
30						
31	No of Contracts	[Market Value * Beta] / Futures Contract Value				
32						
33	No of Contracts	47.00				
34						
35						
36	**(B) Future Date - December**					
37	Contract	-Bid	Ask	Open Interest		Total Volume
38						
39	Dec-20	4,500	4,510	200,000		35,000
40	Mar-21	4,520	4,530	100,000		10,000
41	Mar-22	4,525	4,535	5,000		200
42	Current FTSE	4,550				
43						
44	AAA	800.00	808.00			
45	BBB	510.00	514.00			
46	CCC	349.00	352.00			
47	DDD	502.00	507.00			
48	EEE	1,250.00	1,255.00			

In December, the markets do not appear to be moving to plan and you close out the position by buying futures. The relevant price is the asking price of 4,510 and the December current prices are shown in Figure 10.10. The next question is whether the hedge was successful in eradicating the risk on the portfolio.

Profit and loss

Figure 10.10

	B	C	D	E	F	G
50						
51	**[C] Profit and Loss**					
52		Opening Price	Closing Price	No of Shares / Contracts	Tick	Profit / (Loss)
53						
54	Dec-20 Futures	4,500.00	4,510.00	47.00	5.00	(2,350.00)
55						
56	AAA	728.00	800.00	20,000.00		14,400.00
57	BBB	537.00	510.00	100,000.00		(27,000.00)
58	CCC	367.00	349.00	100,000.00		(18,000.00)
59	DDD	507.00	502.00	150,000.00		(7,500.00)
60	EEE	1,183.00	1,250.00	50,000.00		33,500.00
61						
62	Profit / (Loss on Shares)					(4,600.00)
63						
64	Tradeoff					(6,950.00)

The futures loss is calculated as the change in price multiplied by the number of contracts multiplied by the price per tick:

$$\textit{Futures loss or gain} = (4,500 - 4,510) * 47 * 5 = (2,350)$$

It is also necessary to find the profit or loss on the portfolio based on the simple calculations above. The overall effect is a loss of 6,950 since the shares underperformed the market and the future rose in price. Given that the portfolio did not reflect the index, the futures position could not eliminate the risk of adverse movements. There is more volume in the March contracts so further contracts could be taken out to continue the hedge.

EXERCISE

A company needs to borrow money in six months' time for six months and interest rates are expected to rise. The current data is given in Figure 10.11.

Figure 10.11

Exercise data

	A	B	C	D	E
4					
5		(1) Prices			
6				Price	Interest Rate
7			Spot	9,520.00	4.80
8		1	December	9,508.00	4.92
9		2	March	9,505.00	4.95
10		3	June	9,496.00	5.04
11		4	September	9,499.00	5.01
12					
13		Current Date		Sept	
14		Loan Required		March	
15		Payment per Annum		2.00	
16		Loan Amount		5,000,000.00	
17		Contract Size		1,000,000.00	
18					
19		Number of Contracts		5.00	
20					

The loan is 5,000,000 and the standard contract size 1,000,000, meaning that five contracts are required. Calculate the overall position if the March spot price is 4.95 per cent and the future rises to 9,520 (4.80 per cent). Was there an overall profit or was there a loss?

SUMMARY

Futures contracts differ from forward contracts as exchange contracts with standard size, delivery dates and rules governing the parties to reduce the risk on trading. Futures are available to cover commodities, interest rates, equities and foreign exchange. To understand the margin position on the future and underlying asset it is necessary to set out the payoff for each instrument and then to show the overall profit or loss. While it is possible to hedge with futures, trading does not eliminate risk but merely changes its nature from one based solely on underlying price movements.

Foreign exchange

File: MFMaths3e_11.xls

RISK

Organisations face exposure to foreign exchange risk through adverse movements in rates. With any risk assessment it is necessary to understand the nature of risk and assess whether the effect is material and needing to be hedged or controlled, or is negligible and can be ignored. The costs of hedging may also be important in the decision process. Foreign exchange presents particular risks that can be divided into three categories:

■ Transaction risk arises from differences in interest rates. For example, a manufacturer takes an order and delivers goods in three months' time. In the interim the exchange rate moves adversely against the manufacturer. Figure 11.1 shows the timing of cash flows in a typical transaction involving order, delivery and payment. This does not take account of potential credit and other exterior macro risks which cannot be controlled directly. The fan chart in Figure 11.2 reinforces the view that uncertainty increases with time, where each line represents percentiles away from the middle base case line.

■ Translation exposure relates to the change in accounting income and balance sheet statements caused by changes in exchange rates. This is not a cash flow and is seen in consolidations of overseas subsidiaries as one of the adjustments between the retained earnings and the balance added to retained earnings on the balance sheet. Values change over time from local to domestic currency and changes are shown in the notes to annual accounts under UK and US GAAP (Generally Accepted Accounting Practice).

■ Economic exposure involves changes in expected future cash flows, and hence economic value, caused by a change in exchange rates. While a company may provide only domestic goods or services, it is still exposed to rates since it will purchase goods or services from overseas or companies which acquire items overseas.

Transaction risk

Figure 11.1

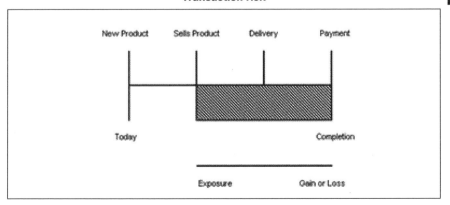

Figure 11.2   **Fan chart showing a possible range of results**

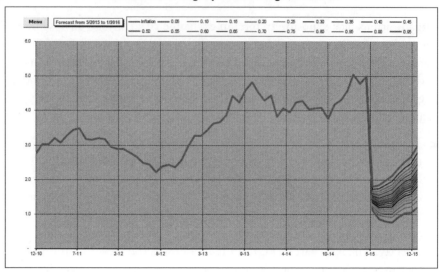

Companies can reduce risks by structuring their affairs before purchasing risk hedging products. Since hedging normally incurs associated costs it may be better to review systems for potential savings. Examples are:

- Natural hedges and internal cash management. For example, sourcing materials in local currency by matching cost and revenue reduces exposure to currency movements. The introduction of the euro has made it easier for European companies to reduce transaction risks associated with importing and exporting goods.

- Reducing or avoiding the amount of trade credit that will be extended as the value that the firm will receive is reduced. Where exporters are strong and can shift the problem of exchange rates onto the importer, risks can be removed.

- Obtaining trade credit or borrowing in the local currency so that the money is repaid with fewer dollars. This matches the investment with the financing and cancels out the costs.

- Netting where cash flows of participating subsidiaries of the same company are netted off so that each subsidiary pays or receives only the net amount of its intra-company purchases and sales.

- Adjusting intra-company accounts between the parent and overseas subsidiary.

- International financing hedges such as bonds and loans.

SPOT RATES

The key risks to be modelled are transaction risks in order to assess the level of exposure and the potential movement in rates. The terminology is as follows:

- Spot exchange rate is the rate today for exchanging one currency for another for immediate delivery. This is the sale of one currency for another currency with delivery two days after the dealing rate.
- Forward exchange rate is the rate today for exchanging one currency for another at a specific future date.

In a previous chapter, it was held that forward interest rates were a function of interest rates over the period. With foreign exchange, the future outright rate is tied to the spot rate and the relative interest rates in the two currencies. The theory holds that there should be interest rate parity between the two rates since you have a choice of investing in one or the other currency. For example, you could:

- buy foreign currency now and place funds on deposit for the length of time required;
- put domestic currency on deposit for the period and then buy foreign currency; or
- buy foreign currency forward at the quoted rate.

The theory states that if interest rate parity holds, the result of both equations should be the same. If it does not hold, there would be an arbitrage opportunity to move funds into one currency or the other. This means that you could make money by investing in one or the other currency by going clockwise or anti-clockwise around the rectangle of variables in Figure 11.3.

Rectangle variables

Figure 11.3

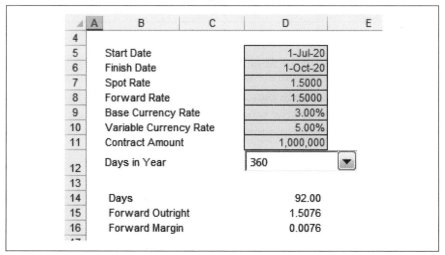

	A	B	C	D	E
4					
5		Start Date		1-Jul-20	
6		Finish Date		1-Oct-20	
7		Spot Rate		1.5000	
8		Forward Rate		1.5000	
9		Base Currency Rate		3.00%	
10		Variable Currency Rate		5.00%	
11		Contract Amount		1,000,000	
12		Days in Year		360	
13					
14		Days		92.00	
15		Forward Outright		1.5076	
16		Forward Margin		0.0076	

The variables for testing this are given below where the example contains differing interest rates and the same spot rate for day and expiry. The choice is therefore to place funds on deposit at 3 per cent and exchange at the spot rate or exchange today and place funds on deposit at 5 per cent. Without modelling the figures, the outcomes must be different and present an opportunity for exchanging today since the variable rate is higher.

Using ACT/360, rows 19 and 20 (see Figure 11.4) calculate the interest by depositing today at 3 per cent. The future value is then exchanged on expiry. The variable deposit shows the effect of exchanging today and there is clearly a gain of 7,667.

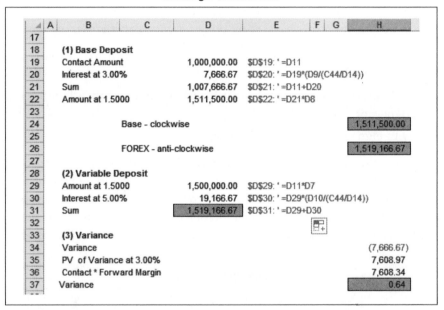

Figure 11.4

Rectangle calculations

To double-check the figures, you could use Data, Data Tools, What-If Analysis, Goal Seek to set the variance to zero, as in Figure 11.5. There are only three inputs, as below. The procedure works backwards through the model to set the variance in cell H34 by changing the forward rate in cell D8. The forward rate to set the variance to zero is 1.5076.

Goal Seek calculation

Figure 11.5

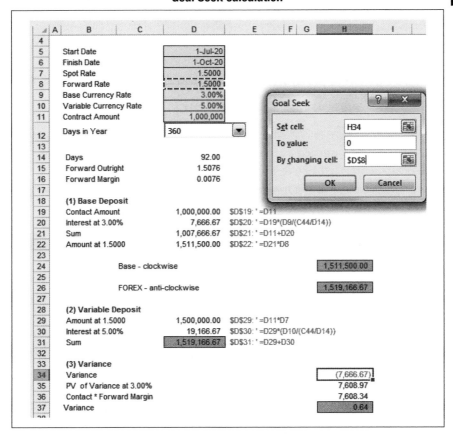

You can also use a formula to derive the forward rate directly. The forward outright is the spot rate required to remove the arbitrage opportunity:

$$Forward\_Outright = \frac{\left(1 + Variable\_Rate * \left(\frac{Days}{Year}\right)\right)}{\left(1 + Base\_Rate * \left(\frac{Days}{Year}\right)\right)}$$

Base rate = Domestic rate
Variable rate = Foreign rate

The forward margin is the difference between the two rates and is given by this formula:

$$Forward\_Margin = \left(\frac{Days * Spot * (Variable\_Rate - Base\_Rate)}{Year + (Days * Base\_Rate)}\right)$$

The base currency interest rate is higher than the foreign rate and therefore one would expect the forward outright to rise. The forward outright in cell I7 is:

```
=Spot*((1+Var_Int*(Days/Days_in_Year))/(1+Base_
Int*(Days/Days_in_Year)))
```

The forward margin in cell I8 is given by the formula:

```
=(Days*Spot*(Var_Int-Base_Int))/(Days_in_Year+
(Days*Base_Int))
```

The rate could be quoted as the spot plus the forward margin to show the two constituents. Cell I9 (see Figure 11.6) contains the formula to show that the correct result with the forward rate has to be the same as using the spot rate today:

```
=(Amount+(Amount*(Base_Int/(Days_in_Year/
Days))))*I7
```

The table using Data, Data Tools, What-If Analysis, Goal Seek with two axes of cells C8 and C9 underlines the sensitivity of the forward rate to the difference in the relative interest rates (see Figure 11.7). With the interest rates the same at 5 per cent, the forward is the same as the spot rate. As the base interest rate falls and the variable rate remains the same, the forward rate increases to remove the arbitrage possibility.

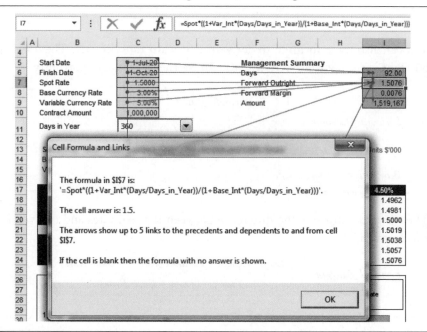

Figure 11.6 **Forward outright and forward margin**

Sensitivity chart

Figure 11.7

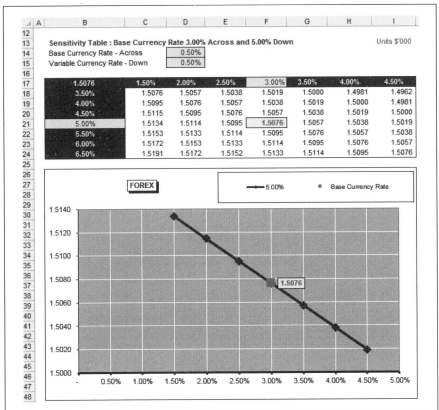

LONGER DATES

The methodology holds over periods beyond one year depending on the efficiency of the long-term swap market. Rather than using simple interest calculations, the formulas use compounding. In Figure 11.8, the spot rate is 1.50 and the rates are again 3 and 5 per cent. The differential is found through compounding:

$Base = (1 + base\ rate)\ \wedge\ No.\ of\ years = 1.1594$

$Rate = (Variable/Base) * Spot$

$Rate = (1.2765/1.1594) * 1.50 = 1.6515$

You can also use an FV function to calculate the rates directly, as in cell G12:

```
=FV (D8, D$11, 0, -1)
```

The same equivalence holds as in the short-term model. Using the rate of 1.6515 as the forward rate, the result is the same as exchange to the overseas rate today and deposit at the variable currency rate.

Figure 11.8

Long-term rates

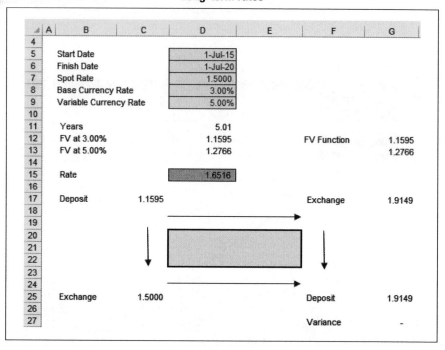

EQUIVALENCE

Using forward rates, exporters can fix rates at the time of order and remove uncertainty on exchange rate fluctuations. The margin can be fixed in domestic currency even though the transaction is in a foreign currency. The choices are:

■ swaps;

■ forwards;

■ futures;

■ options.

On forecasting rates, the difference in interest rates holds to ensure that the outcomes remain in equilibrium. This can also be shown by the four-way equivalence model (see Figure 11.9).

Purchasing power parity: $(1 + inflation\ local)/(1 + inflation\ overseas) =$
spot rate/forward rate

This can be rewritten as:

Forward rate $=$ Spot rate$/[(1 + inflation\ local)/(1 + inflation\ overseas)]$

Equivalent rates

Figure 11.9

	A	B	C	D	E	F	G	H	I
4									
5		Spot Rate			1.5000				
6		Domestic Inflation Rate			2.50%				
7		Overseas Inflation Rate			5.00%				
8		Base Interest Rate			4.00%				
9									
10		**(1) PPP**							
11		Spot / [(1+B Inflation) / (1+F Inflation)]			1.5366	$E$11: ' =E5/((1+E6)/(1+E7))			
12									
13		**(2) Fisher**							
14		(1+B Rate) / [(1+B Inflation) / (1+F Inflation)]							
15		Nominal Rate (Int F)			6.54%	$E$15: ' =(1+E8)/((1+E6)/(1+E7))-1			
16									
17		**(3) Interest Rate Parity**							
18		Spot / [(1+B Rate) / (1+Nominal Rate)]			1.5366	$E$18: ' =E5/((1+E8)/(1+E15))			
19									
20									
21		**Equivalence Model**							
22									
23									
24		(Int F - B Rate) / (1+ B Rate)	2.44%		(Infl F – Infl L) / (1+ Infl L)			2.44%	
25									
26									
27		(Forward - Spot) / Spot	2.44%		(Spot T - Spot) / Spot			2.44%	
28									

The Fisher effect shows the link between real and nominal interest rates in the formula:

Fisher: $(1 + real\ rate) = (1 + nominal\ rate) * (1 + anticipated\ inflation\ rate)$

or, alternatively:

Fisher: $(1 + nominal\ rate) = (1 + real\ rate)/(1 + anticipated\ inflation\ rate)$

The links between inflation and interest rates should hold under this model as in the bottom grid to give the same answer on each corner. For the theory to hold, these equations must result in the same answer:

$(Variable\ interest - base\ interest\ rate)/(1 + base\ interest\ rate)$
$(Overseas\ inflation - domestic\ inflation)/(1 + domestic\ inflation)$
$(Forward\ rate - spot\ rate)/spot\ rate$
$(Spot\ rate\ at\ time\ T - spot\ rate)/spot\ rate$

The theories relating to exchange rates may not always hold due to macro factors. For example:

■ Short-term price elasticity of exports and imports influencing the relationship between a country's exchange rate and its purchasing power parity.

■ Commodity items and products in mature industries being more likely to conform to purchasing power parity where there is more information available than new and technology industries.

■ Frictions such as government intervention in erecting and maintaining trade barriers cause purchasing power parity not to hold.

COMPARISONS AND ARBITRAGE

In the example below (see Figure 11.10), a company has the option of borrowing in sterling, dollars or euros and the rates and margins are in rows 5 to 12. The borrowing is for three months and in sterling the rate is 5.1 per cent. If the company chooses to borrow in another currency, it takes on the currency risk and this is represented by the swap rate.

For dollars, the company borrows 18,000,000 at 2.9 per cent and the repayment is calculated in cell C18:

=C17*(C9+C10)*($C11/$C12)
$18,000,000 * 2.9\% * (91/360)$

The amount in sterling is translated back at the spot rate less the swap rate of 0.0095. This gives a sterling amount of 10,126,752. The yield of 5.084 per cent in cell C25 is:

=(C23/$C13)*($C14/$C11)
$= (126,752/10,000,000) * (365/91)$

Figure 11.10

Comparison

▲ A	B	C	D	E	F	G
4						
5	Spot GBP / USD	1.8000		Spot GBP / EUR		1.4500
6	Swap	0.0095		Swap		0.0100
7	Sterling Interest	4.500%				
8	Sterling Margin	0.600%				
9	USD Interest	2.500%		EUR Interest		2.000%
10	USD Margin	0.400%		EUR Margin		0.350%
11	Period	91 days				
12	Days	360 days				
13	Amount	10,000,000.00				
14	Actual Days	365 days				
15						
16	(1) USD Comparison			(1) EUR Comparison		
17	USD Amount	18,000,000.00		EUR Amount		14,500,000.00
18	Repayment	131,950.00		Repayment		86,134.03
19	Total	18,131,950.00		Total		14,586,134.03
20						
21	Rate	1.7905		Rate		1.4400
22	Sell at 1.7905	10,126,752.30		Sell at 1.4400		10,129,259.74
23	Extra	126,752.30		Extra		129,259.74
24						
25	Yield	5.084%		Yield		5.185%
26						
27	Rates					
28	Borrowing Rate	5.014%		Borrowing Rate		5.114%
29	Convert to Act/365	5.084%		Convert to Act/365		5.185%
30						
31	Sterling Rate	5.100%				
32	Gain / (Loss)	0.016%		Gain / (Loss)		(0.085%)

The figures can be substituted into the same equations for the euro and the yield is 5.185 per cent. This means that it is marginally cheaper to borrow in dollars than in sterling.

EXERCISE

A treasurer has the option of borrowing in dollars or euros. Construct a model to ascertain if there is a potential saving in one of the currencies over 91 days. Also, what is the break-even exchange rate? The data are:

Spot EUR/USD	1.4000
Swap	0.0100
USD Interest	3.000%
EUR Interest	5.000%
EUR Margin	0.500%
Amount	10,000,000.00

SUMMARY

The link between foreign exchange spot and forward rates can be modelled easily using the mathematics in this chapter and the wider links to purchasing power parity and the equivalence model. The formulas can be built up to demonstrate the benefits of borrowing in different currencies as a key component of treasury management strategy.

Options

Exercise

Summary

File: MFMaths3e_12.xls

DESCRIPTION

Options are instruments in some ways similar to futures in that they allow risk to be controlled and traded through dedicated exchanges. An option is a right rather than obligation, so unlike a future you can allow the contract to lapse if there is no gain. This ability to 'walk away' has proved very attractive as part of an overall risk strategy. From early beginnings with the establishment of the Chicago Board Options Exchange (CBOE) in 1973, the volume and diversity of options contracts have grown enormously. Other exchanges such as the London International Financial Futures Exchange (LIFFE) have been developed and the vast range of options contracts now includes:

- shares and indices;
- interest rates;
- currencies;
- commodities.

The key difference between futures and options is the potential for taking advantage of upside gains while limiting the potential downside losses. Options may allow:

- participation in short-term price movements with limited capital outlay trading on margins and risking less capital;
- hedging against a fall in price of an asset and using an option as an insurance policy.

Standard definitions for options are:

- Call: a call option is a contract giving its owner the right (but not the obligation) to buy at a fixed price at any time on or before a given date. Therefore a three-month call option with an exercise price of 250p on a share currently priced at 225p gives you the right to buy that share at 250p at any time before the expiry date.
- Put: a put option is a contract giving its owner the right (but not the obligation) to sell at a fixed price at any time on or before a given date. A three-month put option with an exercise price of 250p on a share currently priced at 225p gives you the right to sell that share at 250p at any time before its expiry date.

The main mathematical tasks are to determine the payoff from different options strategies to show if the option should be exercised or discarded and the main models for pricing options effectively.

TERMINOLOGY

The fixed price at which your option contract is set gives you the right to make a purchase or a sale eventually (exercise your right). This is called the options 'exercise' or 'strike' price. An American option uses the above definitions whereas European options can only be exercised on the expiry date. Since you can allow an option to lapse if it becomes worthless, options can be used for contingent as well as uncertain cash flows to cover risk. For example, you may be confident of taking an order and want to cover an export amount above the normal monthly average. An option could remove some of the risk; however, just as with insurance, the costs increase the closer you come to the market forward rates and therefore there is an eventual trade-off between cover and expenses.

As with futures, contracts and expiry dates are standardised by the exchange, such as in the form below. The contracts here expire in each of the quarters and the columns show the prices and volume traded. This gives an idea of the fluctuation and the liquidity in terms of the current volume.

Expiry	Latest Bid	Latest Offer	Volume Today	High Today	Low Today
01/12/2XXX	4,952	4,951.5	65,320	4,998.5	4,848
18/03/2XXX		4,993	98	4,905	4,865
17/06/2XXX			0		
16/09/2XXX			0		

Unit of trading: Contract valued at £10 per index point (e.g. value £65,000 at 6,500.0)

Delivery months: March, June, September, December (nearest four available for trading)

Quotation: Index points (e.g. 6,500.0)

Minimum price movement
(tick size and value): 0.5 (£5.00)

Last trading day: Third Friday in delivery month

Delivery day: First business day after the last trading day

Trading hours: 08:00–17:30

The table below shows the strike price and the distribution of call and put prices.

Open Interest	Total Daily Volume	Last Trade	Bid	Offer	Strike	Bid	Offer	Last Trade	Total Daily Volume	Open Interest
150					100					
150					110					
1,022					120					130
1,672	24	15.75	14	16	130					2,572
16,774	2,540	5.75	4.25	6.0	140		0.25			4,616
2,298				0.5	150	4.5	6.25	3.0	10.0	1,946
450					160	14.5	16.5			
					170		22.5	250		
					180					

Each contract includes the following:

■ Expiry dates are normally listed according to pre-defined cycles. In practice, contracts stop trading on a specific day of the expiry month ('last trading day'). A number of expiry months are listed at any one time with varying validity.

■ Exercise (strike) prices are made either side of the current price: for options on any given share or index, a range of exercise prices is available. For equity options there is usually an exercise price close to the current share price and a minimum of two exercise prices either side of it.

■ Premiums are the initial amounts paid. When purchasing an option, the premium is the price you pay for the product. If you are writing the option, this is the amount you receive in exchange for entering into the contract to fulfil future commitments.

■ Units of trading constitute individual contract sizes. Individual equity options are usually based on 1,000 shares so that the smallest amount for purchase or sale is 1,000 shares. Other options might be based on an index value priced at GBP per point, or a certain quantity of a physical commodity.

■ Quotation is the price quoted in the market. For UK equity options, the option premium is quoted as pence per share. If the contract is based on 1,000 shares, an option trading at GBP 0.05 will cost the purchaser $0.05 \times 1,000 = $ GBP 50.

■ Minimum price movement is the smallest amount by which the quotation can move. Equity options, quoted in pence per share, can move by a minimum increment of 0.5p. For one contract as a whole, this is valued at the minimum unit of trading of $1,000 \times 0.5p = $ GBP 5.0. This is also known as the 'tick size'.

UNDERLYING ASSET

If you do nothing then the profit or loss on an underlying asset is directly related to the future price. This is a simple profit or loss, as in Figure 12.1. As the price goes above 100 there is a profit and the converse is true below 100.

Figure 12.1

Underlying asset

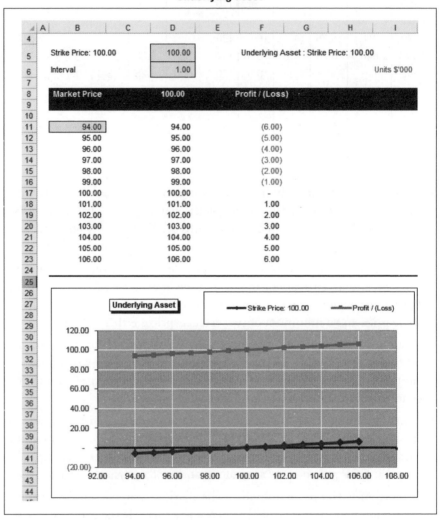

CALL OPTIONS

An option that gives you the right to buy something at a fixed price is called a 'call' option. If you buy that right, it is called a long call; if you sell that right, it is called a short call. Understanding the effect of buying and selling is easier with an Excel model to show the payoff as the underlying price moves closer or further away from the option or strike price (see Figure 12.2). The following examples use stocks; however, the same principles apply to other types of options.

Call option prices

Figure 12.2

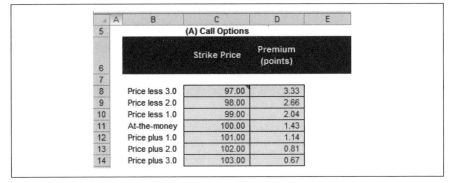

	A	B	C	D	E
5			(A) Call Options		
6			Strike Price	Premium (points)	
7					
8		Price less 3.0	97.00	3.33	
9		Price less 2.0	98.00	2.66	
10		Price less 1.0	99.00	2.04	
11		At-the-money	100.00	1.43	
12		Price plus 1.0	101.00	1.14	
13		Price plus 2.0	102.00	0.81	
14		Price plus 3.0	103.00	0.67	

Figure 12.3 shows a strike price of 100 and with example prices of call options.

Profit and loss table

Figure 12.3

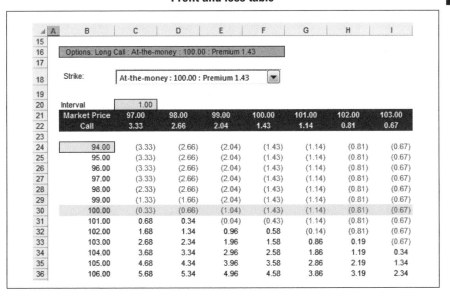

	B	C	D	E	F	G	H	I
16	Options: Long Call : At-the-money : 100.00 : Premium 1.43							
18	Strike:	At-the-money : 100.00 : Premium 1.43						
20	Interval	1.00						
21	Market Price	97.00	98.00	99.00	100.00	101.00	102.00	103.00
22	Call	3.33	2.66	2.04	1.43	1.14	0.81	0.67
24	94.00	(3.33)	(2.66)	(2.04)	(1.43)	(1.14)	(0.81)	(0.67)
25	95.00	(3.33)	(2.66)	(2.04)	(1.43)	(1.14)	(0.81)	(0.67)
26	96.00	(3.33)	(2.66)	(2.04)	(1.43)	(1.14)	(0.81)	(0.67)
27	97.00	(3.33)	(2.66)	(2.04)	(1.43)	(1.14)	(0.81)	(0.67)
28	98.00	(2.33)	(2.66)	(2.04)	(1.43)	(1.14)	(0.81)	(0.67)
29	99.00	(1.33)	(1.66)	(2.04)	(1.43)	(1.14)	(0.81)	(0.67)
30	100.00	(0.33)	(0.66)	(1.04)	(1.43)	(1.14)	(0.81)	(0.67)
31	101.00	0.68	0.34	(0.04)	(0.43)	(1.14)	(0.81)	(0.67)
32	102.00	1.68	1.34	0.96	0.58	(0.14)	(0.81)	(0.67)
33	103.00	2.68	2.34	1.96	1.58	0.86	0.19	(0.67)
34	104.00	3.68	3.34	2.96	2.58	1.86	1.19	0.34
35	105.00	4.68	4.34	3.96	3.58	2.86	2.19	1.34
36	106.00	5.68	5.34	4.96	4.58	3.86	3.19	2.34

At expiry, if the share's price has fallen below the exercise price, the option will be allowed to expire worthless. In this case the option is 'out of the money'. This is the maximum amount that you can lose because an option only involves the right to buy or sell, not the underlying obligation. When it is not in your interest to exercise the option you do not have an obligation and therefore the maximum loss is the initial premium you paid.

The formula in cell C24 is:

```
=IF($B24>C$21,$B24-C$21-C$22,-C$22)
```

When the price is greater than the strike price, the profit is the price less the strike price less the initial cost of the option. Here the option is said to be 'in the money'. The break-even point is the strike price plus the cost of the option. When it is below, the amount lost is only the option premium. In Excel this is best demonstrated as in Figure 12.4 since you are seeking this series shape for a long call.

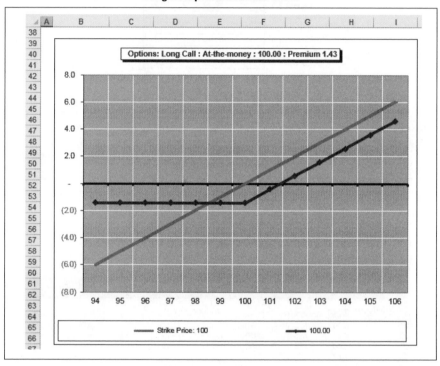

Figure 12.4

Long-call profit and loss chart

With a short or sold call the payoff is the other way around (see Figures 12.5 and 12.6). Here the potential profit is limited to the initial premium received for the selling option. As the price of the underlying security rises, the downside is unlimited since the underlying security has to be delivered. When the asset price is above the strike price, the formula is the strike price minus the asset price plus the premium. Therefore the option acts as a kind of insurance policy against adverse price movements.

The key points on call options are:

■ The most that the buyer of the option can lose is the initial premium.

■ The maximum profit that the writer can make is the amount of the initial premium.

Short-call table

Figure 12.5

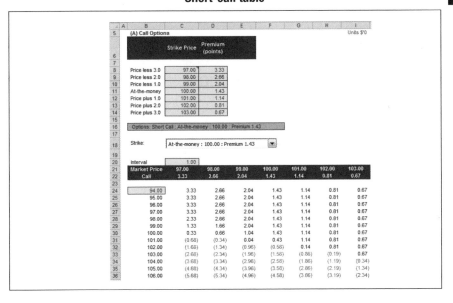

Short-call chart

Figure 12.6

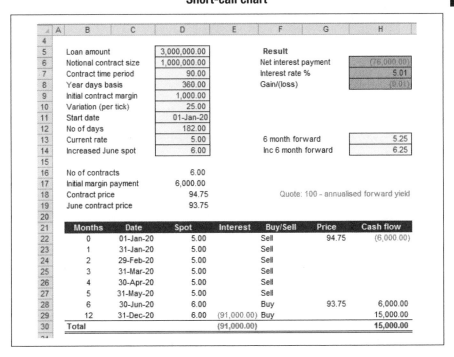

- The break-even point for both seller and buyer is the agreed strike price plus the initial premium.

- The potential profit to the buyer is unlimited and, on the other hand, the potential loss to the writer of the option is unlimited.

■ The holder of the call will exercise the option when the underlying asset price is greater than the strike price and will let it lapse when the price is below the strike price.

PUT OPTIONS

The opposite type of option to a call is a put option and this gives the right to sell at a predetermined price. Buying the right is called a long put and selling the right is called a short put. A put is the reverse of a call, in that the value of the position rises as the price of the underlying share falls since you are selling at the strike price.

Figure 12.7 shows a profit and loss table for a long put.

Figure 12.7 **Long-put table**

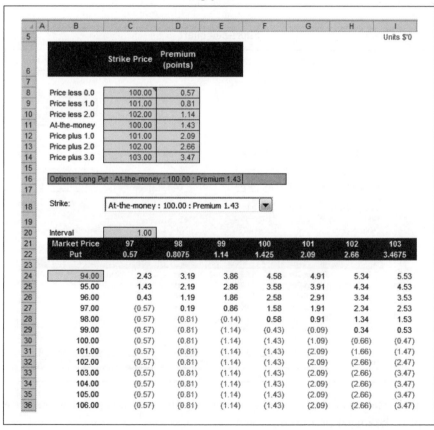

	B	C Strike Price	D Premium (points)	E	F	G	H	I Units $'0
8	Price less 0.0	100.00	0.57					
9	Price less 1.0	101.00	0.81					
10	Price less 2.0	102.00	1.14					
11	At-the-money	100.00	1.43					
12	Price plus 1.0	101.00	2.09					
13	Price plus 2.0	102.00	2.66					
14	Price plus 3.0	103.00	3.47					

Options: Long Put : At-the-money : 100.00 : Premium 1.43

| Strike: | At-the-money : 100.00 : Premium 1.43 | ▼ |

Interval	1.00						
Market Price	97	98	99	100	101	102	103
Put	0.57	0.8075	1.14	1.425	2.09	2.66	3.4675
94.00	2.43	3.19	3.86	4.58	4.91	5.34	5.53
95.00	1.43	2.19	2.86	3.58	3.91	4.34	4.53
96.00	0.43	1.19	1.86	2.58	2.91	3.34	3.53
97.00	(0.57)	0.19	0.86	1.58	1.91	2.34	2.53
98.00	(0.57)	(0.81)	(0.14)	0.58	0.91	1.34	1.53
99.00	(0.57)	(0.81)	(1.14)	(0.43)	(0.09)	0.34	0.53
100.00	(0.57)	(0.81)	(1.14)	(1.43)	(1.09)	(0.66)	(0.47)
101.00	(0.57)	(0.81)	(1.14)	(1.43)	(2.09)	(1.66)	(1.47)
102.00	(0.57)	(0.81)	(1.14)	(1.43)	(2.09)	(2.66)	(2.47)
103.00	(0.57)	(0.81)	(1.14)	(1.43)	(2.09)	(2.66)	(3.47)
104.00	(0.57)	(0.81)	(1.14)	(1.43)	(2.09)	(2.66)	(3.47)
105.00	(0.57)	(0.81)	(1.14)	(1.43)	(2.09)	(2.66)	(3.47)
106.00	(0.57)	(0.81)	(1.14)	(1.43)	(2.09)	(2.66)	(3.47)

The formula in cell C24 is:

```
=IF($B24<C$21,C$21-$B24-C$22,-C$22)
```

This means that if the asset price is less than the strike price, the profit is the strike price less the asset price less the option premium. At expiry, the put is worth nothing if the asset price is more than the exercise price; however, the maximum loss is limited to the option premium. The breakeven point is the strike price less the premium, so the purchaser makes unlimited profit below this price. The profit and loss chart for a long put is given in Figure 12.8.

Long-put chart

Figure 12.8

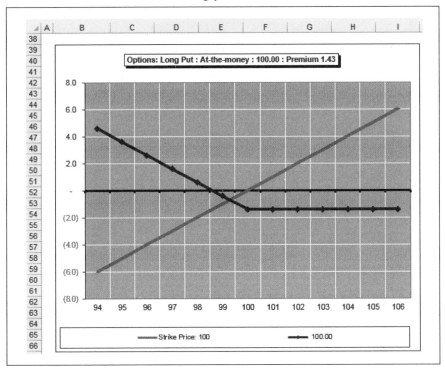

The seller of the put option (short put) has unlimited loss below the break-even point and the maximum profit is limited to the option premium. This can be shown on the table and chart (see Figures 12.9 and 12.10) by changing around the IF statement and checking the series shape.

The key points on put options are as follows:

■ The most that the buyer of the option can lose is the initial premium.

Figure 12.9　　　　　　　　　**Short-put table**

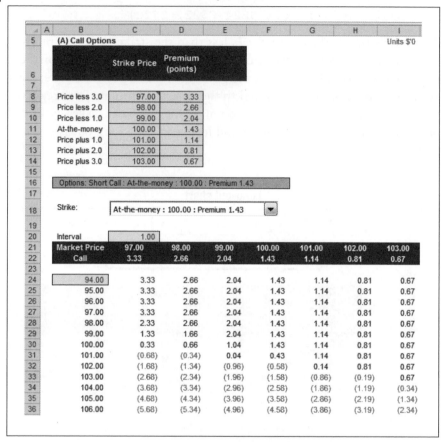

- The maximum profit for the buyer is limited to the strike price less the initial premium.

- The sum of the profits between the buyer and seller is always zero since one offsets the other. The buyer's profit equals the seller's losses.

The holder of the put will exercise the option when the underlying asset price is less than the strike price and will let it lapse when the price is greater than the strike price.

EXAMPLE

The example in Figure 12.11 brings together the four possibilities against a stock strike price of 600. The call is priced at 38.0 and the put at 9.0. Based on prices down the left-hand side, the payoff is listed using each of the IF statements to build up the overall picture. The formulas in row 14 are:

Short-put chart

Figure 12.10

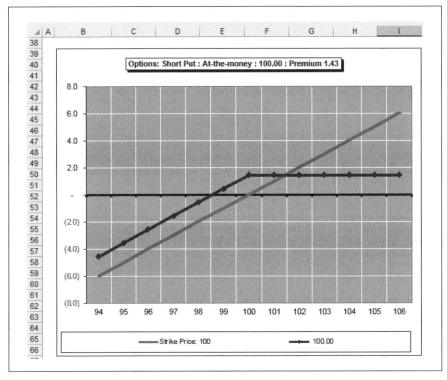

Example option table

Figure 12.11

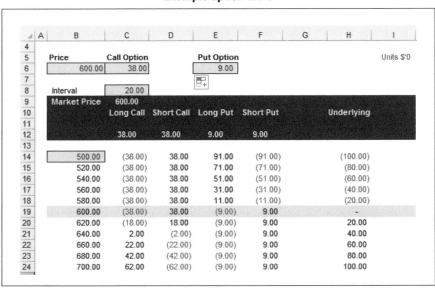

```
Cell C14:  =IF($B14>$C$9,$B14-$C$9-C$12,-C$12)
Cell D14:  =IF($B14>$C$9,$C$9-$B14+D$12,+D$12)
Cell E14:  =IF($B14<$C$9,$C$9-$B14-E$12,-E$12)
Cell F14:  =IF($B14<$C$9,$B14-$C$9+F$12,+F$12)
```

Again, it is better to chart the overall effect (see Figure 12.12). Each of the long positions is mirrored by a short position to each gain or offset by the other party's loss. The line through the middle with no markings is the underlying asset profit and loss around the strike price.

Figure 12.12

Four possible option charts

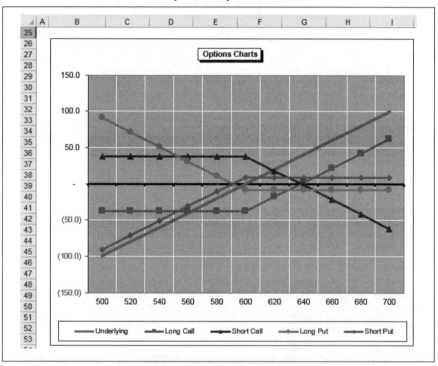

COVERED CALL

This is an example of combining a short call with a stock. In effect you will collect premium income for writing the call, and this is offset against upside potential on the stock. In the example (see Figures 12.13 and 12.14), the strike price is 600 and the current price 550. You gain 38 by writing the call. As the stock price climbs, you make money on the stock and lose money on the option. The upside is limited to 88 due to the dual effect of the profit on the stock and the loss on the option. If the stock goes down in price, the option becomes worthless; however, the premium is retained and this offsets the loss on the underlying stock. The attractiveness of entering into the transaction depends on the attitude to risk and an opinion as to the future direction of the stock.

Covered call

Figure 12.13

	A	B	C	D	E	F	G
4							
5		**Strike**		**Current**	**Call Option**		
6		600.00		550.00	38.00		
7							
8		Interval		20.00			
9			**Short Call**			**Underlying**	**Overall**
10			38.00				
11							
12		500.00	38.00		(50.00)		(12.00)
13		520.00	38.00		(30.00)		8.00
14		540.00	38.00		(10.00)		28.00
15		560.00	38.00		10.00		48.00
16		580.00	38.00		30.00		68.00
17		600.00	38.00		50.00		88.00
18		620.00	18.00		70.00		88.00
19		640.00	(2.00)		90.00		88.00
20		660.00	(22.00)		110.00		88.00
21		680.00	(42.00)		130.00		88.00
22		700.00	(62.00)		150.00		88.00

Covered call payoff

Figure 12.14

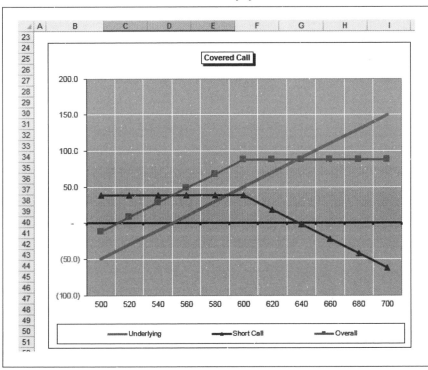

INSURANCE USING A STOCK AND A LONG PUT

The intention is to protect a stock from reductions in value. Buying a put makes money as the stock value goes down and the requirement is to offset the downside. The IF statement for the long put shows the profit as the asset price falls below the strike price. The underlying profit or loss is based on the current price of 550. The long put costs 45 and the overall columns combine the effect of buying the put and the underlying stock. The overall position provides insurance against asset price falls by removing the downside but leaving the upside intact. The chart also confirms the payoff (see Figures 12.15 and 12.16). To keep the insurance in place it would be necessary to buy more options at the existing market price as these contracts expire in order to maintain the cover.

Figure 12.15

Stock and put combination

	B	C	D	E	F	G
4						
5	**Strike**	**Current**	**Put Option**			
6	600.00	550.00	45.00			
7						
8	Interval	20.00				
9		Long Put		Underlying		Overall
10						
11		45.00				
12						
13	500.00	55.00		(50.00)		5.00
14	520.00	35.00		(30.00)		5.00
15	540.00	15.00		(10.00)		5.00
16	560.00	(5.00)		10.00		5.00
17	580.00	(25.00)		30.00		5.00
18	600.00	(45.00)		50.00		5.00
19	620.00	(45.00)		70.00		25.00
20	640.00	(45.00)		90.00		45.00
21	660.00	(45.00)		110.00		65.00
22	680.00	(45.00)		130.00		85.00
23	700.00	(45.00)		150.00		105.00

PRICING MODELS

In this chapter, the examples have used option prices and underlying asset prices without any discussion of the derivation of the pricing. The next sections introduce two widely used models to show the relevant factors and the pricing method. In return for a future obligation the writer of an option receives a premium against a potential future expense commitment, and so there must be some method for assessing value on either side of the bargain. The two models are the binomial model and the Black–Scholes model

Stock plus long put

Figure 12.16

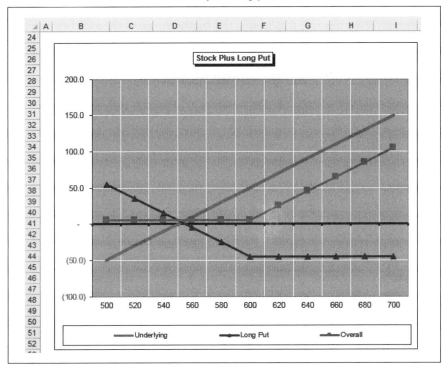

from the paper by Fischer Black and Myron Scholes ('The pricing of options and corporate liabilities', *Journal of Political Economy*, May/June 1973, pp. 637–54).

Pricing options depend on the probability that the asset goes up or down in price. In simple terms, the premium paid to the writer should represent the buyer's expected margin. The buyer can always exercise the option when advantageous and let it lapse when worthless. As in insurance contracts, probability theory should allow some model of expected outcomes and the rewards or costs. The probability of outcome depends on the following:

■ Volatility is a measure of past fluctuation, for example, stock or share prices. Theory assumes that volatile shares are riskier and therefore options should be more expensive due to unexpected outcomes. Standard deviation is used as a proxy for risk, although past volatility may not equal future volatility.

■ Strike price, since the buyer will always exercise when there is an advantage.

■ Maturity, since there is more chance that the option will accrue value. Forecasting is notoriously difficult over longer periods, as evidenced by columnists trying to forecast the FTSE 100 index 12 months ahead.

- Interest rates are important as the writer's premium can be placed on deposit and earn interest up until the point of expiry. Since the option is a form of forward price, this is affected by the shape of the yield curve.

BLACK–SCHOLES MODEL

The Black–Scholes model depends on a number of assumptions:

- Volatility and interest rates do not change over the period of the option. This may be a simplification since volatility and interest rates can and do vary over time.

- Future relative price changes are not dependent on historic or current changes, so that there is no 'memory' in the model which would require changes to the probability of outcome.

- There are no transaction costs such as dealing fees or taxes to distort the pricing.

- The probability distribution of relative price changes is lognormal. This distribution assumes a smaller probability of significant deviations from the mean and reduces the problem of the extremes or 'tails' in dealing with normal distributions.

The calculations look complex but are easier in Excel than using a financial calculator or tables. The formula has to be calculated in stages to reduce the cell complexity (see Figure 12.17). The inputs are:

| Figure 12.17 | | Black–Scholes formula |

⊿	A	B	C	D	E	F	G	H
4								
5		Current Stock Price: S	100.00					Units $'0
6		Standard Deviation: V	20.00%					
7		Annual Risk Free Rate: r	5.00%					
8		Exercise Strike Price: X	95.00					
9		Time To Maturity: T	0.5000					
10								
11		d1	0.6102		(LN(S/X)+(r+0.5*V^2)*T)/(V*SQRT(T))			
12		d2	0.4688		d1-V*SQRT(T)			
13		N(d1)	0.7291		Formula NormSDist(d_1)			
14		N(d2)	0.6804		Formula NormSDist(d_2)			
15		Call Price	9.8727		P*N(d_1)-X*exp(-r*T)*N(d_2)			
16								
17		-d1	(0.6102)					
18		-d2	(0.4688)					
19		N(-d1)	0.2709		Formula NormSDist(-d_1)			
20		N(-d2)	0.3196		Formula NormSDist(-d_2)			
21		Put Price	2.5272		P*N(-d_1)-X*exp(-r*T)*N(-d_2)			

- current stock price (S);
- volatility of the share price as measured by standard deviation (V);
- risk-free rate (r);
- exercise price (X);
- maturity date (T).

The first stage in the model is to calculate *d1* and *d2* using the formulas below:

$d1$: $(LogNormal(Stock\ price/Strike\ price) + (Risk\ free + 0.5 * Vol\wedge2) * T)/$
$(Vol * \sqrt{(Time)})$

$d2$: $d1 - (Vol \times \sqrt{(Time)})$

The function for a standard normal distribution is `NORMSDIST` and this is applied to *d1* and *d2*. The final formula is:

European call option $= Price * N(d1) - Strike\ price * EXP(-Risk\ free * Time) * N(d2)$

European put option $= Price * N(-d1) - Strike\ price * EXP(-Risk\ free * Time) * N(-d2)$

The second Black–Scholes sheet models the sensitivity to the exercise price and volatility. The inputs are the same as those used on the first Black–Scholes sheet and the workings are covered using `Data`, `Group` and `Outline`.

With the call, the price goes up with increases in volatility and with the reduction of the current price away from the strike price. The put option works in the opposite direction: the price increases with volatility but increases towards the strike price (see Figure 12.18).

This is a summary of the changes in variables and option value:

Factor	Call	Put
Increase in asset value	Increase	Decrease
Increase in volatility of underlying asset	Increase	Increase
Increase in strike price	Decrease	Increase
Increase in time to expiry	Increase	Increase
Increase in interest rates	Increase	Decrease

Figure 12.18

Black–Scholes sensitivity

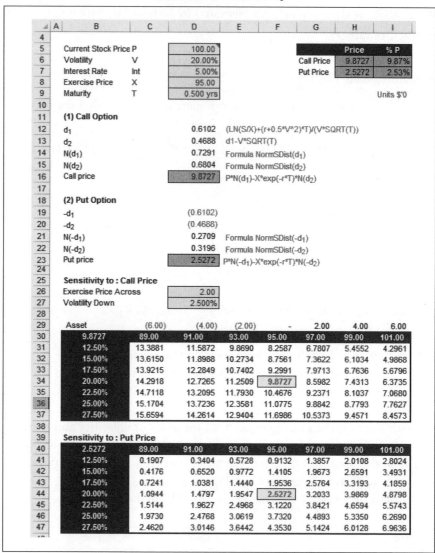

To show the changes graphically, there is a chart of the payoffs (see Figure 12.19).

Sensitivity chart

Figure 12.19

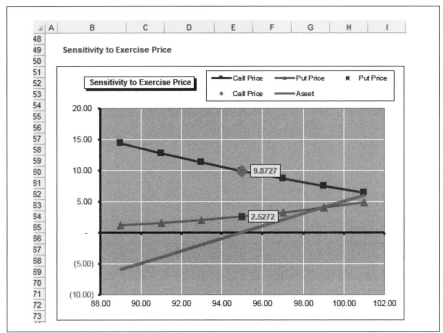

CALL PUT PARITY

There is a mathematical relationship between call and put options known as call put parity. If you have a portfolio where you purchase a share with an exercise price of 60, then purchase a put and immediately sell a call option. If the share price on expiry rises to 100, the net position would be:

Share	*100*
Call option	*−40*
Put option	*0*
Net position	*60*

If the price were below exercise price then the call would be worthless and the put option would be in the money. The call put parity is given by the formula:

Spot + Put = Call + Present value of Exercise price, or
Call premium − put premium = Present value of (forward price − strike price), or
Sell forward + buy call + sell put = 0

As stated with the assumptions, the formula assumes a perfect market with no transaction costs or taxes. The present value is calculated in the model using the basic formula $1/(1 + \text{Interest rate})$ and the periodic interest rate without any tax (see Figure 12.20).

| Figure 12.20 | Call put parity |

⬚ A	B	C	D	E	F	G
4						
5	Call		9.87			Units $'0
6	Put		2.53			
7	Maturity	T	0.500 yrs			
8	Interest Rate	Int	5.00%			
9	Volatility	V	20.00%			
10	Current Stock Price	P	100.00			
11	Exercise Price	X	95.00			
12						
13	Formula		P + Put = Call + Present Value of Exercise Price			
14	P + Put		102.53			
15	Call Price		9.87			
16	PV of X		92.71			
17	C + PV		102.58			
18	Variance		(0.06)			
19	Error on Parity		(0.06)			

GREEKS

The option price on its own is not enough as a single point answer. While models can express simple calculations in the same way as a handheld financial calculator, a superior Excel model should do more. There should be no overall profit from the transactions as discussed in the section above since a movement in one element is offset by the movement in another. Dealers need sensitivity values on options and these sensitivity numbers are known as the Greeks.

For example, as a call option price increases:

- exercise price decreases;
- time to expiry increases;
- stock price increases;
- interest rate increases;
- volatility increases.

On the Greeks sheet, the sensitivities are modelled together with explanations of the formulas (see Figure 12.21).

The definitions of the factors are:

- Delta measures how much the option's price will change when there is a change in the price of the underlying asset. This is the change in the option value/change in underlying asset value. For call options, the result ranges from zero for deep 'out of the money' call options, 0.5 at the money and approaching one for 'deep in the money' options. With puts options the values are close to zero deep out of the money, -0.5 at the money and approaching -1 deep in the money. The delta can be used for

Greeks workings

Figure 12.21

	A	B	C	D	E	F	G	H	I	J
4										
5		Call		9.87		Delta		0.729		Units $'0
6		Put		2.53		Gamma		0.023		
7		Maturity	T	0.500 yrs		Theta		(7.836)		
8		Interest Rate	Int	5.00%		Vega		23.418		
9		Volatility	V	20.00%						
10		Current Stock Price	P	100.00						
11		Exercise Price	X	95.00						
12										
13		Delta		Call	Put	Change in price when underlying price changes				
14		N(d1)		0.7291	(0.2709)					
15										
16		Gamma				Rate at which delta changes				
17		Ln(P/X)		0.0513		Gamma highest when option at the money and				
18		Adjusted return		0.0150		reduces away from the price				
19		Time adjusted volatility		0.1414						
20		d2		0.4688						
21		d1		0.6102						
22		Coefficient		0.3989						
23		(d1^2/2)		0.1862						
24		Exp-(d1^2/2)		0.8301						
25		N'(d1)		0.3312						
26		N'(d1)/(P*Time_Adj_Volatility)		0.0234	0.0234					
27										
28		Theta								
29		d1 at 0% Interest		0.4334		Minimum when share price equals exercise price				
30		r*Call-r*P*Delta-0.5*(V^2)*(P^2)*Gamma		(7.8356)	(3.2028)	For every 1/100 of a year premium moves by -7.836				
31										
32		Vega								
33		N'd1		0.3312		Sensitivity of an option to a change in volatility				
34		P*Sqrt(T)*N'd1		23.4178	23.4178	Most senstive when at the money				
35										
36		Rho								
37		Exp(-Int T)		0.9753						
38		N(d2)		0.6804	0.3196	Change in premium associated with a one basis				
39		Rho		31.5202	(14.8071)	point move in the short-term interest rate				

hedging purposes since it assists with working out the amount of the underlying asset to be bought or sold to cover a position.

■ Gamma measures the rate at which the delta changes with changes in the underlying price and is defined by the change in delta/change in price. A high gamma value means that a moderate change in the underlying price results in a larger change in delta. The gamma value should be positive for long call and put positions and negative for short positions.

■ Theta measures the change in value over time and is defined as the change in the option value/change in time. The value should be negative for a long position and positive for a short position.

■ Vega is the change in the option value which results from increased volatility and this should always be a positive value. This is defined as the change in option value/change in volatility. Increases in volatility increase the value of options since it is the risk or volatility that contributes to the price. The value is highest when at the money and declines as the difference between market and exercise prices increases.

■ Rho measures the change in option premium associated with a one basis point move in the short-term interest rate.

In the workings to the Black Scholes Sensitivity sheet there is a data table with volatility as the axis and this generates the Greeks for the different volatilities. Since the input for volatility is on this sheet, the data table as an array function has to be sited here also. The values are then simply looked up on the Greeks sheet and charted with the range of volatilities (see Figures 12.22 and 12.23).

Figure 12.22 — **Greeks table**

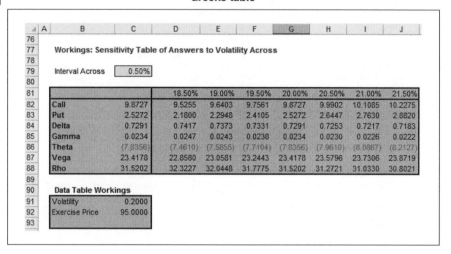

Figure 12.23 — **Greeks chart**

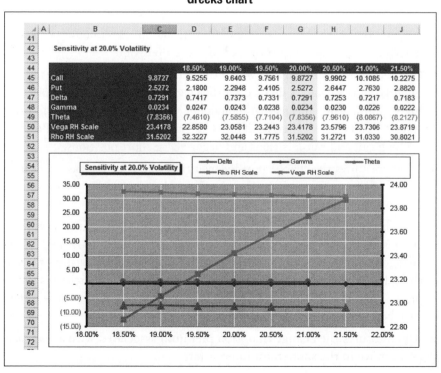

BINOMIAL MODELS

The binomial model can be constructed using a lattice of values based on the price of the underlying asset, risk-free rate, time to maturity and, as with the Black–Scholes model, the volatility in the price of the underlying asset. The model is pricing the level of volatility or risk and should arrive at approximately the same answer. The model is built on the assumption that there are two outcomes for an asset price at a particular point in time. It can rise or fall and there is a distinct probability of either occurrence.

In the example in Figure 12.24, the price today is 95 against an exercise price of 100. There is a 50:50 chance that the asset will go up or down in value. You need call options to hedge possible reduction in value and the number required is given by the hedge ratio.

Binomial payoff

Figure 12.24

			Probability	Value	Percentages
Value today				95.00	
Probability Up			50.00	120.00	1.26
Probability Down			(49.00)	80.00	0.84
Exercise Price (X)				100.00	
Option Value				2.00	
Required Holding (Hedge Ratio)				20.00	
		Step 1 Probability	Share Value	Option Value	Payoff
		50.00	120.00	2.00	80.00
	95.00				
		(49.00)	80.00	-	80.00
Variance					-

This is given in cell E11 as = (Up Value − Down Value)/2. Against a risk-free investment there has to be no gain or loss and given an option value of two, the following must hold:

$$120 - 2 * Hedge\ ratio\ n = 80 - 0 * Hedge\ ratio$$

The model above confirms that this is correct. This logic can be taken forward into the next model with more periods (see Figure 12.25). The valuation has to move through each of the periods and replicate the

Figure 12.25

Single binomial period

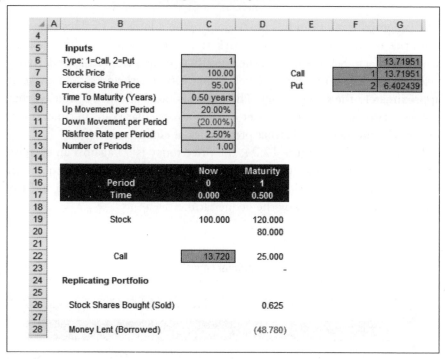

underlying portfolio for the asset being valued. The final value is given by this formula:

*Call value = Value of underlying asset * option delta – borrowing needed to replicate option*

In the example, the asset value can rise or fall by 20 per cent. The formula in cell D19 values the call option at 120 – 95. If the values decline then the option is worthless and therefore cell D20 is zero:

```
=IF(Type=1,MAX(D19-Strike_Price,0),MAX(Strike_
Price-D19,0))
```

The share bought and sold in cell D26 is equal to:

(Call up – Call down)/(Stock up – Stock down)

```
=(D22-D23)/(D19-D20)
```

The money let or borrowed in cell D28 is:

$$=(D23 - Stock\ Shares\ Bought * D20)/(1+(Risk\ Free\ Rate))$$

The call option is derived from:

$$=Stock\ Shares\ Bought * 100 + Money\ Lent = 13.720$$

The model with six periods carries forward the logic and builds up the lattice of the stock growing in value based on the probability of up and down (see Figure 12.26). At six periods, the formula in cell C31 is:

```
=IF($C$5=1,MAX(I21-$C$7,0),MAX($C$7-I21,0))
```

The exercise price is 95.0 and therefore the option has a value of 13.0. The risk-neutral probability is given by:

(Periodic risk free − Down percentage per period)/(Up percentage per period − Down percentage per period)

```
=(H6-C14)/(C13-C14)
```

The formulas work from right to left until C31 where the values in column D are used to derive the option value of 7.346 with no arbitrage.

```
=IF(D32=" "," ",($H$5*D31+(1-$H$5)*D32)/(1+$H$6))
```

The binomial model is perhaps simpler in methodology than the Black–Scholes; however, with few periods, the answers are different and therefore models are needed with many more periods. There is also an example with 50 periods since the values start to converge after about 20 periods (see Figure 12.27).

Six-step binomial period

Figure 12.26

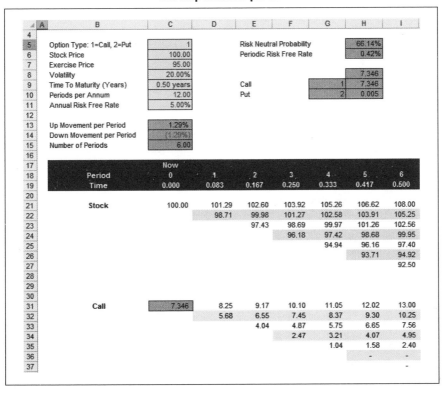

Figure 12.27

Fifty-step binomial model

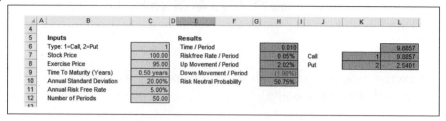

COMPARISON WITH BLACK–SCHOLES

The Black–Scholes Comparison sheet compares the binomial and Black–Scholes answers (see Figures 12.28 and 12.29). The inputs are the same.

Figure 12.28

Comparison inputs

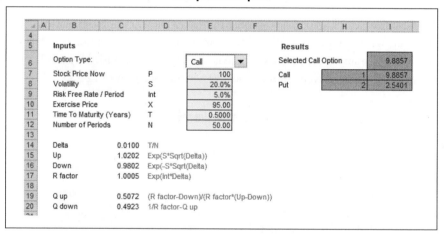

Figure 12.29

Black–Scholes workings

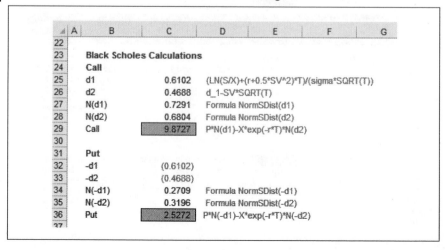

The formulas for the call and put options are (see Figure 12.30):

```
Call =IF(B98<=$E$12,COMBIN($E$12,$B98)*
$C$19^$B98*$C$20^($E$12-$B98)*MAX($E$7*
$C$15^$B98*$C$16^($E$12-$B98)-$E$10,0),0)
```

*Call = Previous Result + COMBIN(N, Period) * Q up ^ Period * Q down ^ (N − Period) * Max(Strike * Up ^ Period * Down ^(N − Period) − Exercise, 0)*

```
Put =IF(B98<=$E$12,COMBIN($E$12,$B98)*
-$C$19^$B98 * $C$20^($E$12-$B98)*MAX($E$10-
$C$15^$B98 * $C$16^($E$12-$B98)*$E$7,0),0)
```

*Put = Previous Result + COMBIN(N, Period) * Q up ^Period * Q down ^ (N − Period) * Max(Exercise − Up^Period * Down^(N − Period) * Strike, 0)*

Binomial formulas

Figure 12.30

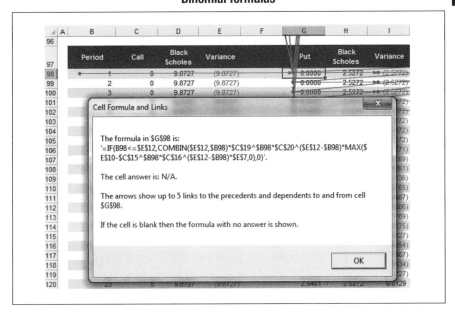

The function COMBIN is used to return the number of combinations for a given number of items (see Figure 12.31). Here the function determines the total possible number of groups from the period number and the total number of periods.

The schedule sets out the cumulative results for the number of steps in the binomial lattice. The maximum number of steps is 50 and, using IF statements, the model will accept a lesser number. The schedule in Figure 12.32 shows the binomial and the Black–Scholes answer for that number of steps together with the variance, which reduces with more steps.

Figure 12.31

COMBIN function formula

- The number of combinations is as follows, where number = n and number_chosen = k:

$$\binom{n}{k} = \frac{P_{k,n}}{k!} = \frac{n!}{k!(n-k)!}$$

where:

$$P_{k,n} = \frac{n!}{(n-k)!}$$

Figure 12.32

Variance schedule

	A	B	C	D	E	F	G	H	I
96									
97		Period	Call	Black Scholes	Variance		Put	Black Scholes	Variance
98		1	0	9.8727	(9.8727)		0.0000	2.5272	(2.5272)
99		2	0	9.8727	(9.8727)		0.0000	2.5272	(2.5272)
100		3	0	9.8727	(9.8727)		0.0000	2.5272	(2.5272)
101		4	0	9.8727	(9.8727)		0.0000	2.5272	(2.5272)
102		5	0	9.8727	(9.8727)		0.0000	2.5272	(2.5272)
103		6	0	9.8727	(9.8727)		0.0000	2.5272	(2.5272)
104		7	0	9.8727	(9.8727)		0.0000	2.5272	(2.5272)
105		8	0	9.8727	(9.8727)		0.0000	2.5272	(2.5272)
106		9	0	9.8727	(9.8727)		0.0001	2.5272	(2.5271)
107		10	0	9.8727	(9.8727)		0.0003	2.5272	(2.5269)
108		11	0	9.8727	(9.8727)		0.0011	2.5272	(2.5261)
109		12	0	9.8727	(9.8727)		0.0036	2.5272	(2.5236)
110		13	0	9.8727	(9.8727)		0.0107	2.5272	(2.5165)
111		14	0	9.8727	(9.8727)		0.0284	2.5272	(2.4987)
112		15	0	9.8727	(9.8727)		0.0686	2.5272	(2.4586)
113		16	0	9.8727	(9.8727)		0.1503	2.5272	(2.3769)
114		17	0	9.8727	(9.8727)		0.2996	2.5272	(2.2275)
115		18	0	9.8727	(9.8727)		0.5444	2.5272	(1.9827)
116		19	0	9.8727	(9.8727)		0.9018	2.5272	(1.6254)
117		20	0	9.8727	(9.8727)		1.3605	2.5272	(1.1667)
118		21	0	9.8727	(9.8727)		1.8638	2.5272	(0.6634)
119		22	0	9.8727	(9.8727)		2.3045	2.5272	(0.2227)
120		23	0	9.8727	(9.8727)		2.5401	2.5272	0.0129
121		24	0.1096	9.8727	(9.7631)		2.5401	2.5272	0.0129
122		25	0.6541	9.8727	(9.2187)		2.5401	2.5272	0.0129
123		26	1.6338	9.8727	(8.2389)		2.5401	2.5272	0.0129
124		27	2.9510	9.8727	(6.9217)		2.5401	2.5272	0.0129
125		28	4.4358	9.8727	(5.4369)		2.5401	2.5272	0.0129
126		29	5.8974	9.8727	(3.9754)		2.5401	2.5272	0.0129
127		30	7.1776	9.8727	(2.6952)		2.5401	2.5272	0.0129
128		31	8.1850	9.8727	(1.6878)		2.5401	2.5272	0.0129
129		32	8.9009	9.8727	(0.9719)		2.5401	2.5272	0.0129
130		33	9.3615	9.8727	(0.5112)		2.5401	2.5272	0.0129
131		34	9.6301	9.8727	(0.2427)		2.5401	2.5272	0.0129
132		35	9.7719	9.8727	(0.1009)		2.5401	2.5272	0.0129
133		36	9.8396	9.8727	(0.0331)		2.5401	2.5272	0.0129
134		37	9.8688	9.8727	(0.0039)		2.5401	2.5272	0.0129
135		38	9.8801	9.8727	0.0074		2.5401	2.5272	0.0129
136		39	9.8840	9.8727	0.0113		2.5401	2.5272	0.0129
137		40	9.8853	9.8727	0.0125		2.5401	2.5272	0.0129
138		41	9.8856	9.8727	0.0128		2.5401	2.5272	0.0129
139		42	9.8857	9.8727	0.0129		2.5401	2.5272	0.0129

The chart in Figure 12.33 shows how the binomial option moves closer to the Black–Scholes result. With fewer steps the binomial model will converge more quickly on the Black–Scholes result.

Call option comparison chart

Figure 12.33

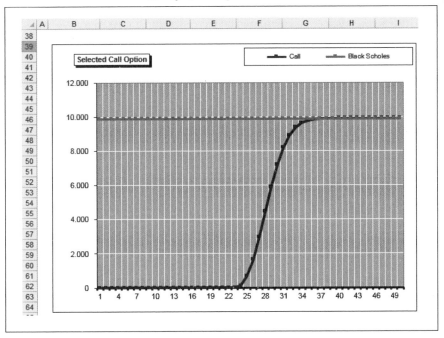

The chart in Figure 12.34 plots the differences between the options and the Black–Scholes model, and in this example the difference reduces to 0.01 by the last period.

Variance chart

Figure 12.34

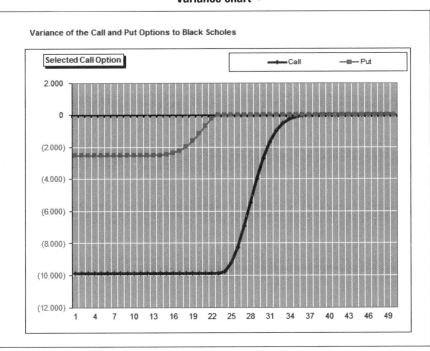

EXERCISE

Produce a spreadsheet to calculate the payoff from this strategy:

(1) Purchased call options

Exercise price	25
Premium	0.5
Number of contracts	4
Minimum number	200
Share price at option expiration	30

(2) Purchased put options

Exercise price	30
Premium	4.5
Number of contracts	4
Minimum number	200

(3) Shares

Purchase price	25
Number of shares	500

SUMMARY

Options pricing and the components of options prices can be viewed as payoffs with gains or losses. Charts show how call or put options become worthless as underlying prices rise or fall. Options can be combined with underlying assets to form payoffs which can hedge risk and the possibility of adverse price movements. The pricing emanates from the key variables of a risk-free rate, exercise price, strike price, time period and volatility. The Black–Scholes and binomial models provide standard methods for pricing call and put options and the sensitivity to change can be computed in the Greeks or sensitivity charts. Options can then be priced more accurately and combined to form trading strategies to reduce losses from increased or reduced volatility.

Real options

File: MFMaths3e_13.xls

REAL OPTIONS

Traditional investment analysis using net present value principles dictates that projects should be accepted if they achieve a positive net value when discounted at a risk-adjusted cost of capital. Since a model of this kind is a simplification of potential real-world scenarios, it follows that no model can include all the complexities of the relevant factors or there are uncertainties about the nature and connectivity of the inputs. For example, cash flow models assume that management can take no action to change cash flows or that an investment is 'all or nothing' and cannot be increased, scaled back or abandoned. Although you can undertake sensitivity analysis, you are often changing one variable at a time while ignoring the interplay of the various factors.

The net present value is typically found as follows:

- value of future free cash flows discounted at the risk-adjusted cost of capital;

- less initial investment;

- equals net present value.

This method could in theory reject projects which could become viable as a result of future action or delay. One modelling approach is to apply options theory to project and investment cash flows in order to assess the value of waiting, obtaining more information or following an alternative course of action. The shape of the payoff will follow either a call or a put option:

- call – option to delay or expand;

- put – option to abandon.

As with valuing and pricing options in the previous chapter, the key variables in the model are:

- Current asset value: S – this is equivalent to the strike price as the current value.

- Standard deviation: V – as volatility and therefore risk increases, the model will price the option at a higher level.

- Annual risk-free rate: r – the alternative risk-free rate.

- Exercise price: X – the exercise price as the cost of building or developing the assets.

- Time to maturity: T – number of time periods. In the example below, this is a year and so the interest rate used is the same as the periodic rate.

For comparison, other inputs are needed:

- Cost of option as the estimated upfront opportunity cost.

- Future asset value as the estimated value of the project at the end of one time period.

- Discount rate as the risk-adjusted weighted average cost of capital.

BLACK–SCHOLES MODEL

Specimen inputs are in the model below. The current asset value is 10.0 against a cost of development of 11.5, so the project fails on net present value grounds. The option cost is 0.5 and the volatility of cash flows is 20.0 per cent. The risk-free rate is 5.0 per cent and the cost of capital 10.0 per cent. The future asset value is estimated at 11.0, so the project should predict if it has a positive value using the Black–Scholes call formula (see Figure 13.1).

Figure 13.1

Black–Scholes inputs

	A	B	C	D	E	F	G	H
4								
5		Current Asset Value: S	10.000					Units $'000
6		Standard Deviation: V	20.00%					
7		Annual Risk Free Rate: r	5.00%					
8		Exercise Price: X	11.000					
9		Cost of Option	0.500					
10		Future Asset Value	11.500					
11		Discount Rate	10.00%					
12		Time To Maturity: T	1.000					
13								
14		d1	(0.1266)		(LN(S/X)+(r+0.5*V^2)*T)/(V*SQRT(T))			
15		d2	(0.3266)		d1-V*SQRT(T)			
16		N(d1)	0.4496		Formula NormSDist(d$_1$)			
17		N(d2)	0.3720		Formula NormSDist(d$_2$)			
18		Call Price	0.6040		P*N(d$_1$)-X*exp(-r*T)*N(d$_2$)			
19		Value - Option Price	0.1040		Price - Option Price			

The model follows the same call formula as in the previous chapter. The first stage in the model is to calculate d1 and d2 and then the option value using the formulas below:

$d1$: $(LogNormal(Asset\ price/Exercise\ price) + (Risk\ free + 0.5 * Vol^\wedge 2) * T)/(Vol * \sqrt{(Time)})$

$d2$: $d1 - (Vol * \sqrt{(Time)})$

$Call\ option = Asset\ price * N(d1) - Exercise\ price * exp(-Risk\ free * Time) * N(d2)$

The call price can then be compared against the initial option price, as in cell C19. Here the option has a net value of 0.1040. The model also checks the cash flows without using the option. In this case the initial outflow is 0.50 and, at the end of the time period, the cash flow is the future asset value less the exercise price (see Figure 13.2).

Present value of future cash flows

Figure 13.2

	A	B	C	D	E	F	G	H
13								
14		d1	(0.1266)		(LN(S/X)+(r+0.5*V^2)*T)/(V*SQRT(T))			
15		d2	(0.3266)		d1-V*SQRT(T)			
16		N(d1)	0.4496		Formula NormSDist(d₁)			
17		N(d2)	0.3720		Formula NormSDist(d₂)			
18		Call Price	0.6040		P*N(d₁)-X*exp(-r*T)*N(d₂)			
19		Value - Option Price	0.1040		Price - Option Price			
20								
21		Date	0	1	2	3	4	
22		Cash Flows	(0.500)	0.500	0.000	0.000	0.000	
23								
24		Present Value	(0.045)					
25								
26		-d1	0.1266					
27		-d2	0.3266					
28		N(-d1)	0.5504		Formula NormSDist(-d₁)			
29		N(-d2)	0.6280		Formula NormSDist(-d₂)			
30		Put Price	1.0675		P*N(-d₁)-X*exp(-r*T)*N(-d₂)			
31								

The formula in cell C24 is:

```
=NPV(C11,D22:G22)+C22
```

This demonstrates that the project should be accepted since the value with the option is greater than the initial cost of the option. The simple net present value views only the accrued benefits and ignores the potential benefit, whereas the project should be accepted if the value of the option is greater than the initial cost of the option.

BINOMIAL MODEL

You can achieve the same result with a binomial model, again with an increased number of inputs (see Figure 13.3). The model achieves similar results to the Black–Scholes model over 50 steps with a variance of 0.0021. The model uses the COMBIN function to return the number of possible combinations or steps:

```
Cell C101: =IF(B101<=$E$15,COMBIN($E$15,$B101)
*$C$22^$B101*$C$23^($E$15-$B101)*MAX($E$7*
$C$18^$B101*$C$19^($E$15-$B101)-$E$10,0),0)
```

Call = Previous Result + COMBIN(N, Period) * Q up ^ Period * Q down ^ (N − Period) * Max(Strike * Up ^ Period * Down ^ (N − Period) − Exercise, 0)

Figure 13.3 | **Binomial model**

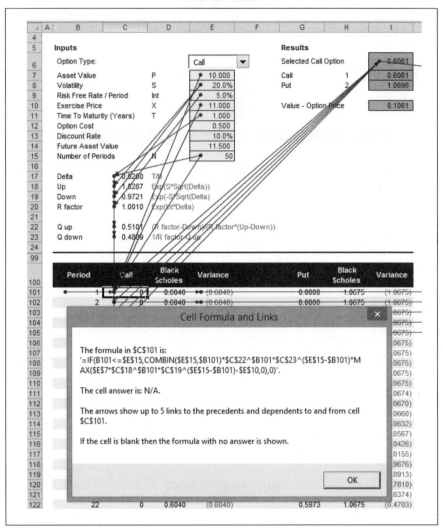

A sensitivity table shows how the option value increases with volatility from the 0.606 value at 20.0 per cent to 1.803 at 50.0 per cent (see Figure 13.4). As the project would only go ahead if profitable, then this alternative increases with volatility. Against the risk-free rate, the method provides a return on risk.

Sensitivity to volatility

Figure 13.4

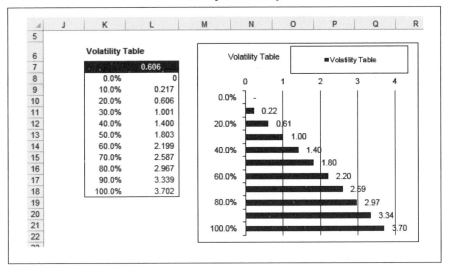

EXERCISE

Use options methodology to value an option to abandon with the data in Figure 13.5. This is a put option where the abandonment leads to a 50 per cent recovery of 500,000.

Exercise inputs

Figure 13.5

	A	B	C	D
4				
5		Years	T	10.0 yrs
6		Risk Free Interest Rate	Int	5.00%
7		Volatility	S	20.00%
8		PV of Future Cash Flows	P	1,500,000.00
9		Capital Value	PV	1,000,000.00
10		Salvage % of Capital Value	X	50.00%
11		Years Remaining	TR	5.0 yrs

The total project lasts ten years and an abandonment option exists for the first five years. The volatility is estimated at 20.0 per cent against a risk-free rate of 5.0 per cent. The annualised yield for the d1 calculation is $1/T$ or 10.0 per cent. The formula for the option value is:

$$=(EXP)(0 - Yield) * TR)) * P * N(d1) - Salvage * (EXP((0 - Int) * TR))$$
$$* N(d2) - (EXP((0 - Yield) * TR)) * P + Salvage * (EXP((0 - Int) * TR))$$

The value of the option can then be compared against the value of abandonment. A sensitivity table will show how the value changes with increased volatility.

SUMMARY

Options methodology can be applied to valuing the possibility of abandonment as a put option or the alternative to expand or delay as a call option. Since the potential gains and losses are being valued, the method avoids some of the pitfalls of the 'all or nothing' approach determined by traditional net present value techniques.

Valuation

File:MFMaths3e_14.xls

VALUATION METHODS

Valuation models use time value of money principles or simpler market principles to value assets, stock and shares or the perceived value of future benefits. Valuation by different methods does not necessarily produce the same answers and the market employs a wide variety of methods in order to ascertain underlying value. The purpose of this chapter is to set out some of the basic mathematics for valuation. Methods fall into these main categories:

- asset and adjusted asset valuations;
- dividend models;
- market methods;
- free cash valuation.

Companies can be valued from several different perspectives: for example, a liquidation value can be very different from a going concern. Alternatively, a stream of dividends is very different from cash flow, although a long-term investor may view a company purely for its income potential. Similarly it depends on whether you are buying or selling. Since a flow of future benefits represents a forecast, the financial model has to include all relevant inputs and demonstrate risk analysis of the key variables. The valuation is very likely a defined range rather than a single point which should then be compared with several valuation methods and with other companies within a peer group.

The printouts in Figures 14.1 and 14.2 show the base data for the model as an abridged income statement and balance sheet with supplementary information. The methods require information about earnings, dividends and cash flows, and this can be extracted from the data. Period 0 is the last historical data and there are five forecast periods.

Income statement

Figure 14.1

	B	C	D	E	F	G	H
		0	1	2	3	4	5
17	Earnings before Interest and Tax (EBIT)	15.00	20.00	23.00	26.00	29.00	32.00
18	Interest Paid	(10.00)	(15.00)	(16.00)	(17.00)	(18.00)	(19.00)
19	Earnings before Tax	5.00	5.00	7.00	9.00	11.00	13.00
21	Tax at 20.0%	(1.00)	(1.00)	(1.40)	(1.80)	(2.20)	(2.60)
23	Net Income	4.00	4.00	5.60	7.20	8.80	10.40
25	Dividends at 25.0%	(1.00)	(1.00)	(1.40)	(1.80)	(2.20)	(2.60)
27	Retained Earnings	3.00	3.00	4.20	5.40	6.60	7.80
29	Supplemental Data						
30	Depreciation	–	(20.00)	(13.00)	(11.00)	(12.00)	(12.00)
31	Capital Expenditure	–	(10.00)	(10.00)	(20.00)	(20.00)	(30.00)
32	Change in Net Working Capital	–	17.37	6.33	6.28	(1.78)	0.17
33	Change in Other Assets	–	10.00	–	9.00	(4.00)	3.00

Figure 14.2	Balance sheet

	A / B	C	D	E	F	G	H
14							
15		0	1	2	3	4	5
34							
35	Balance Sheet						
36	Assets						
37	Net Working Capital	30.00	13.00	7.20	1.60	4.20	5.00
38	Net Fixed Assets	200.00	210.00	220.00	240.00	260.00	280.00
39	Other Assets	20.00	10.00	10.00	1.00	5.00	2.00
40	Total Assets	250.00	233.00	237.20	242.60	269.20	287.00
41							
42	Liabilities						
43	Loan % at 8.0%	50.00	40.00	50.00	60.00	90.00	80.00
44	Bank Loan % at 8.0%	100.00	90.00	80.00	70.00	60.00	80.00
45	Total Debt	150.00	130.00	130.00	130.00	150.00	160.00
46							
47	Equity	100.00	103.00	107.20	112.60	119.20	127.00
48							
49	Total Liabilities and Equity	250.00	233.00	237.20	242.60	269.20	287.00
50							
51	Gearing	150.00%	126.21%	121.27%	115.45%	125.84%	125.98%
52	ROE	4.00%	3.88%	5.22%	6.39%	7.38%	8.19%
53	No of Shares	50.00					
54	Share Price	5.00					
55	Market Value	250.00					
56							
57	CheckSum: No errors	-	-	-	-	-	-

Other variables used in the model are as below:

Tax rate %	*20.00*
Loan %	*8.00*
Bank loan %	*8.00*
Risk free %	*5.00*
Risk premium %	*6.00*
Growth rate %	*5.00*
Future debentures discount rate %	*8.00*
Dividend payout rate %	*25.00*

ASSETS

A glance at the accounts shows a current equity value of 100.0 based on the shareholders' funds or equity. This is simply the accounting net worth, which does take account of many factors which could be important in determining value. Here is a selection of issues:

■ Not based on replacement cost of assets, but on historic cost.

■ Uses historical data and says nothing about the future and the organisation's future earning power.

■ Ignores the value of information and non-financial capital such as knowledge and patents which do not appear on the balance sheet. Non-financial assets in areas such as legal, healthcare, information, consulting and personal services could be more valuable than traditional fixed assets.

■ Accounting approach is based on a range of standards and conventions which can be applied differently and affect value. For example, the choice of depreciation method can enhance or reduce earnings merely by selecting periods or switching from accelerated to straight-line methods.

■ There are a number of items which are 'off balance sheet' and can mask the true level of borrowings or enhance earnings and therefore net worth. Examples include factoring, operating leases, joint ventures, contracted capital expenditure, contingent liabilities (e.g. asbestos), pensions deficits, derivatives and financial instruments, and current and future litigation.

MARKET METHODS

Stock market and earnings methods using share prices, earnings per share and price/earnings per share (P/E) are traditional ways of forming benchmarks or comparisons. The mathematics is very simple and spreadsheets are not really required, although the benchmark is often needed for comparison and price ranges. While the pricing reflects market sentiment about particular stocks which can rise on takeover speculation or fall during a crash, it does represent a fair price between a willing buyer and seller.

The basic calculation is:

*Market value = number of shares * share price*

The model needs:

■ earnings after tax and interest (NPAT);
■ number of shares;
■ calculated earnings per share (EPS);
■ price-earnings per share (P/E) ratio;

The valuation can be derived from either:

■ P/E × earnings per share = share price; or
■ Share price × number of shares = market value.

The net income and number of shares is on the Data sheet, and from this the earnings per share can be calculated as approximately 0.07. The current share price is 5.0, so the P/E ratio is 71.43.

The valuation is therefore P/E * net earnings: 71.43 * 3.50 = 250.0.

Figure 14.3

Market methods

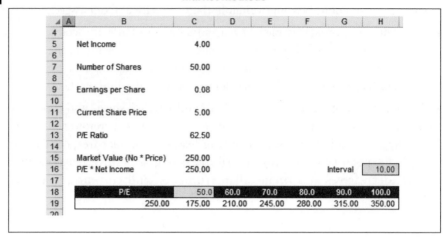

	A	B	C	D	E	F	G	H
4								
5		Net Income	4.00					
6								
7		Number of Shares	50.00					
8								
9		Earnings per Share	0.08					
10								
11		Current Share Price	5.00					
12								
13		P/E Ratio	62.50					
14								
15		Market Value (No * Price)	250.00					
16		P/E * Net Income	250.00				Interval	10.00
17								
18		P/E	50.0	60.0	70.0	80.0	90.0	100.0
19		250.00	175.00	210.00	245.00	280.00	315.00	350.00
20								

The data table in Figure 14.3 shows the sensitivity to the P/E ratio. The formula is:

$$\textit{Value of equity} = \textit{sustainable earning} * \textit{approx. P/E ratio} + \textit{value of non-operating assests}$$

The model would benefit perhaps from some adjustments since you need to identify sustainable earnings:

■ historical and forecast growth pattern, which may not match;

■ resilience ('quality') of earnings;

■ accounting adjustments and their effect on valuation;

■ adjustments for external factors beyond the control of the company;

■ quoted/unquoted adjustment since private companies are often valued as a percentage of the peer group to reflect the non-tradability.

This method also suffers from weaknesses such as the following:

■ A high P/E ratio denotes a share with growth prospects, but this is also dependent on market sentiment for the sector and the market, for example, the recent technology or banking booms followed by collapses.

■ The method is not based on time value of money concepts or real future prospects.

■ Companies invest now for returns in future periods and this is not included in the method. Earnings can be depressed by heavy investment which could generate enhanced cash flow in the future.

■ A company may issue shares at any time and optimism may overvalue shares and stock market sectors.

■ No account is taken of different accounting methods or changes in standards which affect earnings but do not alter the underlying cash flow.

Nevertheless, market methods reflect the value that people are prepared to pay for a specific stock and, in an efficient market, news and other negative information should translate quickly into share price losses.

MULTI-PERIOD DIVIDEND DISCOUNT MODELS

When you buy shares, you are essentially buying into the dividend stream. Unless you sell the shares, the only income is the dividend, and therefore the value could be viewed as the present value of the expected future dividends. The simple perpetuity formula is Gordon's growth model as a shortcut to present-valuing an infinite stream of cash flows. The simple formula is:

$$P_1 = \frac{D_1}{E(R_1) - g}$$

where:

D_1 = Dividend for next period, i.e. $D_0 * (1 + g)$
$E(R_1)$ = Desired return
g = Implied growth = Cost of equity − Dividend yield/$(1 + Dividend yield)$

In Figure 14.4, the dividend is 0.018 and the growth rate is 8.5 per cent. Therefore:

$$Value = (0.020) * (1 + 8.5\%)/(9.42\% - 8.5\%)$$

Dividend model

Figure 14.4

	B	C	D	E	F	G	H	I
4								
5	Assumed Terminal Growth		8.50%					
6	Earnings Retention Rate		75.00%					
7	Cost of Equity		9.42%					
8								
9	Period	0	1	2	3	4	5	6
10								
11	Return on Equity (ROE)	4.00%	3.88%	5.22%	6.39%	7.38%	8.19%	9.42%
12	Dividend Portion		0.97%	1.31%	1.60%	1.85%	2.05%	2.35%
13								
14	Net Income	4.00	4.00	5.60	7.20	8.80	10.40	
15	Dividends	(1.00)	(1.00)	(1.40)	(1.80)	(2.20)	(2.60)	
16								
17	Nominal Dividend / Share	0.020	0.020	0.028	0.036	0.044	0.052	0.056
18								
19	Growth		-	40.00%	28.57%	22.22%	18.18%	
20	Overall Growth Rate		21.06%					
21								
22	Terminal Value							6.16
23								
24	One Stage Value		2.37					
25	Two Stage Value per Share		4.06					
26	Firm Value		202.91					

The simple dividend model assumes a constant rate of growth in perpetuity. It is possible to construct multi-stage models using forecast dividends and different rates of discounting. In the model above, the company forecasts a period of rapid growth over the next five years before dropping back to more modest growth. The dividend rate is 25.0 per cent and the income and dividends are shown on the Data sheet.

The forecast dividends are discounted at the cost of equity and then the final dividend is subjected to the perpetuity formula. The terminal value is:

```
Cell I22: =I17/(C7-C5)
```

The share value is:

```
Cell D25: =NPV(C7,D17:H17)+PV(C7,H9,0,-I22)
```

The valuation by this method is 4.06 per share or 202.91 in total. The model is based on stable growth or dividends which last to infinity. This is a simplification: for example, dividends cannot grow faster than earnings since it is unsustainable that dividends would become greater than earnings over a sufficient number of periods.

The model is also extremely sensitive to the growth rate. As the growth rate converges on the discount rate, the value increases rapidly and will become negative if the growth rate exceeds the discount rate. The chart in Figure 14.5 shows a rapid increase in value followed by a dramatic fall above the growth rate of 8.5 per cent.

| Figure 14.5 | Sensitivity to growth rate |

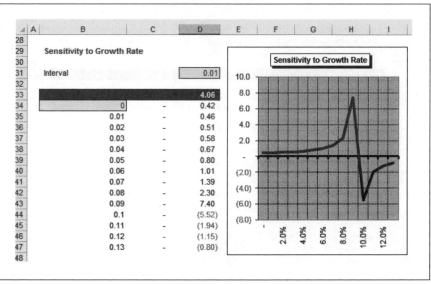

FREE CASH FLOW VALUATION

Free cash methods focus on the forecast cash to be produced by the company and discount the cash flows at a risk-adjusted rate to reflect the mix and relative cost of debt and equity. Given the weaknesses of other methods in using the time value of money or including future prospects, the reasoning behind cash flow is the focus on tangible future benefits which are not modified by accounting methods or standards. The methodology is:

- Forecast operating cash flows and prepare related financial statements as in the Data sheet.
- Calculate a suitable discount rate (cost of capital using a weighted average cost of capital formula for each source of capital).
- Determine a suitable residual value (continuing value using the perpetuity – Gordon's growth model) or some other suitable multiple such as the enterprise value (EV) to the earnings before interest, tax, depreciation and amortisation (EBITDA).
- Calculate the present value of the cash flows and terminal value above at the weighted average cost of capital.
- Add excess cash and cash equivalents and subtract market value of debt.
- Enterprise value less debt plus cash is the equity value.
- Interpret and test results of calculations and assumptions using sensitivity analysis to form a range of potential valuations.

Cost of capital

The model generates the forecast cash flows over five years that belong to all providers of capital. Therefore the discount rate or cost of capital needs to reflect systematic risk and cost of each form of capital. This is the weighted average cost of capital. Equity is calculated using the standard Capital Asset Pricing Model as an extension of portfolio theory. The formula is:

$$E(R_i) = R_f + \beta_i[E(R_m) - R_f]$$

where

$E(R_i) = $ *Expected return on share i*
$R_f = $ *Risk-free rate*
$E(R_m) = $ *Expected return on the market*
$\beta_i = $ *Beta of share i*

The risk-free rate is a suitable, almost risk-free rate such as a 10-year government bond. The historical range in the UK is currently 3 to 5 per cent and the model uses 5 per cent. The risk premium is a measure of the return that investors should demand for investing in shares and thereby accepting a risk rather than investing in a risk-free asset. While returns have varied in individual years over the last 50 years, the range has fluctuated between 10 and 12 per cent on the London stock market. Standard deviation is also substantial, which reflects the volatility of shares over government bonds. The model uses a premium of 6 per cent from the Data sheet.

Beta is a measure of volatility against an index. If a share price is more volatile than the index then the value will be greater than one, and less than one where it is less volatile. To illustrate the calculation of beta, the model contains some share and index prices over a five-year period on the Stock Prices sheet (see Figure 14.6). A simple mean and standard deviation are calculated using the AVERAGE and STDEVP functions:

```
Cell C7: =STDEVP(C10:C70)
```

Figure 14.6

Stock prices

	A	B	C	D
4				
5				
6		Mean	4,306.35	552.20
7		Std Deviation	574.74	289.63
8				
9		Date	Index	Company X
10		01-Dec-20	4,647.75	933.90
11		01-Nov-20	4,517.93	852.00
12		01-Oct-20	4,351.73	841.50
13		01-Sep-20	4,284.45	858.01
14		01-Aug-20	4,293.30	729.91
15		01-Jul-20	4,093.35	584.21
16		01-Jun-20	4,194.90	463.37
17		01-May-20	3,994.20	426.75
18		01-Apr-20	3,722.55	364.21
19		01-Mar-20	3,611.70	388.36
20		01-Feb-20	3,291.98	334.48
21		01-Jan-20	2,969.85	290.92
22		01-Dec-19	3,028.20	236.99
23		01-Nov-19	3,012.30	244.26
24		01-Oct-19	3,239.48	195.54
25		01-Sep-19	3,418.65	193.44
26		01-Aug-19	3,313.28	183.02
27		01-Jul-19	3,215.33	188.82
28		01-Jun-19	3,644.10	176.60
29		01-May-19	3,587.70	184.75
30		01-Apr-19	4,122.45	256.73
31		01-Mar-19	4,536.75	262.36
32		01-Feb-19	4,592.78	268.70
33		01-Jan-19	4,631.63	250.10
34		01-Dec-18	4,375.50	300.12
35		01-Nov-18	4,386.90	326.66
36		01-Oct-18	4,454.33	352.20
37		01-Sep-18	4,387.13	290.92
38		01-Aug-18	4,023.60	291.68
39		01-Jul-18	3,838.95	285.59
40		01-Jun-18	4,587.23	425.07

These prices need to be converted into excess return figures above the risk-free rate (see Figure 14.7). The Beta sheet calculates the return from one period to the next and then subtracts the periodic risk-free rate:

```
Cell C23: =IF(Stock_Prices!C11 <> 0, (Stock_
Prices!C10 - Stock_Prices!C11) / Stock_
Prices!C11,0)

Cell E23: =C23-Beta!$D$6
```

Adjusted stock prices

Figure 14.7

	A	B	C	D	E	F
20						
21		Date	Index	Company X	Above Average Risk Free	
22					Index	Company X
23		01-Dec-20	2.87%	9.61%	2.46%	9.20%
24		01-Nov-20	3.82%	1.25%	3.40%	0.83%
25		01-Oct-20	1.57%	(1.92%)	1.15%	(2.34%)
26		01-Sep-20	(0.21%)	17.55%	(0.62%)	17.13%
27		01-Aug-20	4.88%	24.94%	4.47%	24.52%
28		01-Jul-20	(2.42%)	26.08%	(2.84%)	25.66%
29		01-Jun-20	5.02%	8.58%	4.61%	8.17%
30		01-May-20	7.30%	17.17%	6.88%	16.75%
31		01-Apr-20	3.07%	(6.22%)	2.65%	(6.64%)
32		01-Mar-20	9.71%	16.11%	9.30%	15.69%
33		01-Feb-20	10.85%	14.97%	10.43%	14.55%
34		01-Jan-20	(1.93%)	22.76%	(2.34%)	22.34%
35		01-Dec-19	0.53%	(2.97%)	0.11%	(3.39%)
36		01-Nov-19	(7.01%)	24.92%	(7.43%)	24.50%
37		01-Oct-19	(5.24%)	1.09%	(5.66%)	0.67%
38		01-Sep-19	3.18%	5.69%	2.76%	5.27%
39		01-Aug-19	3.05%	(3.07%)	2.63%	(3.49%)
40		01-Jul-19	(11.77%)	6.92%	(12.18%)	6.50%
41		01-Jun-19	1.57%	(4.41%)	1.16%	(4.83%)
42		01-May-19	(12.97%)	(28.04%)	(13.39%)	(28.46%)
43		01-Apr-19	(9.13%)	(2.15%)	(9.55%)	(2.56%)
44		01-Mar-19	(1.22%)	(2.36%)	(1.64%)	(2.78%)
45		01-Feb-19	(0.84%)	7.44%	(1.26%)	7.02%
46		01-Jan-19	5.85%	(16.67%)	5.44%	(17.08%)
47		01-Dec-18	(0.26%)	(8.13%)	(0.68%)	(8.54%)
48		01-Nov-18	(1.51%)	(7.25%)	(1.93%)	(7.67%)
49		01-Oct-18	1.53%	21.06%	1.12%	20.65%
50		01-Sep-18	9.03%	(0.26%)	8.62%	(0.68%)
51		01-Aug-18	4.81%	2.13%	4.39%	1.72%
52		01-Jul-18	(16.31%)	(32.81%)	(16.73%)	(33.23%)
53		01-Jun-18	0.56%	(8.69%)	0.14%	(9.11%)

The scatter plot in Figure 14.8 is an XY scatter chart without a series line. The series formula is:

```
Chart:  =SERIES(Beta!$E$22,Beta!$E$23:
$E$82,Beta!$F$23:$F$82,1)
```

This plots the excess returns on the index as the X-axis and the company as the Y-axis.

Figure 14.8

Scatter chart

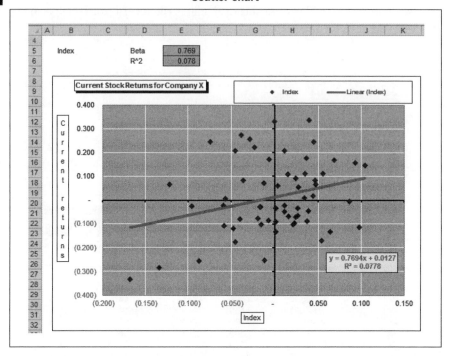

Since this is not very meaningful on its own, a linear trend line has been inserted to show the direction. If you select the series and right click, you have the opportunity to insert a linear trend or other types of trend line. If you click Options you can also insert the regression equation being used and the R-squared (measure of fit) value (see Figure 14.9). This is one way of calculating the beta of a stock since the beta is the slope of the trend line. A simple regression equation is in the form:

$$y = mx + b$$

where

$m = slope$
$x = next\ or\ forecast\ x\ value$
$b = intercept$

The equation here is y = 0.7694x + 0.0127 and so the slope (beta) is 0.7694.

There are other ways of calculating the beta using dynamic functions in Excel. The slope of a regression line is given by the formula:

$$Slope = Covariance_{xy}/Variance_{x}$$

There are the functions COVAR and VARP for calculating these two items, or Excel includes functions called SLOPE and INTERCEPT for calculating the value directly:

Trend line options

Figure 14.9

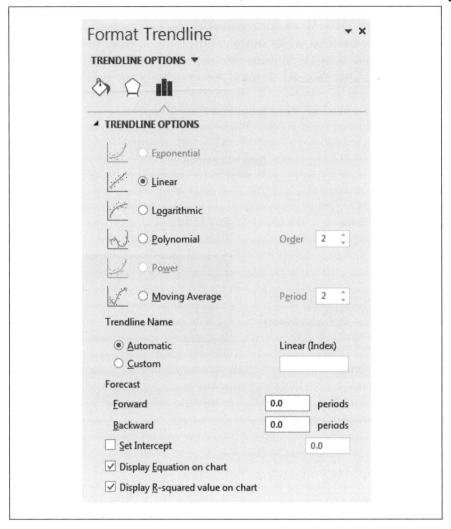

```
Covariance cell D11: =COVAR($E$23:$E$82,
$F$23:$F$82)
Variance cell D12: =VARP(E23:E82)
Slope cell D14: =SLOPE($F$23:$F$82,$E$23:$E$82)
```

These methods all achieve the same value of 0.7694. There is also an advanced array function called LINEST whereby you can calculate the intercept and slope together:

```
Cell D9: =LINEST(Beta!$F$23:$F$82,Beta!$E$23:$E$8
2,,TRUE)
```

To insert the function, the entries to cell D9 are as in Figure 14.10. All the entries are locked using F4 so that the formula can be dragged to the right into cell D10. With both cells selected, you go to the formula bar and insert the function with Control, Shift, Enter in order to enter the two cells as an array or block. Together the two cells calculate the intercept and slope dynamically. The cell on the right is the intercept. Again the answer is 0.7694.

Figure 14.10

Beta calculation

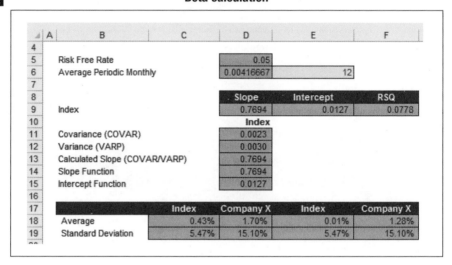

	B	C	D	E	F
4					
5	Risk Free Rate		0.05		
6	Average Periodic Monthly		0.00416667	12	
7					
8			Slope	Intercept	RSQ
9	Index		0.7694	0.0127	0.0778
10			Index		
11	Covariance (COVAR)		0.0023		
12	Variance (VARP)		0.0030		
13	Calculated Slope (COVAR/VARP)		0.7694		
14	Slope Function		0.7694		
15	Intercept Function		0.0127		
16					
17		Index	Company X	Index	Company X
18	Average	0.43%	1.70%	0.01%	1.28%
19	Standard Deviation	5.47%	15.10%	5.47%	15.10%

This provides all the information for the beta calculation, bearing in mind that beta is affected both by volatility and by the company's financial leverage. Since the data is backward looking, the effect of the historical debt/equity needs to be stripped out and then reinserted as a forward debt/equity ratio.

The formulas for leveraging are:

- Asset (un-leveraged) beta: $\text{Beta}_U = \text{Beta}_L / [1 + (1 - \text{tax}) * (D/E)]$
- Equity (leveraged) beta: $\text{Beta}_L = \text{Beta}_U * [1 + (1 - \text{tax}) * (D/E)]$

```
Cell C12: = ($C$11/(1+(1-$C$9)*$C$10))
Cell G12: = (C12*(1+(1-$C$9)*G10))
```

The formulas above un-leverage the beta based on the tax rate of 20.0 per cent and a debt/equity ratio of 60.0 per cent. The forecast debt/equity ratio is 52 per cent and therefore the forward beta is slightly lower than the historical beta (see Figure 14.11).

Beta calculation

Figure 14.11

	A	B	C	D	E	F	G	H	I
4									
5		**(1) Equity**							
6		Risk Free Rate	5.00%		$C$6: ' =Beta!D5				
7		Risk Premium	6.00%		$C$7: ' =Data!C10/100				
8									
9		Tax Rate	20.00%		$C$9: ' =Data!C6/100				
10		Historical Debt/Equity Ratio	60.00%		$C$10: ' =(Data!C43+Data!C44)/(Data!C53*Data!C54)				
11		Calculated Beta	0.7694		$C$11: ' =Beta!D9				
12		Asset Beta	0.5198		$C$12: ' =($C$11/(1+(1-$C$9)*$C$10))				
13		Unleveraged Cost of Equity	8.12%		$C$13: ' =C6+C7*C12				
14									
15		Historical CAPM	9.62%		$C$15: ' =C6+C7*C11				
16		Forecast D/E Ratio	52.00%		$C$16: ' =(Data!D43+Data!D44)/(Data!C53*Data!C54)				
17		Equity Beta	0.7361		$C$17: ' =($C$12*(1+(1-$C$9)*$C$16))				
18									
19		Leveraged Cost of Equity	9.417%		$C$19: ' =C6+C17*C7				
20									
21		**(2) Debt**			$C$21:				
22		Cost of Debt	8.00%		$C$22: ' =((Data!C7/100)*(Data!D43/Data!D45))+((Dat				
23		Tax Rate	20.00%		$C$23: ' =C9				
24									
25		Net of Tax Cost of Debt	6.400%		$C$25: ' =C22*(1-C23)				
26									
27		**(3) Weightings**							
28		Equity	250.00		65.79%	$C$28: ' =Data!C53*Data!C54			
29		Debt	130.00		34.21%	$C$29: ' =Data!D43+Data!D44			
30		Total	380.00		100.00%	$C$30: ' =SUM(C28:C29)			
31									
32		**(4) Weighted Average Cost of Capital**							
33									
34		Equity	6.195%			$C$34: ' =C19*E28			
35		Debt	2.189%			$C$35: ' =C25*E29			
36									
37		WACC	8.385%			$C$37: ' =SUM(C34:C36)			

With the re-leveraged beta, the cost of equity can be calculated with the Capital Asset Pricing Model (CAPM) formula. The cost of debt is the weighted cost of the two facilities multiplied by (1 – tax) at 5.6 per cent. The cost of capital formula (WACC) is the weighting multiplied by the cost for each source of capital. The workings above find the weightings of each source and multiply out the costs:

WACC formula: $D/D + E * Cost\ of\ Debt + E/D + E * Cost\ of\ Equity$

The cost of capital is 8.38 per cent. Based on the figures, the cost of capital declines as leverage increases since the cost of debt is constant. It is likely that increased leverage could lead to an increased cost of debt and therefore the cost of capital could start to rise. The model could easily be extended to pick a rate from a table of leverage and borrowing rates (see Figure 14.12).

Figure 14.12   **Sensitivity to debt ratio**

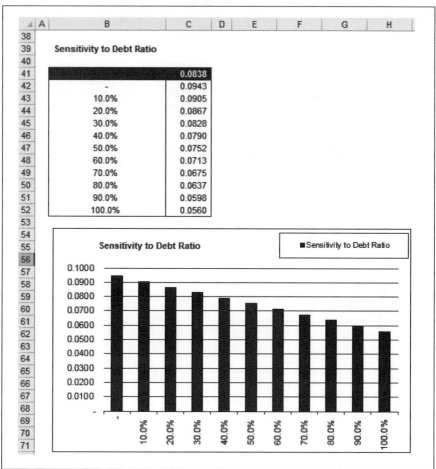

Free cash valuation

The FCF sheet brings together the cash flows, cost of capital and terminal value. The schedule looks up values from the Data sheet and generates a free cash flow (see Figure 14.13). This is the cash available to pay dividends to shareholders and interest to debt or bond holders. The terminal value is calculated in cell I20 using the perpetuity formula:

$$(9.8 * (1 + Growth)) / (WACC - Growth)$$

Other possible methods for calculating the terminal value (which could all yield different answers) include:

- EV/EBITDA or other multiple;
- P/E ratio;
- liquidation value;

Free cash flow valuation

Figure 14.13

	B	C	D	E	F	G	H	I
5	Units $'000		0	1	2	3	4	5
7	Earnings before Interest and Tax (EBIT)		15.00	20.00	23.00	26.00	29.00	32.00
8	Less Tax at 20.0%		(3.00)	(4.00)	(4.60)	(5.20)	(5.80)	(6.40)
9	EBIT * (1 - Tax)		12.00	16.00	18.40	20.80	23.20	25.60
11	Depreciation		-	20.00	13.00	11.00	12.00	12.00
12	Operating Cash Flow		12.00	36.00	31.40	31.80	35.20	37.60
14	Less Capital Expenditure		-	(10.00)	(10.00)	(20.00)	(20.00)	(30.00)
15	Less Change in Net Working Capital		-	17.00	5.80	5.60	(2.60)	(0.80)
16	Less Change in Other Assets		-	10.00	-	9.00	(4.00)	3.00
18	Free Cash Flow		12.00	53.00	27.20	26.40	8.60	9.80
20	Terminal Value: (9.80*(1+Growth))/(WACC-Growth)							304.03
22	Total Cash Flow			53.00	27.20	26.40	8.60	313.83
24	Weighted Average Cost of Capital		8.38					
26	FCF Valuation at 8.38%		308.84					
28	Subtract Debt		(150.00)					
30	FCF Equity Value		158.84					

- replacement cost;
- book value;
- market to book value ratio;
- two- and three-stage perpetuity models with a fade factor to a cost of capital.

The enterprise value of 308.84 is gained by discounting the cash flows and the terminal value at the cost of capital of 8.38 per cent. This is in effect the sum of the market values of both debt and equity. Since the equity value is required, the value of current debt is subtracted leaving an equity value of 158.84.

This schedule approach does not show clearly the various elements of the investment and cash flow model, and one solution is to model it showing the various steps. The graphic in Figure 14.14 is an example of trying to show the components of the equity value. The chart shows the proportion of value that is derived from the terminal value calculation which is over 65.0 per cent. Despite the relative complexity of this method over market multiples, the result is still dependent on key factors such as the terminal value growth rate, leverage and the cost of capital and the forecast cash flows.

| Figure 14.14 | **Proportion of value from cash flows and terminal value** |

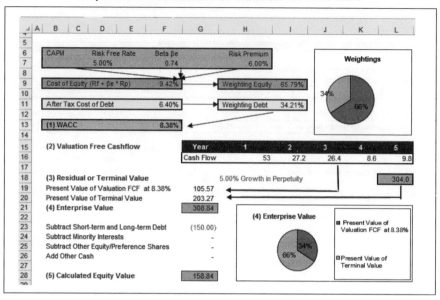

ADJUSTED PRESENT VALUE

The adjusted present value (APV) method is a variant on free cash flows. Instead of deriving a composite value, this pieces together value from different segments to try to show where the value comes from. The free cash method above does not tell how much leverage or cost improvements are worth, and for risk analysis this could help to show the potential risks in achieving a suitable return.

Examples of layers are:

- margin improvement;
- plant closures or cost reductions;
- synergies;
- working capital improvements;
- asset sales;
- high terminal value growth.

In Figure 14.15, the base case valuation is 1.0 per share and further 'layers' show a potential value of 1.60 if all the plans are realised. The model therefore needs to split out each of these components.

The steps as in Figure 14.16 are:

- Develop the free cash forecast as in the last section using discounted cash flow methodology.

Valuation gains (MBO = Management Buyout)

Figure 14.15

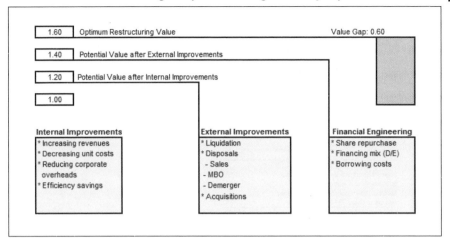

APV framework

Figure 14.16

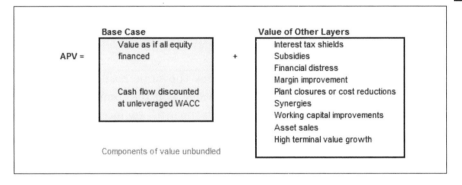

- Discount the cash flows using a cost of equity derived from the unleveraged beta.
- Calculate actual interest tax shield gained from the leverage and discount at the cost of debt.
- Develop free cash flows for all other synergies and benefits of the transaction. These cash flows need to be adjusted for tax.
- Discount each layer using its own appropriate cost of capital to form a series of net present values for each of the revenue gains and costs.
- Add together all elements to obtain the adjusted present value which is equivalent to the firm's enterprise value.
- Subtract the debt to form the equity value as in free cash flow methodology.

Figure 14.17

APV base case

	B	C	D	E	F	G	H	I
4								
5			0	1	2	3	4	5
6								
7	Free Cash Flow of Assets		12.00	53.00	27.20	26.40	8.60	9.80
8								
9	Terminal Value: (9.80*(1+Growth))/(Equity-Growth)							329.91
10								
11	Total Cash Flow		12.00	53.00	27.20	26.40	8.60	339.71
12								
13	Risk Free Rate		5.00					
14	Risk Premium		6.00					
15	Asset Beta		0.52					
16	CAPM Cost of Equity		8.12					
17	Base EV at 8.12%		329.40					
18								
19	Subtract Short-term and Long-term Debt		(150.00)					
20	Subtract Minority Interests							
21	Subtract Other Equity/Preference Shares							
22	Add Other Cash							
23	APV Equity Value		179.40					

The cash flow in Figure 14.17 uses the cost of equity with an un-leveraged beta. This was calculated on the WACC sheet:

Risk-free rate	*5.00%*
Risk premium	*6.00%*
Asset beta	*0.52*
Un-leveraged cost of equity	*8.12%*

The terminal value calculation also uses the same cost of equity (see Figure 14.18). The result is the present value as if the company were fully equity funded. This is the base case before any financial engineering or leverage.

Figure 14.18

Interest shield

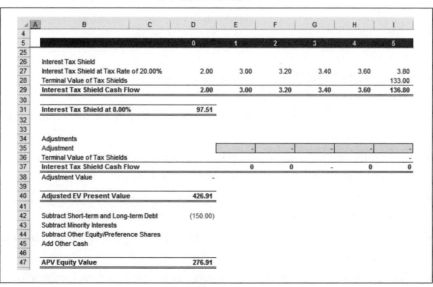

	B	C	D	E	F	G	H	I
4								
5			0	1	2	3	4	5
25								
26	Interest Tax Shield							
27	Interest Tax Shield at Tax Rate of 20.00%		2.00	3.00	3.20	3.40	3.60	3.80
28	Terminal Value of Tax Shields							133.00
29	Interest Tax Shield Cash Flow		2.00	3.00	3.20	3.40	3.60	136.80
30								
31	Interest Tax Shield at 8.00%		97.51					
32								
33								
34	Adjustments							
35	Adjustment			-	-	-	-	-
36	Terminal Value of Tax Shields							-
37	Interest Tax Shield Cash Flow		0	0	-	0	0	
38	Adjustment Value		-					
39								
40	Adjusted EV Present Value		426.91					
41								
42	Subtract Short-term and Long-term Debt		(150.00)					
43	Subtract Minority Interests							
44	Subtract Other Equity/Preference Shares							
45	Add Other Cash							
46								
47	APV Equity Value		276.91					

The next stage is to plot the interest tax shield. This is the interest paid on line 18 of the Data sheet multiplied by the tax rate. The terminal value is also calculated to form a total cash flow which can be discounted at the cost of debt. This procedure can be repeated for other layers of cost or revenue gain. The adjusted present value is then the sum of each of the components as above. This procedure could also be applied to other types of cash model such as investment or project finance where the model needs more flexibility than a single output.

ECONOMIC PROFIT

Economic profit is an alternative way of looking at the returns made by the company. Traditional return on capital measures calculate the return on invested capital, assets or equity. Since the level of capital can be altered by off-balance sheet financing or the level of profit enhanced by switching accounting methods, this method seeks to look at real value generation. Drawbacks with accounting methods include:

■ income recognition, not cash;

■ creative accounting and presentation;

■ drawbacks with selecting projects/transactions on income/capital ratios.

The formula used for economic value added in the model is:

$$EVA = Opening\ capital + (Copy\ of\ capital * Capital\ employed)$$

This will provide a cost of employing capital during the period and any increase must derive from a return on the capital rather than profit. Thus a company increases value by earning over and above the cost of capital and should give rise to:

■ growing by investing in new projects whose return more than compensates for risks taken;

■ curtailing investment in and diverting capital from uneconomic activities.

Capital in a complete model is calculated as the sum of:

■ ordinary equity value;

■ unusual losses/(gains) on balance sheet;

■ preferred stock and minority interests;

■ all debt (book, not market value);

■ present value of non-capitalised leases, less marketable securities;

■ other adjustments to last-in, first-out (LIFO) reserve, goodwill, accounting reserves, capitalised value of marketing, and research and development.

The schedule in Figure 14.19 shows the calculation of economic profit in line 27 based on the calculated cost of capital in the WACC sheet. The total is calculated as the opening capital plus the present value of the gains and losses. At the root is therefore a simple net present value model which reduces future cash flows to a present value to show an overall position.

Figure 14.19

Economic profit

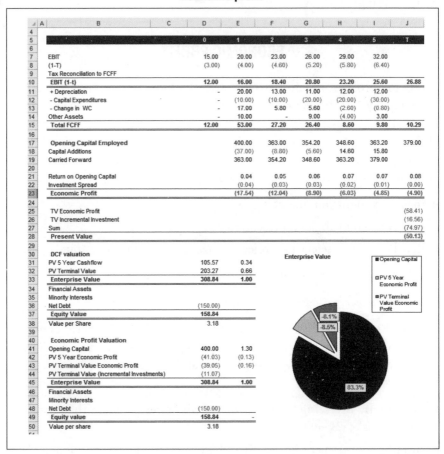

For completeness, there is a comparison chart in the model to demonstrate the different values gained by each method (see Figure 14.20). This shows the cash and dividend models producing lower values than the current market value.

Comparison of values

Figure 14.20

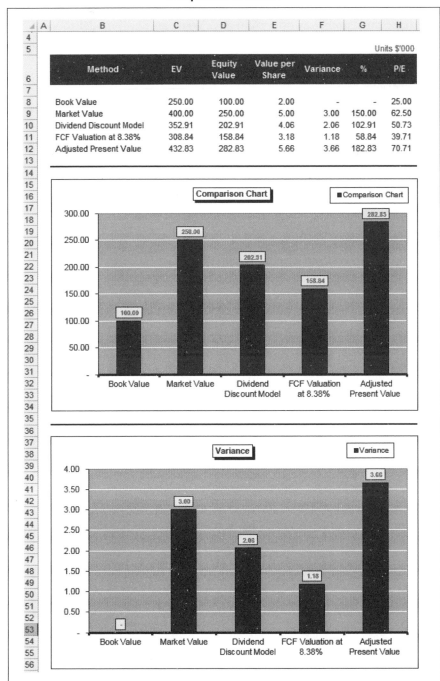

	A	B	C	D	E	F	G	H
4								
5								Units $'000
6		Method	EV	Equity Value	Value per Share	Variance	%	P/E
7								
8		Book Value	250.00	100.00	2.00	–	–	25.00
9		Market Value	400.00	250.00	5.00	3.00	150.00	62.50
10		Dividend Discount Model	352.91	202.91	4.06	2.06	102.91	50.73
11		FCF Valuation at 8.38%	308.84	158.84	3.18	1.18	58.84	39.71
12		Adjusted Present Value	432.83	282.83	5.66	3.66	182.83	70.71

Comparison Chart

Book Value 100.00, Market Value 258.00, Dividend Discount Model 202.91, FCF Valuation at 8.38% 158.84, Adjusted Present Value 282.83

Variance

Book Value –, Market Value 3.00, Dividend Discount Model 2.06, FCF Valuation at 8.38% 1.18, Adjusted Present Value 3.66

EXERCISE

You have the data below on a company. Write an Excel model to value the cash flows, together with two sensitivity tables: a one-dimensional table to WACC and a two-way table to the WACC and growth rate.

WACC	10.00
Growth	1.00
Debt	250.00
Minority Interests	100.00

The annual cash flow forecast begins in one year's time. The final cash flow can be used for a terminal value growth calculation.

Year	1	2	3	4	5	6	7
Cash Flow	100.00	125.00	150.00	175.00	200.00	225.00	250.00

SUMMARY

There are many ways of valuing companies and this section introduces the basic mathematics for using accounting values, dividends, multiples and cash methods. Using perpetuity and discounted cash flow methods, the techniques can be applied to value dividends or cash over initial forecast and longer periods.

Leasing

File: MFMaths3e_15.xls

ECONOMICS OF LEASING

Leasing can be compared with loans except that the sole security is usually the equipment rather than a fixed charge or other security. The financing method has a long history of at least 3,000 years, since the essential benefit allows the borrower the use of assets while paying for them principally to aid cash flow. In the nineteenth century, UK rolling stock leasing companies took advantage of the new joint stock companies legislation in the 1850s to lease wagons to the new rail operating companies, while leasing helped similar companies in the United States in the 1870s. The situation has gone full circle in the UK with post-nationalised operating companies and rail leasing companies opting to lease new rolling stock.

This is one definition of leasing:

> *A lease is an agreement whereby the owner (lessor) allows another party (lessee) to use an asset for a specific period of time in return for a rental. The asset could be fixed or movable plant or real estate. The ownership and use of the asset are separated, allowing one party to fund the purchase of the asset and the other to use the asset in its business or trade.*

Within these definitions, there are three main types of lease:

- Finance lease (or capital lease in the United States) is similar to a loan, where the rentals usually write off the whole of the capital cost over the rental period.

- Operating lease denotes a lease where the lessor relies not only on the rental period for its profits but also retains a significant economic interest in the asset. It has to sell or dispose of the asset on expiry in order to realise 100 per cent of its investment. Thus, it is both a financier and a trader in the asset.

- Lease or hire purchase is similar to a finance lease except that the hirer usually has an automatic right of purchase on expiry. There is usually a nominal purchase fee to pass title.

In the UK, users do not have an automatic right to purchase goods on expiry of a finance lease since the tax depreciation, at the time of writing, normally follows legal ownership. Automatic transfer would turn the contract into a hire purchase arrangement. The position has been complicated where longer-term leases over seven years follow economic ownership to bring the UK more in line with Europe and reduce the perceived lessor benefits of deferred tax allowances. Furthermore, there are potential changes to international accounting standards which would require all leases to be recognised in a similar fashion in annual reports.

In the UK, the usual expiry arrangement is a nominal rental and participation in the sale proceeds to provide the user with almost all the benefits of legal ownership. In continental Europe, tax benefits normally follow economic ownership and finance leases usually allow a simple transfer of ownership on expiry.

The benefits of leasing for clients can be summarised as follows:

■ Spreading the cost of the equipment to match cost savings or revenue gains.

■ Extra source of finance apart from clearing or other banks.

■ Finance of 100 per cent could be available with no deposit.

■ Cost relative to other sources of finance based on a lease versus purchase analysis.

■ Ownership could be available on expiry.

■ Flexibility for upgrades and additions could be greater than on traditional loans.

■ Asset is the only security without charges and other guarantees.

■ Further bank credit, which keeps existing lines clear for other funding.

■ Convenience with sales aid and vendor schemes where finance is available at the point of sale.

■ Responsibility and a lower sign-off are often applicable for rental deals which are not dealt with as fixed asset acquisitions.

■ Balance sheet treatment under accounting standards as an operating lease or rental could allow off-balance sheet financing with no disclosure of the loan and consequent improvement in the gearing and liquidity ratios.

Lessor reasons to lease include the following:

■ Tax benefits such as tax depreciation could be available to the legal owner of the goods, as in the UK or United States.

■ Interest spread between the cost of money and the lessee interest rate.

■ Fees such as document fees added to the first rental, inspection fees or termination fees.

■ Residual values on operating leases where the lessor expects to make a margin on the sale of the goods.

■ Vendor leasing schemes offer a stream business of a known type and risk categories for possibly lower marketing costs than traditional branch structures.

The key calculations for leasing are given below and are discussed in the following sections with worked examples:

■ interest rates;

■ amortisation;

■ accounting;

■ settlements;

■ lessor and lessee evaluation.

INTEREST RATES

Evaluating leases without tax or other cash flows consists of ascertaining the inherent interest rates and calculating other variables. The basic time value of money calculations outlined earlier (see Chapter 2) are based on the variables:

N – *number of periodic payments*
I – *periodic interest*
PV – *present value or capital value*
PMT – *periodic payment*
FV – *future value*

The example used is a 10-year lease with annual payments in arrears with no final or residual value (see Figure 15.1).

Item	Inputs	Notes
N	10	
Payment Interval	12	Annual rentals
I	10%	
PV	−1,000	
PMT	?	
No. of Rents at Start	0	
FV	0	
Advance/Arrears	0	1 = Advance, 0 = Arrears

Payment example

Figure 15.1

	A	B	C	D	E
4					
5		Number of payments	N		10 Rents
6		Interest rate per annum %	INT		10.00
7		Present value	PV		-1,000.00
8		Payment	PMT		0.00
9		Future value	FV		0.00
10					
11		Payment Interval			Annual
12		Payment Toggle	Begin/End		Arrears
13					
14		Answer: Payment			162.75
15					

Cell E14 uses the PMT function and finds a rental of 162.75. This means that an investment today followed by 10 rentals of 162.75 starting in 12 months' time and paid nine more times annually thereafter produces a gross yield of 10 per cent nominal (see Figure 15.2).

Figure 15.2

Workings

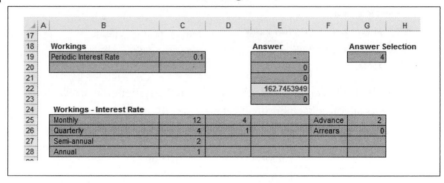

The workings at the base in cells E19:E23 use logic statements to suppress values to zero where values are entered in the inputs above. Since Cell E8 is zero, the payment is computed in cell E22. This example is used below for accounting, settlements and evaluation.

CLASSIFICATION

The general accounting entries for leasing when accounting practice requires disclosure are in the table below. Countries vary on the level of disclosure required and the latest international standard, IAS 17, is designed to provide some standardisation of accounting and reporting disclosure. If leases are not disclosed and are off balance sheet, lessees understate their borrowings and improve liquidity, which could help with meeting borrowing covenants or presenting a lower level of financial risk in annual reports.

Finance Lease		Operating Lease	
Income Statement	Balance Sheet	Income Statement	Balance Sheet
(1) Lessee			
Depreciation (straight line)	Fixed asset	Rentals	No entries*
Amortised interest	Less cumulative depreciation		
	Current debt (<1 year)		
	Long-term debt		
(2) Lessor			
Finance income	Lease debtor		Fixed assets Less depreciation

*Gross rentals payable over the following accounting periods need to be disclosed as a note depending on the local generally accepted accounting practice (GAAP).

The UK method of accounting for leases was originally set out in SSAP 21, *Accounting for leases and hire purchase contracts*, which was published in 1984. This established for the first time the rules for capitalising leases and followed in broad terms the principles set by the US standard FASB 13 in 1976. In addition, it broke new ground by introducing the concept of 'substance over form', meaning that the actuality of the contract should be considered rather than the strict legal form.

Usually SSAP 21 requires users to capitalise lease transactions according to their substance rather than legal ownership. Where a lease transfers 'substantially all the risks and rewards of ownership' to the user, the user capitalises the asset and treats the transaction as if the equipment had been acquired through a borrowing or loan facility. The reality is that economic ownership is passed to the user and is set out in SSAP 21, paragraph 15. This clarified the previous state of affairs whereby a user could have effective economic ownership without reporting the borrowings on the company's balance sheet.

The standard FRS5, *Reporting the Substance of Transactions*, clarifies SSAP 21 and came into force in 1994. There are various phrases to encourage lessees to review the substance rather than the legal form:

- All the aspects and implications should be identified and greater weight given to those more likely to have a commercial effect in practice.
- It will be important to consider the position of all parties to it, including their apparent expectations and motives for agreeing to its various terms.
- A series of transactions that achieves or is designed to achieve an overall commercial effect should be viewed as a whole.

For the purposes of SSAP 21, an operating lease is simply a lease other than a finance lease. This does not transfer 'substantially all the risks and rewards of ownership' and therefore does not need to be capitalised. This means in practice that the lessor maintains a substantial interest in the equipment. The rental agreement does not write off the equipment, and therefore the lessor must deal in the equipment in order to realise 100 per cent of the capital plus charges. The retention of risk is an important concept in determining the position of the parties.

SSAP 21 provides guidance on the transfer of risks and rewards in the simple 90 per cent test:

> *It should be presumed that such a transfer of risks and rewards occurs if at the inception of the lease the present value of the minimum lease payments, including any initial payment, amounts to substantially all (normally 90 per cent or more) of the fair value of the leased asset.*

The latest accounting standard of IAS 17 has been adopted by large companies in the UK. As an international standard, it has to allow for countries which allow direct sale to the lessee on expiry of a lease, which is not normally possible in the UK. Therefore the standard appears more lax since it provides examples of different types of leases but does not include a formal present value test. Accounting standards continue to evolve and it is possible that new standards will be adopted in the next few years to require the capitalisation of all leases in order to remove the potential understatement of borrowings on operating leases. This has not been decided by the accountancy bodies; for example, there is currently an exposure draft proposal to classify leases as Type A requiring capitalisation and Type B allowing rentals to be expensed on a straight-line basis.

The key points of IAS 17 are as follows:

- Finance leases are those that transfer 'substantially all risks and rewards to the lessee'.
- Lessee should capitalise a finance lease at the lower of the fair value and the present value of the minimum lease payments.
- Rental payments should be split into (i) a reduction of liability and (ii) a finance charge designed to reduce in line with the liability.
- Lessee should calculate depreciation on leased assets using useful life, unless there is no reasonable certainty of eventual ownership. In the latter case, the shorter of useful life and lease term would be used.
- Lessee should expense operating lease payments.

For completeness, the US standard includes the tests below. If any of the statements is true, the lease becomes an on-balance-sheet capital (finance) lease.

- Automatic ownership transfer (UK – not a credit sale or conditional sale agreement).

- Bargain purchase option (UK – not a lease or hire purchase contract).

- Lease term represents 75 per cent or more of the asset's economic life (UK – SSAP 21 – does not contain a similar test).

- Present value or more of the minimum lease payments represent 90 per cent of the asset's fair market value reduced by any lessor retained investment tax credit (is similar to UK present value test).

The model therefore needs to double-check the accounting treatment and this is achieved by discounting the rental payments and comparing the present value against the assumed capital value. The key point is that the lessee includes the direct payments and removes the residual value since this is usually the risk of the lessee. Secondly, the lessee uses its marginal cost of funds since it may not know the lessor cost of funds. The model sets out the basic calculations (see Figure 15.3).

Lessee present value calculation

Figure 15.3

	A	B	C
4			
5		N	10
6		I	10.000%
7		Frequency (1,3,6,12)	12
8		PV	(1,000.00)
9		FV	-
10			
11		Begin/End	0
12			
13		PMT	162.75
14			
15		Client Interest Rate	10.000%
16		Fair Market Value (FMV)	1,000.00
17			
18		PV	1,000.00
19		% FMV	100.00%
20		Client Decision Threshold	90.000%
21		PV	Capital Lease
22			

The model on the Classification sheet repeats the rental calculation. The client cost of funds is 10 per cent and the equipment value is assumed to be 1,000. Cell C18 present-values the 10 rentals at 10 per cent and obviously the present value is 1,000. The decision point is input as 90.0 per cent and a simple IF statement in cell C21 decides if the lease is a finance or capital lease.

The next question might be to decide the level of residual value that would reclassify the lease as an operating lease by forcing the present value below 90.0 per cent. This is a one-dimensional data table as in Figure 15.4. At around 25.0 per cent, the present value falls below 90.0 per cent. Of course, these figures assume that the lessor and lessee have the same interest rate and the required residual would fall if the client interest rate were higher.

The other variables that can be structured by the lessor are as follows:

- Lease term, since the minimum period includes the period of the contractual obligation (primary period) plus further periods where the lessee has to continue to lease the asset. A shorter period can reduce the present value since less interest is paid.

- Break clauses or clauses with a 'walk' option are often not clear; however, inclusion of the break clauses reduces the minimum payments' present value below 90 per cent.

- Upgrade clauses, since some computer lessors use 'technology refresh' clauses where the downside is effectively rolled into the next lease. Evaluation of the minimum payments could place the lease off balance sheet; however, a further lease is also required.

- Sometimes renewals require unusually long notice periods such that the user can only with great difficulty lease the equipment for the actual minimum period entered on the lease schedule.

- Rental variations or return provisions sometimes attract extra rentals to compensate the lessor in part for equipment returns.

- For interest rates where the user does not know the exact residual value used by the lessor, the user may use the incremental borrowing rate. This may be subject to discussion on the 'correct' borrowing rate as a marginal rate or a base rate plus a margin.

Figure 15.4	Sensitivity

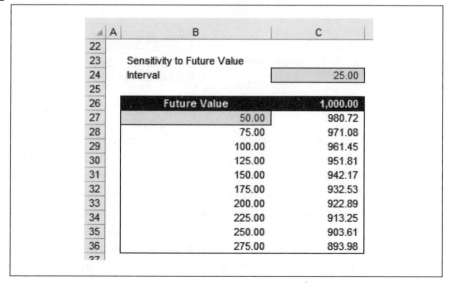

AMORTISATION

Lessees are required to divide finance lease rentals into capital and interest under the accounting standards, and this schedule uses the functions IPMT and PPMT to compute the interest and principal in each period (see Figure 15.5). The interest is therefore the rental less the principal paid:

```
Cell E16: =IF(B16<=$E$5+IF($E$9=0,0,0),PPMT($E$12,
B16,$E$5,$E$7,$E$8,$E$9),0)
Cell F16: =IF(E16=0,0,$E$13-E16)
```

There is also a function called CUMPRINC which calculates the total principal paid over several periods:

```
Cell D16: =-IF(E16=0,0,CUMPRINC($E$12,$E$5,-$E$7,
$B$16,B16,$E$9))
```

Amortisation

Figure 15.5

	A	B	C	D	E	F	G
4							
5		No of Payments	N		10		
6		Interest Rate	I		10.00%		
7		Present Value	PV		-1,000.00		
8		Future Value	FV		0.00		
9		Begin or End of Period	Type		0		
10		Payments per Annum			1		
11							
12		Periodic Interest Rate			10.00%		
13		Payment	PMT		162.75		
14							
15		Period	Function	CUMPRINC	PPMT	Int	Balance
16		1	62.75	62.75	62.75	100.00	(937.25)
17		2	131.77	131.77	69.02	93.73	(868.23)
18		3	207.69	207.69	75.92	86.82	(792.31)
19		4	291.20	291.20	83.51	79.23	(708.80)
20		5	383.07	383.07	91.87	70.88	(616.93)
21		6	484.12	484.12	101.05	61.69	(515.88)
22		7	595.28	595.28	111.16	51.59	(404.72)
23		8	717.55	717.55	122.27	40.47	(282.45)
24		9	852.05	852.05	134.50	28.25	(147.95)
25		10	1,000.00	1,000.00	147.95	14.80	-
26		11	-	-	-	-	-
27		12	-	-	-	-	-
28							
29		Total			1,000.00	627.45	

ACCOUNTING

The accounting sheet builds up the lessee accounting entries. The columns on the income statement are made up of the depreciation on a straight-line basis over 10 years together with amortised interest (see Figure 15.6). The charge is in column G and the total in column H. In the early periods, the total accounting entries are greater than the cash paid.

Figure 15.6

Income statement

	B	C	D	E	F	G	H
4							
5	(A) Profit and loss						
6	Period no	Obligation	Rents paid	Obligation during period	Deprn	Actuarial charge	Total charges
7							
8	0	1,000.00	-	1,000.00	-	-	-
9	1	1,000.00	(162.75)	837.25	100.00	100.00	200.00
10	2	937.25	(162.75)	774.51	100.00	93.73	193.73
11	3	868.23	(162.75)	705.49	100.00	86.82	186.82
12	4	792.31	(162.75)	629.57	100.00	79.23	179.23
13	5	708.80	(162.75)	546.05	100.00	70.88	170.88
14	6	616.93	(162.75)	454.19	100.00	61.69	161.69
15	7	515.88	(162.75)	353.14	100.00	51.59	151.59
16	8	404.72	(162.75)	241.98	100.00	40.47	140.47
17	9	282.45	(162.75)	119.71	100.00	28.25	128.25
18	10	147.95	(162.75)	(14.80)	100.00	14.80	114.80
19	11	0.00	-	0.00	-	-	-
20	12	0.00	-	0.00	-	-	-
21							
22			(1,627.45)		1,000.00	627.45	1,627.45

The balance sheet shows the net book value as the original value plus the cumulative depreciation from the income statement (see Figure 15.7). The liabilities are the present value less the amortised capital, leaving the difference as a timing difference. The timing difference disappears by the end of the lease period.

The model has check totals since the depreciation has to add up to the initial capital value and the total charges have to equal the total interest payable. Similarly, IF statements control inclusion of the entries and therefore calculation in other columns, for example:

```
Cell F9: =IF(B9<=Amortization!$C$6-Amortization!$
F$33,ABS(Amortization!$C$8)/Amortization!$C$6,0)
```

All of the loan and lease cash flows can be built up in the same way by using such IF statements. A rental is included if the period number is

Balance sheet

Figure 15.7

		(B) Balance sheet		
	Period no	Net book asset value	Liabilities	Timing diff.
	0	1,000.00	1,000.00	-
	1	900.00	937.25	(37.25)
	2	800.00	868.23	(68.23)
	3	700.00	792.31	(92.31)
	4	600.00	708.80	(108.80)
	5	500.00	616.93	(116.93)
	6	400.00	515.88	(115.88)
	7	300.00	404.72	(104.72)
	8	200.00	282.45	(82.45)
	9	100.00	147.95	(47.95)
	10	-	0.00	(0.00)
	11	-	0.00	(0.00)
	12	-	0.00	(0.00)

less than or equal to the total number of periods. If the period number is equal to the total number of periods plus one, the residual or future value is included.

SETTLEMENTS

Since the main security under the lease is the market or written-down value of the equipment, it is important for the lessor to plot the current or declining value to be able to set this against the settlement outstanding. In an ideal world, the equipment would always be worth more than the capital outstanding; however, equipment rarely follows an amortisation curve and tends to decline rapidly in the early stages and then flatten out. Compare this with motor vehicles, which tend to fall more in value in the first two years than in the following three years. Equipment considerations include:

■ asset usage, where excessive use will shorten economic life;

■ technology considerations, since rapid change tends to render equipment obsolete;

- economic factors, since demand for used equipment is usually greater in a buoyant economy;

- government regulations, since health and safety or other considerations can increase the price of remarketing or finding second users for equipment;

- developed secondary market, for example, with cars where value can be ascertained quickly;

- lessee factors, since some users tend to retain rather than return equipment;

- portfolio issues, where lessors do not want excessive weightings in equipment types, lessee categories or regions.

Lessors should be interested in these factors to try to improve the value of the underlying lease security:

- manufacturer and model, since specialised equipment tends to decline more rapidly in value;

- quantity, since some lessors prefer integrated pieces of equipment rather than large numbers of unidentifiable equipment, for example, 100 office desks;

- age, if the equipment is already used;

- cost, including hard and soft costs such as installation;

- functions and capabilities;

- special features which tend to reduce value;

- standard physical life;

- normal wear and tear or economic life;

- replacement and maintenance costs;

- technology upgrades and associated costs.

The model needs to calculate the settlement and compare it with the forecasted value of the equipment in each period (see Figure 15.8). The total rentals outstanding are the periodic rental multiplied by the total number of rentals plus any residual or future value. Column D reduces by one rental in each period and the check is the zero balance at the end of the rental period. The settlement is based on the outstanding cash flow discounted at a termination rate. The inherent rate in the lease is 10 per cent and the discount rate used in cell D9 is 5 per cent. This means that there is effectively a penalty of 5 per cent.

```
Cell E13:  =NPV($D$9,C14:$C$25)
```

Settlements

Figure 15.8

	B	C	D	E	F	G	H	I
5	Capital Value		1,000.00		Results			Units $'000
6	Quarterly Rental		162.75		Maximum Exposure		(404.62)	
7	Number of Rentals		10.00		% Capital		40.46	
8	Final Rental		-					
9	Discount Rate		5.00%					
10								
11	Period	Rental	Rents Outstanding	Discounted Amount	Value Deduction	Written Down	Net Value	(Exposure) or Cover
12								
13	-	-	1,627.50	1,256.71	-	-	1,000.00	(256.71)
14	1	162.75	1,790.25	1,156.80	15.00%	(150.00)	850.00	(306.80)
15	2	162.75	1,953.00	1,051.89	15.00%	(150.00)	700.00	(351.89)
16	3	162.75	2,115.75	941.73	15.00%	(150.00)	550.00	(391.73)
17	4	162.75	2,278.50	826.07	12.50%	(125.00)	425.00	(401.07)
18	5	162.75	2,441.25	704.62	12.50%	(125.00)	300.00	(404.62)
19	6	162.75	2,604.00	577.10	10.00%	(100.00)	200.00	(377.10)
20	7	162.75	2,766.75	443.21	10.00%	(100.00)	100.00	(343.21)
21	8	162.75	2,929.50	302.62	5.00%	(50.00)	50.00	(252.62)
22	9	162.75	3,092.25	155.00	5.00%	(50.00)	-	(155.00)
23	10	162.75	3,255.00	-	-	-	-	-
24	11	-	3,255.00	-	-	-	-	-
25	12	-	3,255.00	-	-	-	-	-
26								
27		1,627.50	31,736.25		100.00%	(1,000.00)	4,175.00	(248.67)

The periodic value reductions are in column G and the equipment value reduces in column H. The calculation is simply a percentage value reduction. The exposure in column I is composed of the equipment value less the settlement. In this case the equipment value reduces quickly in the early stages. The chart in Figure 15.9 clearly shows the risks to the lessor in entering into the lease. If the lessee goes bust during the middle stages of the lease, the lessor will lose about 40 per cent of the value.

Exposure chart

Figure 15.9

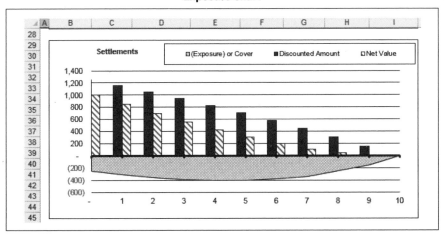

Alternatively, Figure 15.10 shows the difference between the written-down value and the amortised capital outstanding. The written-down value bends downwards while an amortisation curve bends upwards. The line chart on the right-hand scale shows the difference at its maximum in the middle of the period and emphasises the difference between the two methods.

Figure 15.10

Comparison of written-down value (WDV) and amortisation

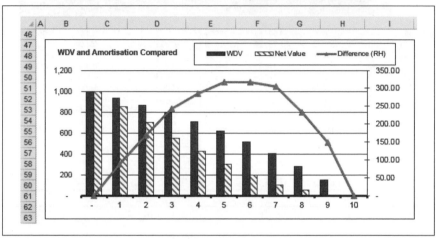

LESSOR EVALUATION

There are many ways of evaluating leases, such as simple sum of digits or the net actuarial method based on post-tax cash flows. The example used here is a 10-year lease at a rate of 10 per cent which produces a rental of 162.75 per annum. The question arises of whether the rental is high enough to reward the lessor adequately for the capital invested. Ten per cent represents only the nominal rate in the deal and is not related to any return value or measure of return. The lessor variables are:

■ number of lease rental payments;

■ rental pattern such as ascending, step down, skip or other non-regular payment structure;

■ number of periodic lease payments in advance or deposit;

■ tax rate and tax method;

■ yield required by lessor;

■ cost of borrowing;

■ initial direct costs;

■ equipment cost and any discounts available;

- closing, brokerage or other fees;
- refundable security deposit (if applicable);
- residual value, final or balloon rentals.

One solution is to view the lease as an investment opportunity, plot the cash flows and calculate the internal rate of return. The required yield must be a weighted average cost of capital derived from the required equity return, cost of debt, tax rate and leverage. When the calculated return is equal to the cost of capital then the rental must be high enough to reward each provider of capital in proportion to their capital introduced.

The first stage is to set out the cash flows and test the existing rental to see if it is high enough. In the inputs in Figure 15.11, the debt ratio is 90.0 per cent with the cost of debt and equity set at 7.5 and 10.0 per cent, respectively. The model computes the required return on capital as 6.40 per cent in cell J7:

```
Cell J7: =((D11*(1-D14))*D10)+(D12*(1-D10))
```

The initial rental is in cell J6 as 162.75:

```
Cell J6: =PMT(D8,D6,-ABS(D5),D9,D7)
```

Figure 15.11

Lessor entries

	A	B	C	D	E	F	G	H	I	J	K	L	M	N
5		Equipment cost		1,000			**Summary**							
6		Lease term		10 yrs			Calculated rental:			162.75				
7		Advance/arrears		0			Weighted cost of capital:			6.40%				
8		Lease rate		10.00%										
9		Residual		0			Required rental			163.07				
10		Debt ratio		90.00%			Street rate			10.05%				
11		Cost of debt (pretax)		7.50%			MIRR			4.25%				
12		Desired return on equity		10.00%										
13		Reinvestment rate		2.00%										
14		Tax rate:		20.00%										
15														
16				1	2	3	4	5	6	7	8	9	10	
17		SG&A expenses:		10.00	10.00	10.00	10.00	10.00	10.00	10.00	10.00	10.00	10.00	
18		Bad debt expense:		5.00	5.00	5.00	5.00	5.00	5.00	5.00	5.00	5.00	5.00	
19														
20		**(A) Initial Calculation**												
21			0	1	2	3	4	5	6	7	8	9	10	Total
22		Initial Cash	(1,000.00)											
23		Rent		162.75	162.75	162.75	162.75	162.75	162.75	162.75	162.75	162.75	162.75	1,627.45
24		Depreciation		(100.00)	(100.00)	(100.00)	(100.00)	(100.00)	(100.00)	(100.00)	(100.00)	(100.00)	(100.00)	(1,000.00)
25		SG&A	-	(10.00)	(10.00)	(10.00)	(10.00)	(10.00)	(10.00)	(10.00)	(10.00)	(10.00)	(10.00)	(100.00)
26		Bad debts	-	(5.00)	(5.00)	(5.00)	(5.00)	(5.00)	(5.00)	(5.00)	(5.00)	(5.00)	(5.00)	(50.00)
27		**Taxable income**	**(1,000.00)**	**47.75**	**47.75**	**47.75**	**47.75**	**47.75**	**47.75**	**47.75**	**47.75**	**47.75**	**47.75**	**477.45**
28		Taxes @ 20%	-	(9.55)	(9.55)	(9.55)	(9.55)	(9.55)	(9.55)	(9.55)	(9.55)	(9.55)	(9.55)	(95.49)
29		Net income	(1,000.00)	38.20	38.20	38.20	38.20	38.20	38.20	38.20	38.20	38.20	38.20	381.96
30		Depreciation	-	100.00	100.00	100.00	100.00	100.00	100.00	100.00	100.00	100.00	100.00	1,000.00
31		**ROA cash flow**	**(1,000.00)**	**138.20**	**138.20**	**138.20**	**138.20**	**138.20**	**138.20**	**138.20**	**138.20**	**138.20**	**138.20**	**1,381.96**
32														
33		IRR%:		6.36%										
34														
35		Difference:		(0.04%)										
36		WACC + Diff.:		6.44%										

During the period, the lessor needs to take into account administration and other costs and factor these into the rental (see Figure 15.12). These are listed in lines 17 and 18 and will be incremental cash outflows from the lease. The first cash flow grid is populated with the known cash flows, which comprise the initial capital value, the rentals, overheads and bad

Figure 15.12	Tax written-down value

⊿ A	B	C	D	E	F	G	H
65							
66	Capital Allowances Workings included in Tax						
67	FYA		WDV Percent	WDV		Capital Tax Cashflow	
68	WDA						
69	CA	1	10.00%	(100.00)		20.00	
70	CA	2	10.00%	(100.00)		20.00	
71	CA	3	10.00%	(100.00)		20.00	
72	CA	4	10.00%	(100.00)		20.00	
73	CA	5	10.00%	(100.00)		20.00	
74	CA	6	10.00%	(100.00)		20.00	
75	CA	7	10.00%	(100.00)		20.00	
76	CA	8	10.00%	(100.00)		20.00	
77	CA	9	10.00%	(100.00)		20.00	
78	CA	10	10.00%	(100.00)		20.00	
79	Sales proceeds					-	
80				(1,000.00)		200.00	
81							

debts. The tax depreciation is set at 10 per cent a year for simplicity; however, this could be changed manually in the workings table at the bottom. Different countries use accelerated or straight-line methods for assessing the allowable write-off values.

The depreciation needs to be subtracted so that taxable income can be calculated in line 27 in Figure 15.11. Tax is set at 20 per cent and net income is in line 29. Since depreciation is not a cash flow this is added back to form the return on assets cash flow in line 31. If the rental values are correct the internal rate of return should be the same as the cost of capital. The internal rate in cell C33 is 6.36 per cent, which is 0.11 per cent lower than the required level:

```
Cell C31: =IRR(C31:M31,0.1)
```

The required rental can be computed directly using a factors method without having to resort to Solver or Goal Seek. If you are using a financial calculator, the steps are:

- Calculate the net outflow of costs at the inception of the lease =PV factor:
  - Calculate the final residual value (if applicable).
  - Compute the present value of the net residual value.
  - Present-value any other cash flows you know about.
- Compute the PV of the unknown periodic lease payments, letting $1 equal each payment:
  - With multiple rentals on signing and in advance, add the number in advance to the factor = Rental factor
- Calculate PMT: PV factor / Rental factor

The result is the periodic rental. The left-hand block in Figure 15.13 present-values all the known cash flows of equipment, depreciation, overheads and bad debts. The discount rate is of course the cost of capital in cell J7. The after-tax values are needed since the return on assets cash flow is after tax. The net of tax value of the depreciation is the present value multiplied by the tax rate. On the other hand, the present value of costs can be multiplied by $(1 - \text{tax})$. The result is the addition on cell D43 of the after-tax present value of all known cash flows.

The rental factor is on the right-hand side and is a simple time value of money calculator (see Figure 15.13). The present value of five rentals of $1 in arrears at a rate of 6.40 per cent is required and the PMT function yields a factor of 7.223. This again has to be multiplied by $(1 - \text{tax})$ to form the net factor 5.778.

Rental confirmation

Figure 15.13

	B	C	D	E	F	G	H	I	J	K	L	M	N
37													
38	After tax NPV value				Calculation of rental								
39	Equipment		(1,000.00)		N		10						
40	Depreciation		144.45		INT		6.40%						
41	SG&A		(57.78)		PMT		-1.00						
42	Bad debts		(28.80)		FV		0.00						
43	NPV		(942.22)		Toggle		0.00						
44													
45	Net of tax factor / NPV				PV		7.223						
46	Calculated Rental:		163.07		Net of Tax		5.778						
47													
48													
49	(B) Calculated Rental												
50			0	1	2	3	4	5	6	7	8	9	10	Total
51	Initial cash	(1,000.00)											
52	Rent		163.07	163.07	163.07	163.07	163.07	163.07	163.07	163.07	163.07	163.07	815.34
53	Depreciation		(100.00)	(100.00)	(100.00)	(100.00)	(100.00)	(100.00)	(100.00)	(100.00)	(100.00)	(100.00)	(500.00)
54	SG&A	-	(10.00)	(10.00)	(10.00)	(10.00)	(10.00)	(10.00)	(10.00)	(10.00)	(10.00)	(10.00)	(50.00)
55	Bad debts	-	(5.00)	(5.00)	(5.00)	(5.00)	(5.00)	(5.00)	(5.00)	(5.00)	(5.00)	(5.00)	(25.00)
56	Taxable income	(1,000.00)	48.07	48.07	48.07	48.07	48.07	48.07	48.07	48.07	48.07	48.07	240.34
57	Taxes @ 20%	-	(9.61)	(9.61)	(9.61)	(9.61)	(9.61)	(9.61)	(9.61)	(9.61)	(9.61)	(9.61)	(48.07)
58	Net income	(1,000.00)	38.45	38.45	38.45	38.45	38.45	38.45	38.45	38.45	38.45	38.45	192.27
59	Depreciation	-	100.00	100.00	100.00	100.00	100.00	100.00	100.00	100.00	100.00	100.00	500.00
60	ROA cash flow	(1,000.00)	138.45	138.45	138.45	138.45	138.45	138.45	138.45	138.45	138.45	138.45	692.27
61													
62	IRR%:	6.40%											

The rental is 942.22/5.778 which equals 163.07 and which can then be inserted into the cash flow (see Figure 15.13). The yield is tested in cell C62 and this is 6.4 per cent. Therefore the minimum rental that should be charged for this rental and cost profile is 163.07. The nominal rate charged to the client using the RATE function is 10.05 per cent.

The rentals are based on the inputs at the top of the sheet. Since equity is more expensive than after-tax debt, reducing the leverage to 50.0 per cent increases the cost of capital to 7.63 per cent and the required rental to 181.46 per cent. The client or street rate increases to 12.61 per cent (see Figure 15.14). Therefore the lease can be evaluated using simple nominal rates or as a spread between the buying and selling rate on the money. For a more accurate evaluation, all the incremental cash flows need to be considered to ensure that the lease returns a yield equal to or greater than the risk-adjusted cost of capital. This method provides one way of including all the associated costs and pricing the lease accordingly.

Figure 15.14

Leverage at 50 per cent

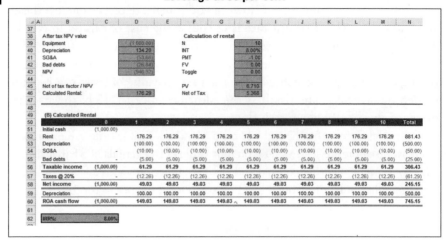

LESSEE EVALUATION

Lessees vary in how they evaluate leases against cash or other forms of finance. Quoted annual percentage rates can be misleading and parts of the decision process could include:

■ total cost and cash flow;

■ overall financial strategy;

■ capital structure or accounting treatment as an operating or finance lease;

■ liquidity considerations such as a required small deposit;

■ debt capacity and capital adequacy with existing lenders;

■ flexibility and upgrades offered on the lease to fit in with planned facility upgrades;

■ low penalties for early termination considerations;

■ simple ownership and end of period options;

■ simple and unrestrictive documentation;

■ administrative convenience as part of a sales-aid programme;

■ other 'soft' factors and preferences for leasing over buying. In the United States more than 30 per cent of equipment is acquired through leasing; the UK figure is around 25 per cent.

Multiplying out the charges or calculating a simple or flat rate of interest as in cells H6 and H7 in Figure 15.15 does not provide much information. The nominal rate of interest is 10 per cent but this can only be compared with the pre-tax marginal cost of borrowing of 12.0 per cent in cell D10. On a pre-tax basis, leasing would appear to be more cost effective than borrowing.

Lease versus purchase cash flows

Figure 15.15

	(A) Rents		(B) Equipment				

Capital Value — 1,000.00   Results   Units $'000
Quarterly Rental — 162.75   Total Charges — 627.50
Number of Rentals — 10.00   Simple Interest Rate — 6.28%
Final Rental — -   Interest rate — 10.00%
Period in Tax Year — 1   PV test — 919.57
Discount Rate — 12.00%   Classification — Capital
Tax Delay — 1   Net Present Value at 9.6% — 956.81
Tax Rate — 20.00%   Leasing Gain — 4.32%

Period	Rental	Tax (Paid)/Recd	Tax WDV	Deprn Percent	Tax Deprn	Cash Flow	Net Cash Flow
-	-		1,000.00	10.00%	100.00	-	-
1	(162.75)	-	900.00	10.00%	100.00	(20.00)	(182.75)
2	(162.75)	32.55	800.00	10.00%	100.00	(20.00)	(150.20)
3	(162.75)	32.55	700.00	10.00%	100.00	(20.00)	(150.20)
4	(162.75)	32.55	600.00	10.00%	100.00	(20.00)	(150.20)
5	(162.75)	32.55	500.00	10.00%	100.00	(20.00)	(150.20)
6	(162.75)	32.55	400.00	10.00%	100.00	(20.00)	(150.20)
7	(162.75)	32.55	300.00	10.00%	100.00	(20.00)	(150.20)
8	(162.75)	32.55	200.00	10.00%	100.00	(20.00)	(150.20)
9	(162.75)	32.55	100.00	10.00%	100.00	(20.00)	(150.20)
10	(162.75)	32.55	-	-	-	(20.00)	(150.20)
11	-	32.55	-	-	-	-	32.55
12	-	-				-	-
	(1,627.50)	325.50		100.00%	1,000.00	(200.00)	(1,502.00)

A more inclusive method is to plot the after-tax cost of leasing versus borrowing using the incremental cash flows with the applicable tax regime and discounted at an after-tax cost of borrowing. The tax delay is set at one year, so columns C and D plot the rentals payable and the tax relief at 30.0 per cent:

```
Cell D19: =-OFFSET(C19,-$D$11,0)*$D$12
```

Tax depreciation is included as a negative since this is relief not available if the lessee decides to lease. The advantage of including this in the leasing cash flow is the need for only one net present value, rather than separate present values for leasing and buying. The tax depreciation is set at 10 per cent per annum, so the tax depreciation is 100 at the tax rate of 20.0 per cent (see Figure 15.15). There are 10 cash flows of 20 starting one year after the agreement date. Since the rentals are annual in arrears the tax relief on rentals is available later than the relief on capital. The overall cash flow in column I in each period is the rental plus the tax relief on rental and on capital.

The pre-tax rate is 12.0 per cent and since the cash flows are after tax, the discount rate is multiplied by $(1 - \text{tax})$. At a rate of 9.6 per cent, the net present value of leasing is 956.81 (see Figure 15.16), representing a gain of 4.32 per cent for leasing. The schedule also includes a sensitivity table using the TABLE function since the relative attractiveness changes with amendments to the discount rate. The break-even point appears to be 11.5 per cent.

Figure 15.16

Sensitivity to discount rate

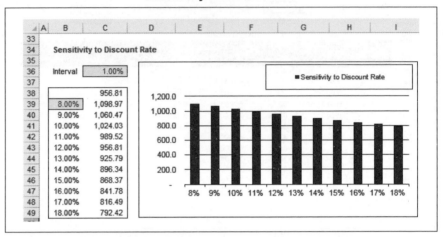

	A	B	C	D	E	F	G	H	I
33									
34		Sensitivity to Discount Rate							
35									
36		Interval	1.00%						
37									
38			956.81						
39		8.00%	1,098.97						
40		9.00%	1,060.47						
41		10.00%	1,024.03						
42		11.00%	989.52						
43		12.00%	956.81						
44		13.00%	925.79						
45		14.00%	896.34						
46		15.00%	868.37						
47		16.00%	841.78						
48		17.00%	816.49						
49		18.00%	792.42						

EXERCISE

Complete a spreadsheet to evaluate a lease from a lessor's standpoint using these data:

Capital cost	*100,000.00*
Residual value	*10.00%*
Period	*5.00 years*
SG&A (overheads)	*(50.00) per annum starting in year 1 (inception is year 0)*
Bad debt	*(10.00) per annum starting in year 1*
Other fees payable by the lessor on signing	*(1,000.00)*
Debt/equity percentage	*75.0%*
Debt	*10.0%*
Equity	*15.0%*
Tax	*20.0%*

The tax regime uses a 20.0 per cent declining balance method, which is the DB function in Excel.

Calculate the required rental and client interest rate and produce a table of the sensitivity to leverage using the same methodology as in this chapter (see Figure 15.17).

Tax writing-down allowances

Figure 15.17

Year	B/F	Allowance	C/F
–	(100,000.0)		(100,000.0)
1	(100,000.0)	20,000.0	(80,000.0)
2	(80,000.0)	16,000.0	(64,000.0)
3	(64,000.0)	12,800.0	(51,200.0)
4	(51,200.0)	10,240.0	(40,960.0)
5	(40,960.0)	8,192.0	(32,768.0)
6	(32,768.0)	32,768.0	–
		100,000.00	

Tax Allowances Workings — 20%

SUMMARY

Leasing uses discounting mathematics and cash flow models to determine the pre-tax yield in a lease and establish the accounting treatment under international accounting standards. With amortisation tables, the accounting statements can be constructed to generate the entries. Settlements are useful to determine potential losses and use discounted present values to compare the lessor settlement with the written-down market value. Using investment cash flows, lessors can evaluate leases against a cost of capital and lessees can compare the relative after-tax benefits of leasing against other forms of finance.

Basic statistics

File: MFMaths3e_16a.xls, MFMaths3e_16b.xls

METHODS

Statistics deals with collecting, analysing, interpreting and presenting numerical data. The purpose of this chapter is to introduce some mathematical techniques for analysing and understanding data useful in finance. While these methods are time consuming with a financial calculator, Excel provides a set of functions and wizards for analysing data sets quickly. For example, you may wish to assess measures of dispersion from sets of historical data so that you can make forecasts or infer outcomes for the future.

The techniques in the chapter are:

- describing, understanding and summarising sets of data;
- determining the probabilities through distributions and how to use them;
- sampling and estimating results from samples;
- making hypotheses about data sets and testing them;
- looking for relationships or linkages through correlation and regression.

DESCRIPTIVE STATISTICS

When you plot sets of data as scatter charts or tables, it is difficult to understand the data or recognise patterns, and therefore you need methods to try to understand key elements about the data. You want to know the 'shape' or the 'spread' of the data. For instance, you may want to know both the return and the risk or range of possible answers on an investment. The two key elements are:

- central tendency – the 'middle' of the data;
- dispersion – how much the data is spread.

Measures of central tendency are arithmetic mean (average), geometric mean, median and mode. These measures show the values around which the data appears to cluster. Measures of dispersion include the range (maximum less minimum), mean absolute deviation, variance and standard deviation. In corporate finance, dispersion is often used as a proxy for risk since corporate finance theory assumes that financial institutions and individuals are 'risk averse' and look for returns which do not deviate greatly from the expected returns. Statistical theory can assist in analysing patterns in sets of data.

Populations

The first file for this chapter (MFMaths3e_16a.xls) includes a sheet called Data with four stock indices as raw data and annual gains or losses as percentages on the right (see Figure 16.1). A population comprises all the members or items in a group or set, for example, the earnings per share of all the stocks traded on an exchange. Since all the data rather than a sample are present, measures of central tendency and dispersion can be calculated for the whole population and you can be sure of accurate results.

Figure 16.1

Data set

A	B	C	D	E	F	G	H	I	J	K
4										
5	No	1	2	3	4		1	2	3	4
6	1	1,414.60	1,414.60	206.30	259.60					
7	2	1,437.00	1,451.50	206.80	260.90		1.6%	2.6%	0.2%	0.5%
8	3	1,545.90	1,577.10	221.90	275.90		7.6%	8.7%	7.3%	5.7%
9	4	1,670.80	1,697.80	233.90	292.70		8.1%	7.7%	5.4%	6.1%
10	5	1,662.50	1,757.20	230.50	304.80		(0.5%)	3.5%	(1.5%)	4.1%
11	6	1,604.80	1,698.50	242.40	321.30		(3.5%)	(3.3%)	5.2%	5.4%
12	7	1,651.80	1,773.00	245.80	320.20		2.9%	4.4%	1.4%	(0.3%)
13	8	1,560.10	1,692.20	231.10	284.40		Formula:		(5.0%)	(11.2%)
14	9	1,663.20	1,765.10	247.90	298.40		=(C7-C6)/C6		7.3%	4.9%
15	10	1,557.80	1,667.50	226.30	270.00				(3.7%)	(9.5%)
16	11	1,634.20	1,753.90	239.00	284.00		4.9%	5.2%	5.6%	5.2%
17	12	1,638.60	1,800.00	244.20	290.90		0.3%	2.6%	2.2%	2.4%
18	13	1,681.00	1,819.90	237.20	277.80		2.6%	1.1%	(2.9%)	(4.5%)
19	14	1,810.20	1,992.60	269.10	328.40		7.7%	9.5%	13.4%	18.2%
20	15	1,981.20	2,128.40	279.20	360.50		9.4%	6.8%	3.8%	9.8%
21	16	1,999.50	2,192.20	286.70	367.10		0.9%	3.0%	2.7%	1.8%
22	17	2,052.50	2,221.90	283.40	364.70		2.7%	1.4%	(1.2%)	(0.7%)
23	18	2,205.00	2,359.20	285.10	372.50		7.4%	6.2%	0.6%	2.1%
24	19	2,286.10	2,558.20	299.00	373.50		3.7%	8.4%	4.9%	0.3%
25	20	2,362.90	2,712.10	313.70	387.70		3.4%	6.0%	4.9%	3.8%
26	21	2,251.70	2,587.80	324.80	414.20		(4.7%)	(4.6%)	3.5%	6.8%
27	22	2,368.00	2,755.70	316.80	406.00		5.2%	6.5%	(2.5%)	(2.0%)
28	23	1,751.80	1,966.20	246.80	295.10		(26.0%)	(28.6%)	(22.1%)	(27.3%)
29	24	1,581.90	1,756.00	225.30	269.30		(9.7%)	(10.7%)	(8.7%)	(8.7%)
30	25	1,714.70	1,976.00	242.10	307.50		8.4%	12.5%	7.5%	14.2%
31	26	1,792.80	2,105.90	252.10	313.30		4.6%	6.6%	4.1%	1.9%
32	27	1,770.80	2,102.10	262.80	340.30		(1.2%)	(0.2%)	4.2%	8.6%
33	28	1,744.50	2,077.30	253.90	341.50		(1.5%)	(1.2%)	(3.4%)	0.4%
34	29	1,804.20	2,158.10	256.30	346.80		3.4%	3.9%	0.9%	1.6%
35	30	1,786.40	2,166.70	257.20	341.70		(1.0%)	0.4%	0.4%	(1.5%)

Often it is not possible or too costly to include an entire group. A sample is a subset of the whole population. A set of 50 stocks from the London Stock Exchange could be a sample and a characteristic of that sample is normally termed a statistic (rather than a parameter for a population).

Data sets and frequency distributions

Data are often presented in tables from which it is difficult to understand patterns in the data. Figure 16.2 show a chart of the first index on the Select Chart sheet, which will be used as an example through the next sections. A data set of this kind is best described by a frequency table or histogram so that you can see the number of years in which the index rose by 10 per cent, 15 per cent and so on. The resulting chart will then exhibit a distribution of values around the central value or mean and also shows the dispersion from the central value.

Data scatter chart

Figure 16.2

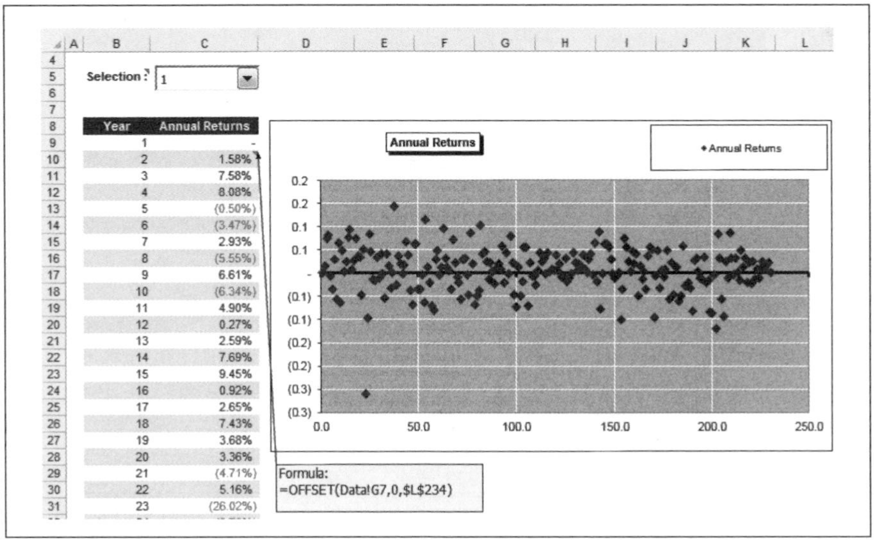

The first stage in the histogram is to define the intervals for counting the results which fall within those intervals. In Figure 16.3 this is 3 per cent. Values for the years can then be counted and placed in the individual bins or categories as below.

Using a spreadsheet, the chart in Figure 16.4 can be constructed from the frequency table using the FREQUENCY function in Excel or the histogram function in the Analysis ToolPak. This is an array function which must be selected as a block and entered with Control, Shift and Enter. This clearly shows the spread of values of the period (see Returns Histogram sheet). The next stage in trying to understand the data is to calculate measures of central tendency and dispersion for comparison purposes.

Figure 16.3

Frequency table

	A	B	C	D	E	F
4						
5		**Arithmetic Average**				
6			1	2	3	4
7		Average	0.7%	0.8%	0.9%	1.2%
8		Geomean	0.5%	0.5%	0.5%	0.5%
9		Std Deviation	4.7%	5.3%	4.5%	8.8%
10						
11						
12		**Frequency Table**				
13						
14		Interval	3.00%			
15						
16		**Bins**	1	2	3	4
17		(15.0%)	1	2	1	7
18		(12.0%)	0	2	1	7
19		(9.0%)	5	6	3	7
20		(6.0%)	13	9	11	15
21		(3.0%)	24	27	19	19
22		-	51	41	48	37
23		3.0%	65	66	72	43
24		6.0%	46	46	51	41
25		9.0%	19	20	19	17
26		12.0%	4	6	3	15
27		15.0%	1	4	1	8
28		18.0%	0	0	0	8
29		21.0%	0	0	0	4
30						
31		**Total No**	229	229	229	228

Figure 16.4

Frequency histogram

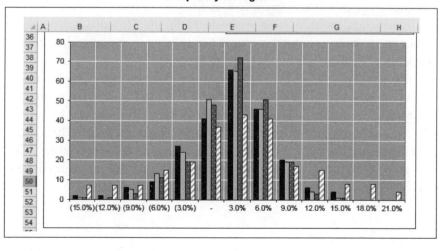

Quartiles and percentiles offer an alternative method to histograms for describing the data in tabular form (see Figure 16.5). The terminology is:

- quartiles – divided in quarters;
- quintiles – fifths;
- deciles – tenths;
- percentiles – hundredths or per cent.

Quartiles and percentiles

Figure 16.5

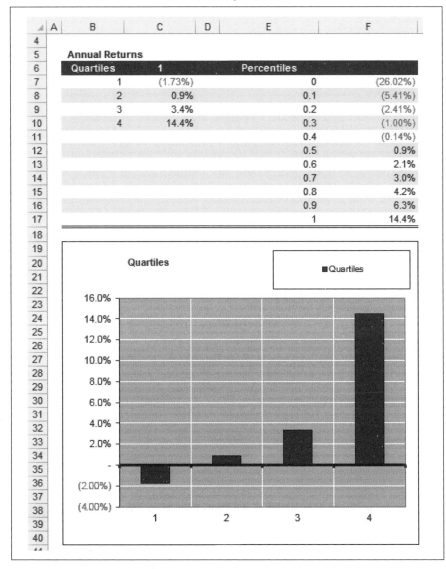

To calculate percentiles manually, the data have to be sorted in ascending order and the result is a cumulative distribution. To find the values, the general formula is $(n + 1) * y/100$ where y is the required percentage.

Mean

The arithmetic mean or average is the key measure of central tendency, which identifies the centre of a data set. The calculation is the sum of the values divided by the number of data points or observations:

$$\overline{X} = \frac{\sum_{i=1}^{N} X_i}{N}$$

The notation $\overline{X}$ is used to denote a sample mean and μ is used for an entire population. In the case of the data the average is:

Addition	149.18%
Number	229
Average	0.65%

In this case the average return is 0.65 per cent over the period, but this covers wide discrepancies in the individual years, as illustrated in the frequency table.

Some general points about the arithmetic mean are:

- All interval and ratio data sets possess an arithmetic mean.
- All data values must be included in the calculation for it to be accurate.
- The sum of the deviations from the mean is always equal to zero.
- A data set always has only one arithmetic mean.

The geometric mean is used as an alternative to calculate returns over successive periods or to measure compound growth rates, for example, on shares. The Excel function is GEOMEAN and AVERAGE for the arithmetic mean. The formula is:

$$G = \sqrt[N]{X_1 * X_2 \ldots \ldots X_N}$$

This is the same as $(X_1 * X_2 * X_N)$ ^ $1 / N$, as in the cell shown in Figure 16.6.

Figure 16.6 **Mean and geomean**

◢ A	B	C	D	E	F
4					
5	Arithmetic Average				
6		1	2	3	4
7	Average	0.7%	0.8%	0.9%	1.2%
8	Geomean	0.5%	0.5%	0.5%	0.5%
9	Std Deviation	4.7%	5.3%	4.5%	8.8%

The geometric mean will always be less than the arithmetic mean and the difference between the two increases with the volatility of the underlying data. This is best illustrated with an example. If you bought stock for 1,000 in a company and after one year the stock was trading at 2,000, then after two years the stock drops back to 1,000, this means that there is no real gain. The formula is:

Geometric mean $= ((1 + 100\%) * (1 - 50\%))^{\wedge}(1/2) - 1 = 0$

	Prices	% Gain
Stock Example	1,000.00	
	2,000.00	100.00%
	1,000.00	(50.00%)
Sum		50.00%
N		2.00
Mean		25.00%
Geomean		–

Mode

The mode is an alternative measure of central tendency and is the most frequently occurring value. A data set may not contain a mode if there are no values present more than once. This is the case with the example data where no value is repeated and an ISERROR function is used with MODE.

Median

The MEDIAN function derives the mid-point of the data when the data are arranged in ascending or descending order: 50 per cent of observations lie above the value and 50 per cent below. The average can be affected by the outliers in the data and, in these cases, the median is a more accurate measure since it is not affected by the outliers. If the shape of the data is completely symmetrical then the median and mean will be the same.

Range

While mean, median and mode provide measures of central tendency, it is often more important to understand the variability in a data set. There is no specific function for the range and this is best calculated using the functions MAX and MIN for maximum and minimum.

Figure 16.7

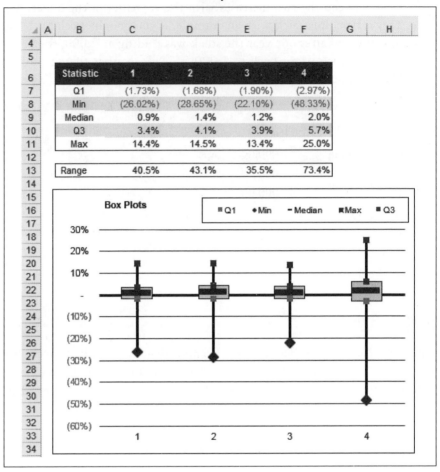

An alternative to showing the range is to use box plots to provide a graphical representation of the distributions (see Box Plots sheet). This is not a standard Excel chart and the data have to be set out exactly as in the grid. Figure 16.7 shows a table containing the first and third quartile together with the minimum and maximum. This can be represented as a chart with the outliers representing the minimum and maximum as a box at the first and third percentiles. The bar in the middle of the box is the median. The plot clearly shows the range where index 4 shows a greater range or volatility than the other three.

Variance and standard deviation

Variation is always present in a data set and therefore individual measures such as the mean or median can lead to misleading answers. If two data sets have the same mean or median, how do you compare them? You also need to know the amount of variation or how the values cluster around the mean. With risk, return is only half of the story and you need some measure of variability as well.

Standard deviation is the most commonly used measure of variability. This is the typical distance from any point in the data set to the centre. In the example data set (see Figure 16.1), standard deviation is a proxy for risk since you want to know the likely return on each of the indices and typically how your return might vary from the mean. This can be built up from the mean absolute deviation and variance as follows (see Figure 16.8).

Variance, media, skew and kurtosis

Figure 16.8

	B	C	D	E	F	G	H	I	J	K
		1	2	3	4		1	2	3	4
Addition	845,579.1	916,996.5	160,765.2	230,927.5		149.18%	193.57%	198.88%	275.08%
Number	230.00	230.00	230.00	230.00		229.00	229.00	229.00	229.00
Mean	3,676.43	3,986.94	698.98	1,004.03		0.65%	0.85%	0.87%	1.20%
St Dev	1,521.82	1,594.27	392.17	837.43		4.73%	5.33%	4.54%	8.81%
Median	3,472.55	3,905.85	548.35	687.10		0.87%	1.35%	1.20%	1.97%
Mode	-	-	299.00	-		-	-	-	-
Range	5,517.60	5,645.20	1,306.40	4,133.20		40.45%	43.13%	35.54%	73.36%
Kurtosis	(1.07)	(1.29)	(1.28)	3.92		3.96	4.03	2.77	4.55
Skew	0.39	0.22	0.44	1.95		(0.87)	(1.01)	(0.83)	(1.00)

The mean absolute deviation (MAD) is the average of the deviations in individual observations from the mean. This is simply the addition of the variance to the mean divided by the number of observations:

$$MAD = \frac{\sum_{i=1}^{n} |X_i - \mu|}{n}$$

The next stage in computing the variance is to take the individual variances and square them to remove the negative values. The formula for variance is:

$$Variance \ \sigma^2 = \frac{\sum_{i=1}^{n} |X_i - \mu|^2}{n}$$

From the figures above, the result for stocks is much higher than bills or bonds, demonstrating that stocks are more risky investments. You appear to make more return for accepting more risk.

The standard deviation is the square root of variance, which reduces the variance to the same units as the original data set. Again σ and μ relate to a population while s and $\overline{X}$ relate to a sample. The formulas for the population and sample standard deviations are:

$$\sigma = \sqrt{\frac{\sum_{i=1}^{n} |X_i - \mu|^2}{n}}$$

$$s = \sqrt{\frac{\sum_{i=1}^{n} |X_i - \overline{X}|}{n - 1}}$$

These calculations are simpler using the Excel functions VAR and STDEV. The standard deviation is the key measure of dispersion and is used to describe the volatility in a data set. The mean or median provides the central value, while the standard deviation shows how much the result could vary from the centre based on the historic results.

The standard deviation can be used to provide insight about the number of observations that lie within any number of standard deviations from the mean. Chebyshev's inequality states that, for any population or sample, the percentage of observations that lie within k standard deviations of the mean is at least:

$1 - 1/k^2$ *for all* $k > 1$.

This means that, with the standard deviation, you can compute the minimum dispersion, and this is independent of the shape of the distribution (see Figure 16.9).

Figure 16.9

Chebyshev's inequality

	A	B	C	D
77				
78		Chebyshev's Inequality : 1 – 1/k^2		
79		K	Percentage	
80		1.25	36.00%	
81		1.50	55.56%	
82		1.75	67.35%	
83		2.00	75.00%	
84		2.25	80.25%	
85		2.50	84.00%	
86		2.75	86.78%	
87		3.00	88.89%	
88		3.25	90.53%	
89		3.50	91.84%	
90		3.75	92.89%	
91		4.00	93.75%	

Comparisons between standard deviations are meaningless unless they are normalised, since you usually want to know the relative dispersion. For example, two projects have a similar net present value and a standard deviation of 100. The first project has a capital cost of 1,000 and the second 5,000. The standard deviation must be converted to a coefficient of variation so that the figures can be compared. This is achieved by dividing the standard deviation by the reference value: $\sigma / \overline{X}$.

Skew

Measures of dispersion show the likelihood of a result differing from the central value, whereas measures of symmetry provide more information on whether deviations are likely to be positive or negative. You know the mean or median and the standard deviation, and these measures provide insight on the shape of the distribution. If a distribution is symmetrical around its mean, then there is an equal chance of a positive or negative deviation. In a normal distribution the series is bell shaped and symmetrical around the mean. The main properties are as follows:

- The median and arithmetic mean are equal.

- Approximately 66 per cent of points lie between plus or minus one standard deviation of the mean. The figures for two and three standard deviations are 95 and 99 per cent.

- The series can be described by its mean and standard deviation.

The function SKEW provides a value for the degree of symmetry. Non-symmetrical distributions can be positively or negatively skewed:

- Positive skew means leaning to the right.

- Negative skew means that there are more outliers to the left forming a bias in this direction.

In a symmetrical normal distribution (the middle diagram in Figure 16.10), the mean, median and mode are the same. With a positive (right leaning) distribution, the order is mode, median and then mean. If the skew is negative (left leaning), the order is mean, median and then mode. Values in excess of 0.5 are normally considered to be large values.

The formula for skew is:

$$S = \frac{1}{n} \sum_{i=1}^{n} \left(\frac{X_i - \mu}{\sigma} \right)^3$$

Figure 16.10   **Skew – positive (right), symmetrical and negative**

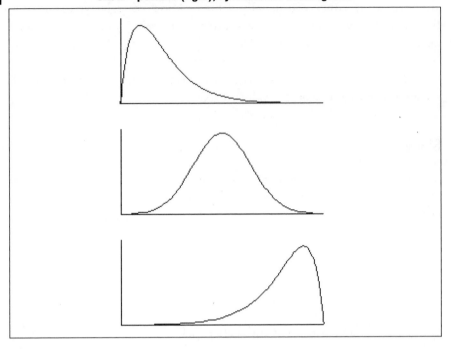

Kurtosis

Kurtosis can be computed with the function KURT and describes the shape of the distribution: leptokurtic describes a distribution that is more peaked than a normal distribution, while platykurtic means less peaked.

The formula for kurtosis is:

$$K = \frac{1}{n}\sum_{i=1}^{n}\left(\frac{X_i - \mu^4}{\sigma^4}\right)$$

As indicated in Figure 16.11, a value of less than three indicates a round distribution, while a normal distribution is three. Greater than three indicates a peaked distribution. A distribution is said to display excess kurtosis if the value is greater than three. Excess kurtosis is therefore kurtosis minus three. Kurtosis is an important calculation in risk management since it is often assumed that distributions are normal and they do not display excess kurtosis. Empirical studies show that this is not always true, and risk is mostly contained not in the centre around the mean and median but at the extremes in the tail of a distribution.

Kurtosis – values of <3, 3 and >3

Figure 16.11

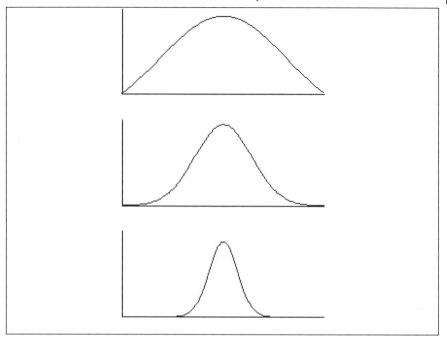

There are Excel functions for all the descriptive statistics; however, the simplest way of generating them is to use the descriptive statistics in the Data Analysis option on the Data menu. This is installed as part of the Analysis ToolPak in Add-ins (see installation instructions). You select the data with or without the header row and nominate an output area usually as a separate worksheet. The example in Figure 16.12 is from the Descriptive Statistics sheet.

Descriptive statistics

Figure 16.12

	B	C	D	E	F	G	H	I	J	K
4										
5		1	2	3	4		1	2	3	4
6										
7	Mean	3,676.43	3,986.94	698.98	1,004.03		0.65%	0.85%	0.87%	1.20%
8	Standard Error	100.35	105.12	25.86	55.22		0.31%	0.35%	0.30%	0.58%
9	Median	3,472.55	3,905.85	548.35	687.10		0.87%	1.35%	1.20%	1.97%
10	Mode	#N/A	#N/A	299.00	#N/A		#N/A	#N/A	#N/A	#N/A
11	Standard Deviation	1,521.82	1,594.27	392.17	837.43		0.05	0.05	0.05	0.09
12	Sample Variance	2,315,926.11	2,541,695.16	153,800.04	701,290.13		0.00	0.00	0.00	0.01
13	Kurtosis	(1.07)	(1.29)	(1.28)	3.92		3.96	4.03	2.77	4.55
14	Skewness	0.39	0.22	0.44	1.95		(0.87)	(1.01)	(0.83)	(1.00)
15	Range	5,517.60	5,645.20	1,306.40	4,133.20		0.40	0.43	0.36	0.73
16	Minimum	1,414.60	1,414.60	206.30	259.60		(26.02%)	(28.65%)	(22.10%)	(48.33%)
17	Maximum	6,932.20	7,059.80	1,512.70	4,392.80		14.43%	14.48%	13.45%	25.02%
18	Sum	845,579.10	916,996.50	160,765.20	230,927.50		149.18%	193.57%	198.88%	275.08%
19	Count	230	230	230	230		229.00	229.00	229.00	229.00
20	Largest(1)	6,932.20	7,059.80	1,512.70	4,392.80		14.43%	14.48%	13.45%	25.02%
21	Smallest(1)	1,414.60	1,414.60	206.30	259.60		(26.02%)	(28.65%)	(22.10%)	(48.33%)
22	Confidence Level(95.0%)	197.72	207.13	50.95	108.80		0.62%	0.69%	0.59%	1.15%

PROBABILITY DISTRIBUTIONS

Examining past defaults or losses may allow predictions about future events. Probability theory requires the assignment of a probability value to all possible outcomes. This is the percentage odds that the outcome is expected to happen. For example, a stock price in six months' time is shown in Figure 16.13.

Figure 16.13

Expected value

▲	A	B	C	D	E	F
4						
5		Expected Value				
6		Time	Price	A	B	C
7		Price today	100.00			
8						
9		Probability		0.50	0.20	0.30
10		Price		80.00	120.00	90.00
11		Price * p		40.00	24.00	27.00
12						
13		Price	91.00			

Based on the probabilities, the expected value is 91.00. While you can create a model with a single point answer, there is likely to be a range of outcomes in the real world. The first section described distributions and this section introduces the most widely used probability distributions.

Terms used to describe probability distributions include continuous and discrete:

- Continuous random variables have infinite outcomes between upper and lower numbers since values are measured right along the scale. Return on capital could be expected between 10 and 15 per cent and between these values there are infinite possibilities of the exact answer.

- Discrete random variables have a distinct number of possible outcomes between an upper and lower boundary. For example, there are X number of stocks in a portfolio.

The two key properties or rules for the probability of X, written as $p(X)$, are:

- $0 \leq p(X) \leq 1$ = the probabilities must be between 0 and 1.
- $\Sigma p(X) = 1$ = the sum of all the probabilities must add up to one.

This means that a probability must be less than or equal to one and greater than or equal to zero. Secondly, the sum of the individual probabilities must equal one. The main method of interpreting statistical results is by comparison. There are three main distributions that are used in modelling: uniform, binomial and normal distributions.

Uniform distribution

A uniform distribution means that there is an equal chance of a particular outcome. This is equivalent to a random chance between values. For a discrete distribution, it could be written as:

$$X(1, 2, 3, 4, 5), p(X) = 0.2$$

There are defined outcomes between the boundaries whereas there will be an infinite number with continuous variables. Figures 16.14 and 16.15 show both types based on 50 randomly produced values. The discrete values are integers between one and five while the continuous values contain decimals between the upper and lower boundaries.

Uniform distribution

Figure 16.14

	B	C	D	E	F	G	H
4							
5	High	1					
6	Low	5					
7	Interval	1					
8					Frequency		
9	Test	Discrete	Continuous		Score	Discrete	Continuous
10	1	5.00	1.76		1.0	9	0
11	2	4.00	1.04		1.5	0	7
12	3	2.00	2.80		2.0	9	10
13	4	3.00	1.73		2.5	0	7
14	5	4.00	1.09		3.0	16	5
15	6	2.00	2.62		3.5	0	3
16	7	3.00	1.26		4.0	7	6
17	8	5.00	2.44		4.5	0	4
18	9	3.00	1.84		5.0	9	8
19	10	1.00	2.32				

Uniform distribution chart

Figure 16.15

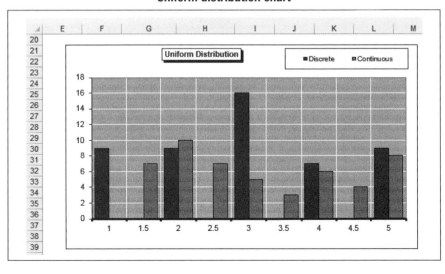

The relevant Excel functions are RAND and RANDBETWEEN, as in cells C10 and D10. RANDBETWEEN produces an integer between a high and low number. RAND generates a random number correct to a number of decimal places between zero and one.

```
Cell C10: =RANDBETWEEN($C$5,$C$6)
Cell D10: =RAND()*($C$6-$C$5)+$C$5
```

Binomial distribution

The binomial distribution is used to denote successes or failures or to construct tables of how assets may move over successive discrete periods. For example, binomial trees can be used to build up pricing for derivatives over a series of time periods. An asset either rises or falls in value over a time period and rarely keeps the same value. The probability of success for each trial is constant and the trials are independent of each other. The final outcome depends on a series of trials. The formula is set out in Figure 16.16 which uses simple multiplication.

Figure 16.16

Binomial example

⊿ A	B	C	D	E	F	G
4						
5			Probability	Value	Percentages	
6	Value today			5,000.00		
7	Probability Up		0.60	5,500.00	1.10	
8	Probability Down		0.40	4,500.00	0.90	
9	Steps		2.00			
10						
11						
12			Step 1 Probability	Step One	Step 2 Probability	Step 2	V*P
13							
14					0.36	6,050.00	2,178.00
15			0.60	5,500.00			
16					0.24	4,950.00	1,188.00
17		5,000.00					
18					0.24	4,950.00	1,188.00
19			0.40	4,500.00			
20					0.16	4,050.00	648.00
21							
22		Expected Value Σp(x)x			1.00		5,202.00

The probability of the stock rising from 5,000 to 5,500 is 60 per cent and the probability of a decline to 4,500 is 40 per cent. The probabilities for the second period are calculated as below. In the first line, the stock is expected to rise in both periods and the probability is 0.6 multiplied by 0.6. The value rises by 10 per cent in each period and the weighted value is the probability multiplied by the value. Figure 16.17 shows the process of multiplication to obtain the expected value.

Probability table

Figure 16.17

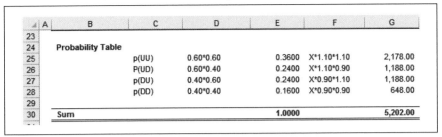

	A	B	C	D	E	F	G
23							
24		Probability Table					
25			p(UU)	0.60*0.60	0.3600	X*1.10*1.10	2,178.00
26			P(UD)	0.60*0.40	0.2400	X*1.10*0.90	1,188.00
27			p(DU)	0.40*0.60	0.2400	X*0.90*1.10	1,188.00
28			p(DD)	0.40*0.40	0.1600	X*0.90*0.90	648.00
29							
30		Sum			1.0000		5,202.00

Normal distribution

The normal distribution is the most important distribution in finance since it forms the basis of many credit and portfolio models. There are many real-world examples of normally distributed data and a normal distribution is assumed in many statistical tests. The key characteristics of the distribution are the following:

- There is a hump in the middle with tails to the left and right.
- The distribution can be described by its mean and variance.
- Skew is zero, which means that it is completely symmetrical around the mean.
- Kurtosis is three and therefore excess kurtosis is equal to zero.

Since the distribution is symmetrical, you can predict the percentage of results that are likely to fall within one or more standard deviations from the mean:

- 34 per cent between 0 and 1 standard deviation either side of the mean, so 68 per cent fall within one standard deviation above and below the mean;
- 45 per cent of the area either side falls between 0 and 1.65 standard deviations, and so this equates to 90 per cent of observations;
- 47.5 per cent either side falls within 0 and 1.96 standard deviations, so 95 per cent of observations fall either side of the mean;
- 49.5 per cent either side falls between 0 and 2.58 standard deviations from the mean, so the equivalent figure is 99 per cent.

Figures 16.18 and 16.19 represent an ideal world; however, the entire population may not be available in the data set, and so the population parameters must be substituted with the sample mean and sample standard deviation. Confidence intervals are therefore important to understand the probability. For example, using 20 years of data, the average return on a stock has been 10 per cent with a standard deviation of 5 per cent.

You might wish to know the 90 per cent confidence interval for the return in the following year. The calculation is:

$$10\% \pm 1.65(5\%) = 10\% \pm 8.25\% = 1.75\% \text{ to } 18.25\%$$

Figure 16.18

Two standard deviations covering 95 per cent of the area

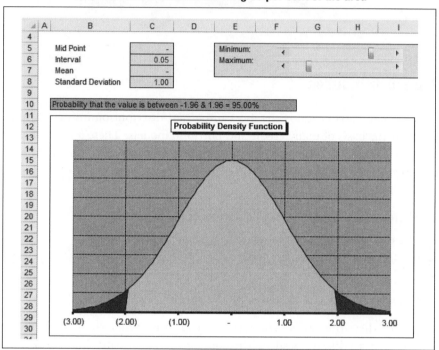

Figure 16.19

Number of standard deviations and percentages (using NORMSDIST function)

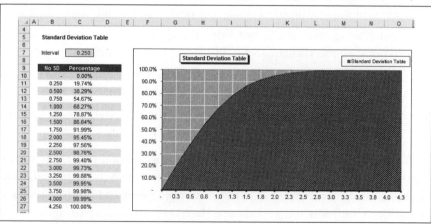

The Excel functions for distributions are:

NORMDIST   *Normal cumulative distribution*

NORMINV   *Inverse of the normal cumulative distribution*

NORMSDIST   *Standard normal cumulative distribution*

NORMSINV   *Inverse of the standard normal cumulative distribution*

```
Cell C48 on Normal_Distribution:
=NORMDIST(B48,$C$7,$C$8,FALSE)
```

Often it is useful to convert a distribution into a standard normal deviation for comparison purposes and this is usually referred to as a z value. The calculation is:

$$z = [data\ point - population\ mean]/standard\ deviation = [x - \mu]/\sigma$$

The steps are:

- Find the mean and the standard deviation (AVERAGE and STDEV).
- Take the value and subtract the mean.
- Divide the result by the standard deviation.

From the mechanics of calculating the z value:

- Almost all standard scores (99.7%) fall between the values of plus and minus three.
- A negative score means that the value is below the mean and a positive score means the value is above the mean.
- A standard score of zero means that the original score was the mean.
- Scores from a standardised normal distribution have special values since the mean is zero and the standard deviation is one.

Using the example of a mean of 10 per cent and a standard deviation of 5 per cent, this would show the probability that values will fall between 6 and 14. This is 57.6 per cent and the table in Figure 16.20 shows further combinations of values.

```
Cell E11:  =(D7-D$5)/D$6
Cell F11:  =NORMSDIST(E11)+NORMSDIST(E11)-1
```

In cell E11, the factor $= [14 - 10] / 5 = 0.80$. This equates to a probability of 57 per cent using NORMSDIST within a normal distribution table. This is divided into two to represent the lower half of the distribution. The difference is the same above the mean, so the overall probability is 57.6 per cent. Figure 16.21 shows other values around the upper and lower values.

```
Cell B10 on Normal_Distribution: ="Probability that
the value is between
```

```
"&TEXT(MIN(Normal_Distribution!G49:G50),"0.00")&"&
"&TEXT(MAX(Normal_Distribution!G49:G50),"0.00")&" =
"&TEXT(G51,"0.00%")
```

Figure 16.20

Standard normal distribution

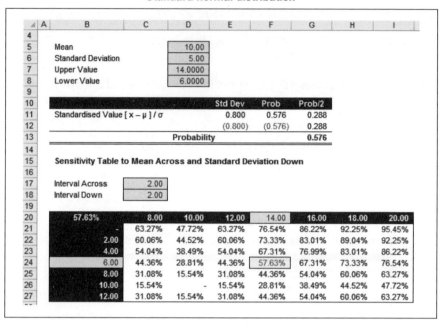

Figure 16.21

Area under series 57.6 per cent

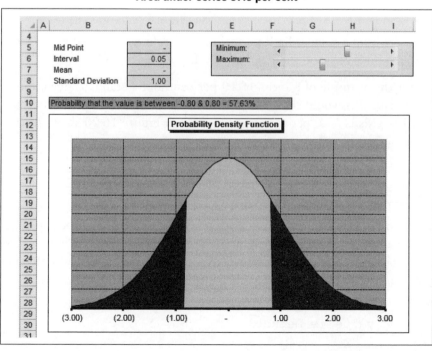

A table of z values is given in Figure 16.22 which contains values using the probability density function for Z. The values show that the probability of observing a z value is less than a given value. The numbers down the left-hand side are whole values and the values across add the decimal places.

The value for 0.80 is 0.7881 for the positive value and therefore the total calculation is:

$$Probability = F(0.7881) - F(-0.7881)$$
$$Probability = 0.7881 - (1 - 0.7881) = 57.6 \text{ per cent}$$

Therefore the probability of a value between 6 and 14 per cent is 57.6 per cent.

Z table (cumulative probability)

Figure 16.22

⊿ A	B	C	D	E	F	G	H	I	J	K	L
4											
5	Mean		-		**Values from Standard Normal**				10.00		
6	Standard Deviation		1.0000						5.00		
7	Upper Value		14.0000						0.80		
8	Lower Value		6.0000						(0.80)		
9											
10	Upper (z)		0.7881	$D$10: ' =NORMDIST(J7,$D$5,$D$6,TRUE)							
11	Lower (z)		0.7881	$D$11: ' =1-NORMDIST(J8,$D$5,$D$6,TRUE)							
12	Total Probability		0.5763	$D$12: ' =D10-(1-D11)							
13											

	-	0.01	0.02	0.03	0.04	0.05	0.06	0.07	0.08	0.09
-	0.5000	0.5040	0.5080	0.5120	0.5160	0.5199	0.5239	0.5279	0.5319	0.5359
0.10	0.5398	0.5438	0.5478	0.5517	0.5557	0.5596	0.5636	0.5675	0.5714	0.5753
0.20	0.5793	0.5832	0.5871	0.5910	0.5948	0.5987	0.6026	0.6064	0.6103	0.6141
0.30	0.6179	0.6217	0.6255	0.6293	0.6331	0.6368	0.6406	0.6443	0.6480	0.6517
0.40	0.6554	0.6591	0.6628	0.6664	0.6700	0.6736	0.6772	0.6808	0.6844	0.6879
0.50	0.6915	0.6950	0.6985	0.7019	0.7054	0.7088	0.7123	0.7157	0.7190	0.7224
0.60	0.7257	0.7291	0.7324	0.7357	0.7389	0.7422	0.7454	0.7486	0.7517	0.7549
0.70	0.7580	0.7611	0.7642	0.7673	0.7704	0.7734	0.7764	0.7794	0.7823	0.7852
0.80	0.7881	0.7910	0.7939	0.7967	0.7995	0.8023	0.8051	0.8078	0.8106	0.8133
0.90	0.8159	0.8186	0.8212	0.8238	0.8264	0.8289	0.8315	0.8340	0.8365	0.8389
1.00	0.8413	0.8438	0.8461	0.8485	0.8508	0.8531	0.8554	0.8577	0.8599	0.8621
1.10	0.8643	0.8665	0.8686	0.8708	0.8729	0.8749	0.8770	0.8790	0.8810	0.8830
1.20	0.8849	0.8869	0.8888	0.8907	0.8925	0.8944	0.8962	0.8980	0.8997	0.9015
1.30	0.9032	0.9049	0.9066	0.9082	0.9099	0.9115	0.9131	0.9147	0.9162	0.9177
1.40	0.9192	0.9207	0.9222	0.9236	0.9251	0.9265	0.9279	0.9292	0.9306	0.9319
1.50	0.9332	0.9345	0.9357	0.9370	0.9382	0.9394	0.9406	0.9418	0.9429	0.9441
1.60	0.9452	0.9463	0.9474	0.9484	0.9495	0.9505	0.9515	0.9525	0.9535	0.9545
1.70	0.9554	0.9564	0.9573	0.9582	0.9591	0.9599	0.9608	0.9616	0.9625	0.9633
1.80	0.9641	0.9649	0.9656	0.9664	0.9671	0.9678	0.9686	0.9693	0.9699	0.9706
1.90	0.9713	0.9719	0.9726	0.9732	0.9738	0.9744	0.9750	0.9756	0.9761	0.9767
2.00	0.9772	0.9778	0.9783	0.9788	0.9793	0.9798	0.9803	0.9808	0.9812	0.9817
2.10	0.9821	0.9826	0.9830	0.9834	0.9838	0.9842	0.9846	0.9850	0.9854	0.9857
2.20	0.9861	0.9864	0.9868	0.9871	0.9875	0.9878	0.9881	0.9884	0.9887	0.9890
2.30	0.9893	0.9896	0.9898	0.9901	0.9904	0.9906	0.9909	0.9911	0.9913	0.9916
2.40	0.9918	0.9920	0.9922	0.9925	0.9927	0.9929	0.9931	0.9932	0.9934	0.9936
2.50	0.9938	0.9940	0.9941	0.9943	0.9945	0.9946	0.9948	0.9949	0.9951	0.9952
2.60	0.9953	0.9955	0.9956	0.9957	0.9959	0.9960	0.9961	0.9962	0.9963	0.9964
2.70	0.9965	0.9966	0.9967	0.9968	0.9969	0.9970	0.9971	0.9972	0.9973	0.9974
2.80	0.9974	0.9975	0.9976	0.9977	0.9977	0.9978	0.9979	0.9979	0.9980	0.9981
2.90	0.9981	0.9982	0.9982	0.9983	0.9984	0.9984	0.9985	0.9985	0.9986	0.9986
3.00	0.9987	0.9987	0.9987	0.9988	0.9988	0.9989	0.9989	0.9989	0.9990	0.9990

SAMPLING/CENTRAL LIMIT THEOREM

Often an entire population is not available, incomplete or too expensive to collect, so it is necessary to use a sample and draw conclusions from it as if it were the whole population. Simple random sampling means that each data point has an equal likelihood of being included in the sample data set. From the sample, you determine how much you expect sample means to vary without using the whole population.

The underpinning statistical theory is the Central Limit Theorem which holds that the sample distribution mean is normal as long as the sample sizes are large enough. The Central Limit Theorem states that if you have a sample taken from a probability distribution with a mean μ and a standard deviation σ, the sampling distribution of $\overline{X}$ is approximately normal with a mean of μ and a standard deviation of $\sigma / \sqrt{n}$.

A key point is that the sampling distribution $\overline{X}$ is normal irrespective of the original probability distribution. As the sample size increases, the approximation to a normal distribution becomes closer. Specific inferences about the population mean can be made from the sample mean regardless of the population's distribution. The sample needs to be sufficiently large, and this in practice means one with more than 30 data points. For example, a portfolio of one share is risky; however, with a random portfolio of 30 shares from an index, individual risk reduces and you start to approximate market risk. You remove the individual (unsystematic) risk and are left with market (systematic) risk.

When you use a sample you need a measure of the possible error, and this is provided by the standard error given that the whole population is known. The formula is:

$$\sigma \overline{x} = \frac{\sigma}{\sqrt{n}}$$

In practice, the population standard deviation is usually not known and therefore the sample standard deviation is calculated with this formula:

$$s = \sqrt{\frac{\sum_{i=1}^{n} |X_i - \overline{X}|^2}{n - 1}}$$

The standard error (see Figure 16.23) is therefore:

$$S\overline{x} = \frac{s}{\sqrt{n}}$$

The table in Figure 16.23 shows the reduction in the standard error as the number of results increases. In the file (MFMaths3e_16b.xls), the example population in Figure 16.24 is a simulated set of data on the Sampling_Data sheet consisting of 1,000 net present values and discount rates. From this, 100 random samples are extracted and analysed. The Excel file recalculates with a new sample every time you press F9. Column D, Random refers to the selected line number in the population distribution and is generated

Standard error table

Figure 16.23

	A	B	C	D	E	F
197						
198		Standard Deviation		3.0000		
199						
200		Results		Standard Error		
201		1.00		3.0000	$D$201: ' =D$198/SQRT($B201)	
202		10.00		0.9487		
203		50.00		0.4243		
204		100.00		0.3000		
205		200.00		0.2121		
206		500.00		0.1342		
207		1,000.00		0.0949		
208		1,500.00		0.0775		
209		2,000.00		0.0671		
210		5,000.00		0.0424		
211						

Sample data

Figure 16.24

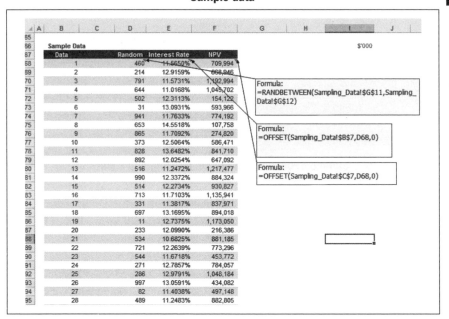

automatically between the upper and lower numbers. The line number is then entered into an OFFSET function to look up the correct line. The values change every time you press F9.

```
Cell D68: =RANDBETWEEN(Sampling_Data!$G$11,
Sampling_Data!$G$12)
```

A scatter chart of the sample does not yield much information (see Figure 16.25) and the data need to be restated as a frequency table and histogram chart, as in Figure 16.26. The table on the left displays the results within the bin ranges and the chart (see Figure 16.27) displays the bell-shaped curve proving the Central Limit Theorem. The results on the right show the mean, standard deviation and standard error for the population and the sample together with the differences between the results. While the standard deviation is reasonably close, the standard error for the sample is higher than for the population.

Figure 16.25

Sample scatter chart

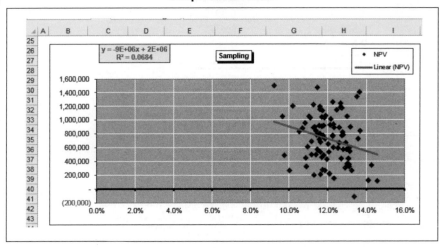

Figure 16.26

Sample frequency and results on Sampling sheet

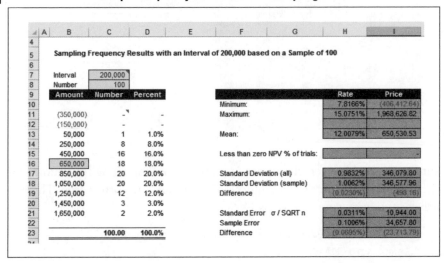

Sample chart

Figure 16.27

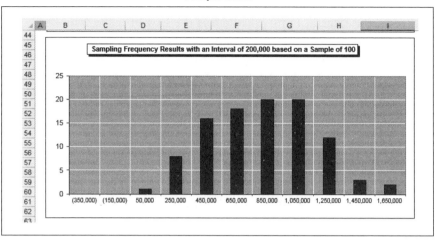

Having taken a sample and found the mean and standard deviation and standard error, a confidence value would also be useful to show how much you could rely on the result. The table in Figure 16.28 denotes the confidence intervals for 80 to 99 per cent. The z value is the number of standard deviations from the mean, as in the last section. The next column multiplies this value by the standard error $(\sigma \sqrt{n})$ to derive a monetary value. This is then added or subtracted from the sample mean to show the upper and lower values within the confidence level. There is 90 per cent confidence that values will fall between 602,364 and 698,696.

Confidence intervals

Figure 16.28

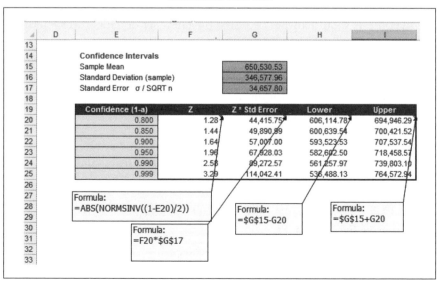

Large numbers

Linked to the Central Limit Theorem is the Law of Large Numbers. This states that a distribution nears its theoretical distribution as the number of observations increases. The table in Figure 16.29 shows the differences between the population and sample standard errors for the rate and net present value. The differences tend to reduce above 30 observations and allow the analyst to be more confident that the sample is representative of the whole population.

Figure 16.29

Standard differences on rate and price

Standard Error Difference on Rate and Price		
Trials	(0.06%)	(21,162.83)
10	(0.0687%)	(22,887.36)
20	(0.0663%)	(23,567.63)
30	(0.0764%)	(25,043.14)
50	(0.0694%)	(22,475.11)
75	(0.0636%)	(23,484.13)
100	(0.0712%)	(21,240.07)

HYPOTHESIS TESTING

Hypothesis testing involves techniques for testing if a claim is valid based on the known data. You formulate a hypothesis, collect data and then test the data to see whether they support or contradict the hypothesis. If you formulate a hypothesis after collecting the data, you risk having a biased test, because the hypothesis could be designed to fit the collected data and therefore prove the hypothesis as true. To prevent the use of a biased test, the hypothesis should always be tested on a new set of data. You should:

- State the hypothesis and define what you are testing.
- State the alternatives and select an appropriate test statistic.
- Specify the level of significance.
- State the decision rule regarding the hypothesis.

With these stages completed, you can collect the sample and calculate the sample statistic. On the basis of the statistic, a conclusion and decision can be made based on the results of the test. These are the elements in a test:

- null hypothesis, H_0 – typically this states there is no change;
- alternative hypothesis, H_a;
- test statistic based on a level of significance;
- rejection region.

The null hypothesis (H_0) represents the default theory, which will be accepted unless there is evidence that this is incorrect. The alternative hypothesis is the one that is automatically accepted if the data do not support the null hypothesis, for example:

- the parameter is not equal to the claimed value (sometimes written as H_a: $\mu \neq 5$);
- the parameter is greater than the claimed value (H_a: $\mu > 5$).
- the parameter is less than the claimed value (H_a: $\mu < 5$).

For example, you are analysing aspects of banking defaults. The null hypothesis would be that cash flow in the previous three years has no effect on occurrences of default; the alternative hypothesis is that cash flow does have an effect and is a key factor (either in a positive or negative direction).

The test statistic is a statistic calculated from the data that you use to decide whether to accept or reject the null hypothesis. The rejection region specifies those values of the test statistic under which you should reject the null hypothesis (and accept the alternative hypothesis).

In hypothesis testing, you can make two types of errors which are defined as:

- Type I error: Rejecting the null hypothesis when the null hypothesis is actually correct. The probability of Type I error is often denoted by the Greek letter α (alpha).
- Type II error: Failing to reject the null hypothesis when the alternative hypothesis is true. The probability of Type II error is usually identified with the Greek letter β (beta).

Your Decision	H_0 = False	H_0 = True
Reject H_0	Correct decision	Type I error (α)
Fail to Reject H_0	Type II error (β)	Correct decision

You can never be sure that decisions do not suffer from either Type I or Type II error, but you can attempt to reduce the probability of error. Generally, the probability of Type I error is more important, because rejecting the null hypothesis usually results in some fundamental change. In the credit example above, erroneously rejecting the null hypothesis that the cash flow is not important could affect future credit decisions or lead to a downgrading in this factor when reviewing current cases.

Type II error becomes important in the design of a study, where you want to ensure that the analysis will detect a difference between the null and alternative hypothesis if such a difference exists. A study of the credit cases should be large enough to detect the importance of cash flow by selecting sufficient numbers of companies from a range of industries.

How low should the value of α be? The accepted value of α is 0.05; in other words, the probability of incorrectly rejecting the null hypothesis should be 5 per cent or less.

Example: two-tailed test

In this example, studies have shown that the number of slow payers in a portfolio of credit agreements follows a normal distribution with mean of 100 and standard deviation of 30. You decide to test a group of 25 batches that used a different credit scoring process. The average number of slow payers in these batches is 90. Does this represent a significant decrease in the rate of delinquency or is it simply a sample average that just happens to be lower than expected?

Following the methodology above, the hypotheses are:

- H_0: there is no change in the number of slow payers;
- H_a: the number of slow payers has changed under the alternative credit scoring process.

Or

- H_0: the mean number of slow payers in the credit scoring process $= 100$;
- H_a: the mean number of slow payers in the credit scoring process $<> 100$.

To evaluate the data, you need a test statistic. To do this, you can calculate the Z value, which is:

$$Z = \frac{\bar{x} - \mu}{\sigma / \sqrt{n}}$$

where $\bar{x}$ is the sample mean, μ is the mean value under the null hypothesis, σ is the population standard deviation and n is the sample size. In the example, $\bar{x} = 90$, $\mu = 100$, $\sigma = 30$ and $n = 25$.

Z follows a standard normal distribution, so once you calculate the value of Z, you can determine whether this represents an extreme value on the standard normal curve. If the value is extreme, you would reject the null hypothesis and accept the alternative. In this example, the value of Z is:

$$Z = \frac{90 - 100}{30 / \sqrt{25}} = \frac{-10}{6} = -1.67$$

After calculating the test statistic, you need to evaluate it against the hypothesis by ascertaining if -1.67 is an extreme value. You therefore need to find the probability of a value on the standard normal curve lying beyond

1.67 units from 0. You are interested in extreme values in either direction in order to reject the hypothesis.

The probability of the standard normal value being −1.67 or less is equal to 0.0478. Because the standard normal curve is symmetric, the probability of a value being 1.67 or more is also equal to 0.0478. Therefore the probability of a value lying 1.67 units or more from 0 is equal to 2 × 0.0478 or 0.0956. This means that there is a 9.6 per cent chance that the results simply are derived from random events (see Figure 16.30).

Inputs and results (from the Hypothesis Testing sheet)

Figure 16.30

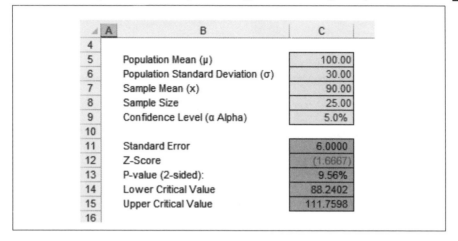

The probability is the confidence of 5 per cent divided by two. The standard deviation is 6 and therefore the lower level becomes 88.24 (see Figure 16.31).

NORMINV function in cell H45

Figure 16.31

Function Arguments		? X
NORMINV		
Probability	Hypothesis_Testing!C9/C41	= 0.025
Mean	C5	= 100
Standard_dev	Hypothesis_Testing!C6/SQRT(Hy	= 6

= 88.24021609

This function is available for compatibility with Excel 2007 and earlier.
Returns the inverse of the normal cumulative distribution for the specified mean and standard deviation.

Probability is a probability corresponding to the normal distribution, a number between 0 and 1 inclusive.

Formula result = 88.24021609

Help on this function   OK   Cancel

Based on a value of 1.667, you can read off the answer from the table in Figure 16.32. The major units are down and minor units are across. The result of 0.0956 comes between 1.66 and 1.67. The lower value then becomes 88.24 and the upper value 111.75.

Figure 16.32

Probability table

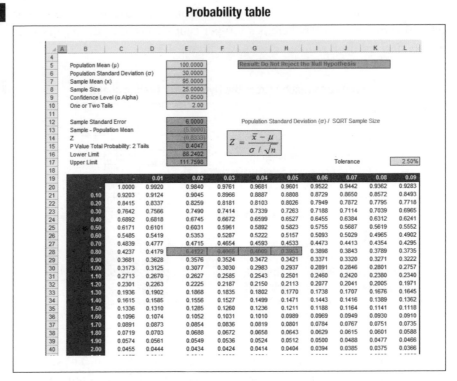

If you reject the null hypothesis and accept the alternative hypothesis that the alternative credit scoring changes the number of slow payers, then there is a 4.0 per cent chance of being wrong (Type I error). Since you usually set the confidence level value of α (the probability of Type I error) to 0.05, you decide that the results are not significant enough to consider rejecting the null hypothesis. In that case, the rejection level has been calculated as 88.24 against the sample average of 90. This can be seen graphically in Figure 16.33.

Acceptance

You can use α to calculate a rejection region, a range of values for which you would reject the null hypothesis. The complement of the rejection region is the acceptance region, which includes only those values that support accepting the null hypothesis. If the null hypothesis is true, only α per cent of the values should lie in the rejection region and $(1 - \alpha)$ per cent of the values should lie in the acceptance region.

Distribution of averages

Figure 16.33

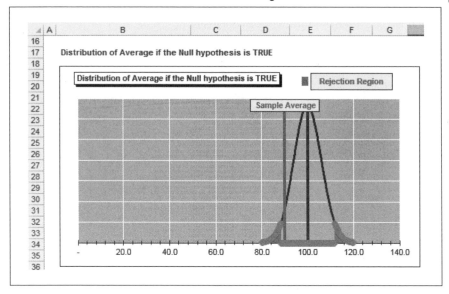

The boundaries of the acceptance region for the Z test as a formula are:

$$\left(\mu - Z_{1-\alpha/2}\frac{\sigma}{\sqrt{n}}, \mu + Z_{1-\alpha/2}\frac{\sigma}{\sqrt{n}}\right)$$

where μ is the mean under the null hypothesis, σ is the known standard deviation, n is the sample size and Z is the Z value. When $\alpha = 0.05$, $Z_{1-0.05/2} = 1.96$.

In the example, the acceptance region for the average number of slow payers in a sample of 25 batches is:

$$= \left(100 - 1.96 \times \frac{30}{\sqrt{25}}, 100 + 1.96 \times \frac{30}{\sqrt{25}}\right)$$
$$= (100 - 11.76, 100 + 11.76)$$
$$= (88.24, 111.76)$$

The upper and lower values of this boundary are called the critical values. Any value that lies outside the critical values supports rejecting the null hypothesis.

Example: one-tailed test

There is the possibility of performing one-tailed and two-tailed tests. In the latter, you test both tails, while in the former you are only interested in the high or low end of the distribution. There could be aspects of the alternative credit scoring that absolutely ruled out the possibility of an increase in the number of slow payers. If that were the case, you could use one-tailed test in which we consider the following hypotheses:

- H_0: the mean number of slow payers is 100;
- H_a: the mean number of slow payers is <100.

In a two-tailed test, you assume that departures from the null hypothesis can go in either direction; in a one-tailed test, you assume that these departures go in only one direction. By adding this extra assumption, you can increase the power of the statistical test since the required p-value is halved.

In the example (see Figure 16.34), the test statistic was -1.67. If you assume that the number of slow payers can only decrease under the new credit scoring process, then you need only consider the probability that a standard normal value is less than -1.67. The probability of that happening is 0.0478, which results in a probability of Type I error of 4.78 per cent. This is less than the 0.05 value you had set as the limit for significance. You would then reject the null hypothesis and accept the alternative hypothesis, concluding that the new credit scoring process does result in a decrease in the number of slow payers.

Figure 16.34

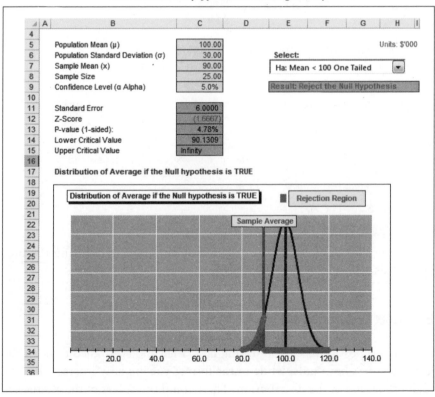

One-tailed test (Hypothesis Testing sheet)

Because it is easier to achieve 'significant' results in one-tailed tests, they should be used with more caution than two-tailed tests and only when warranted by the situation. You should state your alternative hypothesis before doing your analysis (rather than deciding on a one-tailed test after seeing the results with the two-tailed test). It is not valid to gain an unsatisfactory result and then use a one-sided test to gain the result you hoped for.

The *t*-distribution

The tests above assume that the standard deviation of the population is known; however, there may be occasions when this is unknown or you have a small sample but still want to test it. While you could substitute the sample standard deviation (s) for the population standard deviation (σ), there are problems mathematically with this approach. If s is lower than σ, then you will tend to overestimate the significance of the results against the test statistic. If s is higher than σ, then you will tend to underestimate the significance of the results and could falsely reject the null hypothesis. One solution is to use the *t*-distribution as an approximation. You can use this distribution when:

- the sample is large, which in practice means more than 30 data points;
- the sample is small but you are sure that the distribution of the population is normal or approximates to normal.

The derived value for the test statistic based on the *t*-distribution is the *t*-statistic. For a hypothesis test, a *t*-statistic with $n - 1$ degrees of freedom is derived as below. The degrees of freedom are defined as the number of observations minus one:

$$t_{m-1} = \frac{\bar{x} - \mu_0}{s/\sqrt{n}}$$

μ_0 = *hypothesised sample mean*
$\bar{x}$ = *sample mean*
n = *sample size*

As shown in Figure 16.35, the distribution becomes 'more' normal with more degrees of freedom. With about 30 degrees of freedom, the distribution is almost identical to the normal distribution. You can test the difference between the two distributions on the Comparison sheet (see example at the end of the section).

Figure 16.35

The *t*-distribution

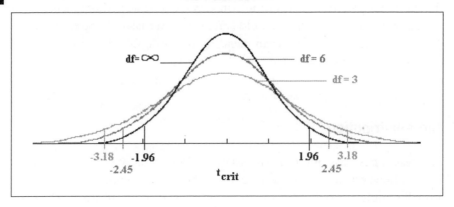

The example in Figure 16.36 uses the data from the previous section. The assumed sample standard deviation is again:

- Standard deviation $(s)/\sqrt{sample\ size}$

The *t*-value is, using the above formula: $[90 - 100]/[30/\sqrt{25}] = 1.67$.

The 1.67 can be looked up from the table in Figure 16.37 which has the sample size down and the *t*-statistic across. The *t*-value and the sample size intersect at about 10.8 per cent. This is higher than the 5 per cent confidence interval. Based on this information the sample result (mean of 90) is not significant against the *t*-statistic. The calculated lower limit is 87.62:

$$Lower\ value = 100 - [2.0639 * 30/\sqrt{25}] = 100 - 12.38 = 87.62$$

Figure 16.36

The *t*-distribution inputs

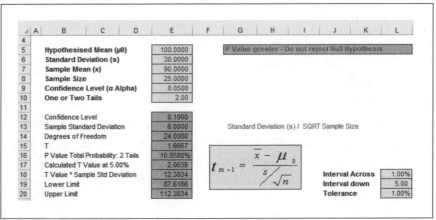

The *p*-value table

Figure 16.37

	A	B	C	D	E	F	G	H	I	J	K	L
65												
66		Probability P Value Table										
67		Tolerance	0.03	2.50%								
68		Interval Across	0.25	0.25								
69												
70		T Value Across and Sample Size										
71		0.1086	0.67	0.92	1.17	1.42	1.67	1.92	2.17	2.42	2.67	2.92
72		5.00	54.15%	41.12%	30.82%	22.95%	17.09%	12.78%	9.62%	7.30%	5.60%	4.34%
73		10.00	52.17%	38.32%	27.33%	19.03%	12.99%	8.75%	5.84%	3.88%	2.58%	1.71%
74		15.00	51.58%	37.48%	26.28%	17.84%	11.78%	7.59%	4.80%	2.99%	1.84%	1.13%
75		20.00	51.30%	37.08%	25.78%	17.28%	11.20%	7.04%	4.32%	2.59%	1.52%	0.88%
76		25.00	51.13%	36.84%	25.48%	16.94%	10.86%	6.73%	4.04%	2.36%	1.35%	0.76%
77		30.00	51.03%	36.69%	25.29%	16.72%	10.63%	6.52%	3.86%	2.22%	1.24%	0.68%
78		35.00	50.95%	36.58%	25.15%	16.57%	10.48%	6.37%	3.74%	2.12%	1.16%	0.62%
79		40.00	50.89%	36.50%	25.04%	16.45%	10.38%	6.26%	3.64%	2.04%	1.11%	0.58%
80		45.00	50.85%	36.43%	24.96%	16.36%	10.27%	6.18%	3.57%	1.99%	1.07%	0.56%
81		50.00	50.81%	36.38%	24.90%	16.29%	10.20%	6.11%	3.52%	1.94%	1.04%	0.53%
82		55.00	50.78%	36.34%	24.85%	16.23%	10.14%	6.06%	3.47%	1.91%	1.01%	0.51%
83		60.00	50.76%	36.31%	24.80%	16.18%	10.09%	6.01%	3.43%	1.88%	0.99%	0.50%
84		65.00	50.74%	36.28%	24.77%	16.14%	10.05%	5.97%	3.40%	1.85%	0.97%	0.49%
85		70.00	50.72%	36.25%	24.74%	16.11%	10.01%	5.94%	3.37%	1.83%	0.95%	0.48%
86		75.00	50.71%	36.23%	24.71%	16.08%	9.98%	5.91%	3.35%	1.81%	0.94%	0.47%
87		80.00	50.69%	36.21%	24.69%	16.05%	9.95%	5.89%	3.33%	1.80%	0.93%	0.46%
88		85.00	50.68%	36.19%	24.66%	16.03%	9.93%	5.87%	3.31%	1.78%	0.92%	0.45%
89		90.00	50.67%	36.18%	24.65%	16.01%	9.91%	5.85%	3.29%	1.77%	0.91%	0.45%
90		95.00	50.66%	36.17%	24.63%	15.99%	9.89%	5.83%	3.28%	1.76%	0.90%	0.44%
91		100.00	50.65%	36.15%	24.62%	15.97%	9.87%	5.82%	3.27%	1.75%	0.89%	0.44%

It is also possible to show this table the other way around with the confidence levels across the top and the sample size down. Based on a sample size of 25 and a confidence level of 5 per cent, the critical *p*-value is in the table in Figure 16.38. This is the *t*-value of the *t*-distribution as a function of the probability and the degrees of freedom. You will note that the values fall as the sample size increases.

The *t*-value table

Figure 16.38

	A	B	C	D	E	F	G	H	I	J	K	L
21												
22		Confidence Level Across and Sample Size Down										
23		2.0639	1.00%	2.00%	3.00%	4.00%	5.00%	6.00%	7.00%	8.00%	9.00%	10.00%
24		5.00	4.6041	3.7469	3.2976	2.9985	2.7764	2.6008	2.4559	2.3329	2.2261	2.1318
25		10.00	3.2498	2.8214	2.5738	2.3984	2.2622	2.1504	2.0554	1.9727	1.8992	1.8331
26		15.00	2.9768	2.6245	2.4149	2.2638	2.1448	2.0462	1.9617	1.8875	1.8213	1.7613
27		20.00	2.8609	2.5395	2.3456	2.2047	2.0930	2.0000	1.9200	1.8495	1.7864	1.7291
28		25.00	2.7969	2.4922	2.3069	2.1715	2.0639	1.9740	1.8965	1.8281	1.7667	1.7109
29		30.00	2.7564	2.4620	2.2822	2.1503	2.0452	1.9573	1.8813	1.8142	1.7540	1.6991
30		35.00	2.7284	2.4411	2.2650	2.1356	2.0322	1.9457	1.8708	1.8046	1.7451	1.6909
31		40.00	2.7079	2.4258	2.2524	2.1247	2.0227	1.9371	1.8630	1.7975	1.7386	1.6849
32		45.00	2.6923	2.4141	2.2427	2.1164	2.0154	1.9305	1.8571	1.7921	1.7336	1.6802
33		50.00	2.6800	2.4049	2.2351	2.1099	2.0096	1.9253	1.8524	1.7878	1.7296	1.6766
34		55.00	2.6700	2.3974	2.2289	2.1046	2.0049	1.9211	1.8486	1.7843	1.7264	1.6736
35		60.00	2.6618	2.3912	2.2238	2.1002	2.0010	1.9177	1.8454	1.7814	1.7237	1.6711
36		65.00	2.6549	2.3860	2.2195	2.0965	1.9977	1.9147	1.8427	1.7789	1.7215	1.6690
37		70.00	2.6490	2.3816	2.2159	2.0933	1.9949	1.9122	1.8405	1.7769	1.7195	1.6672
38		75.00	2.6439	2.3778	2.2127	2.0906	1.9925	1.9101	1.8385	1.7751	1.7179	1.6657
39		80.00	2.6395	2.3745	2.2100	2.0882	1.9905	1.9082	1.8368	1.7735	1.7164	1.6644
40		85.00	2.6356	2.3716	2.2076	2.0861	1.9886	1.9065	1.8353	1.7721	1.7152	1.6632
41		90.00	2.6322	2.3690	2.2054	2.0843	1.9870	1.9051	1.8340	1.7709	1.7141	1.6622
42		95.00	2.6291	2.3667	2.2035	2.0826	1.9855	1.9038	1.8328	1.7698	1.7130	1.6612
43		100.00	2.6264	2.3646	2.2018	2.0812	1.9842	1.9026	1.8317	1.7688	1.7121	1.6604

It is also possible to construct a 95 per cent confidence range for the example. The amount is:

$$Amount = calculated\ t - value * standard\ deviation / \sqrt{sample\ size\ (n)}$$
$$Amount = 2.0639 * 30 / \sqrt{25} = 12.38$$
$$Lower\ limit = 100 - 12.38 = 87.62$$
$$Upper\ limit = 100 + 12.38 = 112.38$$

The expected value should therefore not be greater or less than these values. The sample mean is 90 and within the calculated range of confidence. To prove the similarity between the t- and normal distributions, Figure 16.39 plots the two distributions and the variance based on six degrees of freedom. The distributions are broadly similar and these variances reduce as the degrees of freedom rise to 20 and above.

Figure 16.39   **Variance**

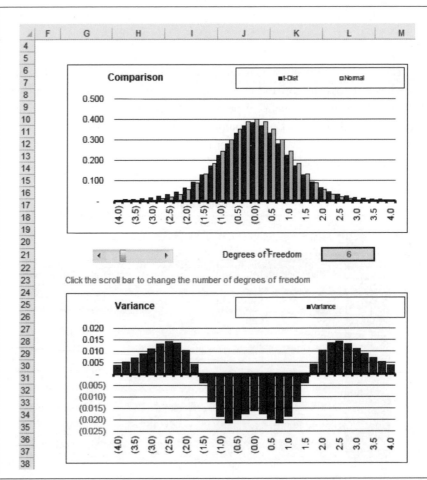

This section has introduced more complex hypothesis testing outlining the methodology and using *z* tests and *t*-distributions showing a worked example and the decision based on the test statistic. In each case you state the hypothesis, select an appropriate test statistic, specify the level of significance and state the decision rule regarding the hypothesis. With these stages completed, you can collect the sample and calculate the sample statistic using one of the above tests. On the basis of the statistic, you can make a decision on the results of the test.

CORRELATION AND REGRESSION

Correlation and regression comprise a set of techniques to analyse relationships between variables. Bankruptcy and defaults ratios such as *Z* scores may be explained by a series of ratios such as gearing or market to book. Alternatively you may think there is a link between sales volume and economic growth. Correlation and regression present the strength of the relationship between variables in mathematical terms. Correlation measures the direction and extent of a linear association between variables while regression summarises the relationship between a dependent variable and one or more independent variables. Both techniques build on the mathematical calculations so far, and Excel provides all the functions and extra techniques in the Analysis ToolPak and functions list.

Correlation

While in regression the emphasis is on predicting one variable from the other, in correlation the emphasis is on the degree to which a linear model may describe the relationship between two variables. In regression you want to find out the extent of the relationship. You want to know if a change in variable A produces a negative or positive change in variable B.

The correlation coefficient can be easily built up on a spreadsheet grid or calculated directly with functions. The example below uses data from the Correlation_Data sheet where sales are matched with two factors. The objective is to test the degree of relationship through correlation and regression.

The table in Figure 16.40 shows an extract of data and a grid for building up the answer in stages. The answer could involve:

- positive covariance, indicating that the variables move in the same direction;
- negative covariance, meaning that the variables move in opposite directions.

This means that if X increases, Y decreases. For example, as price increases, demand is usually reduced. Correlation can only be a value between −1 and +1.

Figure 16.40   **Covariance and correlation grid**

	B	C	D	E	F	G	H
32							
33						SST	
34	Variable 1 X	Sales Y	(X-Xx)	(X-Xx)^2	(Y-Yy)	(Y-Yy)^2	(X-Xx) * (Y-Yy)
35	4.06	306,853.07	0.96	0.93	(104,628.01)	10,947,019,934	(100,697.19)
36	4.17	340,958.93	1.07	1.15	(70,522.14)	4,973,372,335	(75,524.32)
37	4.05	340,626.00	0.95	0.91	(70,855.07)	5,020,441,522	(67,594.36)
38	3.98	364,276.73	0.88	0.77	(47,204.34)	2,228,249,785	(41,524.74)
39	3.75	306,061.80	0.65	0.43	(105,419.27)	11,113,223,346	(68,810.38)
40	3.76	345,290.73	0.67	0.44	(66,190.34)	4,381,161,207	(44,055.00)
41	3.64	344,295.60	0.54	0.29	(67,185.47)	4,513,887,927	(36,285.57)
42	3.34	365,372.33	0.25	0.06	(46,108.74)	2,126,015,973	(11,362.60)
43	3.35	320,751.20	0.26	0.07	(90,729.87)	8,231,910,049	(23,338.50)
44	3.34	356,805.53	0.24	0.06	(54,675.54)	2,989,414,755	(13,200.35)
45	3.00	358,996.73	(0.09)	0.01	(52,484.34)	2,754,606,023	4,903.06
46	3.10	394,611.80	0.00	0.00	(16,869.27)	284,572,408	(83.17)
47	2.87	335,069.53	(0.23)	0.05	(76,411.54)	5,838,723,558	17,656.37
48	2.73	382,652.60	(0.37)	0.14	(28,828.47)	831,080,917	10,721.87
49	2.54	385,904.93	(0.56)	0.31	(25,576.14)	654,138,975	14,291.17
50	2.53	423,255.07	(0.57)	0.33	11,773.99	138,626,902	(6,720.82)
51	2.65	365,031.33	(0.45)	0.20	(46,449.74)	2,157,578,415	20,891.67
52	3.22	411,889.87	0.12	0.01	408.79	167,111	49.39
53	3.29	416,840.60	0.20	0.04	5,359.53	28,724,518	1,052.77
54	3.55	454,916.73	0.45	0.20	43,435.66	1,886,656,495	19,597.32
55	3.41	386,281.87	0.31	0.10	(25,199.21)	635,000,054	(7,773.47)
56	2.97	436,676.53	(0.12)	0.02	25,195.46	634,811,167	(3,128.51)
57	2.85	437,341.67	(0.25)	0.06	25,860.59	668,770,249	(6,389.36)
58	2.68	469,642.80	(0.42)	0.18	58,161.73	3,382,786,363	(24,559.92)
59	2.62	414,309.87	(0.48)	0.23	2,828.79	8,002,068	(1,346.98)
60	3.05	462,844.07	(0.05)	0.00	51,362.99	2,638,157,008	(2,320.04)
61	3.08	460,096.27	(0.02)	0.00	48,615.19	2,363,436,951	(883.31)
62	2.86	497,817.47	(0.24)	0.06	86,336.39	7,453,972,686	(20,942.57)
63	2.90	436,321.60	(0.20)	0.04	24,840.53	617,051,728	(5,028.21)
64	2.96	478,046.07	(0.13)	0.02	66,564.99	4,430,898,239	(8,980.91)
65	2.73	483,738.20	(0.36)	0.13	72,257.13	5,221,092,247	(26,234.35)
66	2.60	516,306.27	(0.50)	0.25	104,825.19	10,988,321,002	(52,273.12)
67	2.53	449,861.87	(0.57)	0.33	38,380.79	1,473,085,240	(21,889.31)
68	2.55	510,308.33	(0.55)	0.30	98,827.26	9,766,827,173	(54,431.03)

The first stage in calculating correlation is to calculate covariance. The covariance formula is:

$$Covariance = \frac{(X_i - \overline{X})(Y_i - \overline{Y})}{n - 1}$$

n = sample size

$\overline{X}$ = mean of variable X observations (referred to as Xx in the table below)

$\overline{Y}$ = mean of variable Y observations (referred to as Yy in the table below)

For each element in X and Y you add the differences between the element and the mean. The sum can then be divided by the number of data points minus one to derive the covariance.

The raw score values of the X and Y variables are presented in the first two columns of the table in Figure 16.40. The second two columns are the X and Y columns transformed using the z-score transformation:

$$z_X = \frac{X - \overline{X}}{s_X}$$

$$z_Y = \frac{Y - \overline{Y}}{s_Y}$$

The mean is subtracted from each raw score in the X and Y columns and then the result is divided by the sample standard deviation.

Using the full data set below with 36 observations, the sum of $(X - Xx) *$ $(Y - Yy)$ is (798,415). This is divided by the number of observations minus one. The covariance is $-22,122$. The value is not very meaningful on its own since the result is sensitive to the scale of the two variables. The covariance is therefore converted into a correlation coefficient as a measure of how the values move together. The formula is:

$$r_{xy} = \frac{covariance - X - \overline{Y}}{(s_x)(s_y)}$$

In the formula above, s is the standard deviation of either X or Y using this formula from an earlier section:

$$sample\ standard\ deviation = s = \sqrt{\frac{\sum_{i=1}^{n} |X_i - \overline{X}|^2}{n - 1}}$$

The table for variable 1 (see Figure 16.41) shows the interim calculations of variance, standard deviation, covariance and the final correlation coefficient.

Correlation

Figure 16.41

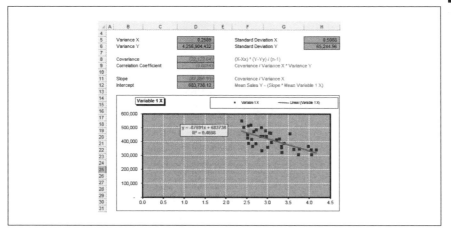

The effect of converting covariance to correlation means that the possible values are reduced from minus one to plus one.

The coefficient is -0.6854, which indicates a negative linear relationship. Other values are:

Correlation Coefficient	Interpretation
$r = +1$	Perfect positive correlation
$0 < r < +1$	Positive linear relationship
$r = 0$	No linear relationship
$r = -1$	Perfect negative correlation
$-1 < r < 0$	Negative linear relationship

The slope is calculated from Covariance xy / Variance x in cell D11:

```
Cell D11: =D8/(E72/(D74))
```

The intercept can be calculated manually as:

*Mean Sales Y − (Slope * Mean Variable 1 X)*

```
Cell D12: =D76-(D11*B76)
```

One other method of interpretation is to draw a scatter plot of the two variables and place a trend line through the data points (Correlation Charts sheet above). Here Variable X is the X axis while sales are plotted on the Y axis. The negative relationship shows up in the negative slope of the trend line through the data points.

The sign of the correlation coefficient ($+$ or $-$) defines the direction of the relationship, either positive or negative. A positive correlation coefficient means that as the value of one variable increases, the value of the other variable increases; as one decreases, the other decreases. A negative correlation coefficient indicates that as one variable increases, the other decreases, and vice versa.

Taking the absolute value of the correlation coefficient measures the strength of the relationship. A correlation coefficient of $r = 0.60$ indicates a stronger degree of linear relationship than one of $r = 0.30$. Likewise a correlation coefficient of $r = -0.60$ shows a greater degree of relationship than one of $r = -0.30$. Thus a correlation coefficient of zero ($r = 0.0$) indicates the absence of a linear relationship and correlation coefficients of $r = +1.0$ and $r = -1.0$ indicate perfect linear relationships. The other variable shows a positive correlation with the trend line sloping upwards, as in Figure 16.42.

The scatter plots in Figure 16.42 illustrate how the correlation coefficient changes as the linear relationship between the two variables is altered. When $r = 0.0$ the points scatter widely about the plot, falling above and below the line in equal distance. As the linear relationship increases, the data becomes more tightly packed around the trend line. With a correlation coefficient of plus or minus one ($r = \pm 1.00$), the data points fall on a straight line.

Scatter plot with positive correlation

Figure 16.42

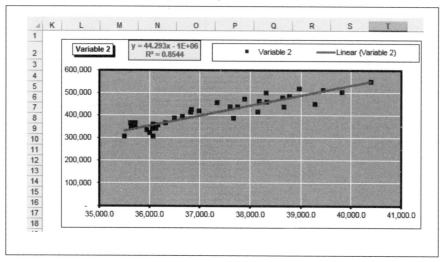

Correlation and hypothesis testing

You can also check the significance by testing the hypothesis that there is some correlation between the variables:

$Ho: = 0$ *versus Ha: P* $\neq 0$

The *t*-distribution formula uses $n - 2$ degrees of freedom:

$$t = \frac{r\sqrt{n - 2}}{\sqrt{1 - r^2}}$$

To make a decision, the calculated *t*-statistic is compared with the critical *t*-value for the number of degrees of freedom and level of significance. Using the data above, the *t*-statistic is -5.4889. Looking up the *t*-statistic from the table in the *t*-distribution section above yields the value 2.0322. This is a significance of 0.05 and 34 degrees of freedom. The conclusion is therefore to reject the hypothesis since the calculated *t*-statistic is greater than the test statistic (see Figure 16.43).

The above example calculates a negative correlation; however, you do need to be careful not to make erroneous decisions based on the data, for example:

■ Correct interpretation of a correlation coefficient requires the assumption that both variables, X and Y, use correct respective measurement scales. Excel will produce a correlation coefficient regardless of whether or not the numbers are 'meaningful' against the measurement scale.

■ Spurious correlation – the appearance of a relationship where no relationship exists. Certain data sets may be highly correlated but the relationship may not be causal.

Figure 16.43

Test statistic

⊿	A	B	C	D	E
4					
5		Test statistic	(r*SQRT(n-2))/(SQRT(1-r^2))	(5.4889)	
6					
7					
8		Degrees of Freedom	=Correlation!D74-2	34.0000	
9		Probability		0.0500	
10		T Statistic	'=TINV(D9,Correlation!D74-2)	2.0322	
11					
12		Test		Accept - greater than T Statistic	

- Outliers – these extreme values can affect the data, and one technique is to remove extreme values before undertaking any analysis.

- Non-linear relationships – correlation plots linear relationships and in certain situations the data may exhibit a strong non-linear relationship. Plotting the chart may reveal more information on the shape and strength of the relationship.

Regression

Regression analysis can assist with summarising and explaining the relationship between one variable (dependent) and one or more independent variables. The purpose is to explain the variation in the dependent variable by reference to the change in independent variables, for example, in forecasting. The previous section calculated the correlation between the variables and found a strong relationship, and regression provides a formula to explain the relationship.

The formula for a linear trend line uses the least squares method to fit the line to the data:

$Y = mx + b$

m = *estimated slope coefficient of the trend line* (*SLOPE function*)

x = *value on x line for the observation*

b = *the intercept where the trend line crosses the y axis* (*INTERCEPT function*)

The regression line is one of several that could be drawn through the data and the effect of this formula is to minimise the sum of the errors from the data to the trend line. By varying the variables of slope and intercept the line minimises the errors between the line and the data points:

$$Slope\ (m) = Covariance_{xy}/Variance\ X = -22,122/0.2517 = -87,890$$

The intercept using the slope coefficient for Variable 1 is:

$$Mean\ Y - (Slope * Mean\ X)$$
$$Intercept:\quad 411,481 - (-87,890.9 * 3.09767) = 683,738$$

Excel functions and the Analysis ToolPak provide straightforward tools for calculating these statistics. The Regression Functions sheet demonstrates the various functions from variance to correlation for Variable 1, while the Data Analysis Regression sheet shows the output from the Data Analysis option for both variables in the Correlation_Data sheet.

The Regression Functions sheet demonstrates each of the functions and compares the variance, standard deviation, correlation, slope and intercept with the results from the manual methods on earlier sheets (see Figure 16.44). The standard error and R^2 factors are discussed in the following sections.

Excel functions compared with manual methods

Figure 16.44

	B	C	D	E
4				
5	Formulas	Function	Result	Variance
6	Variance X	VAR	0.259	(0.00000)
7	Variance Y		4,256,904,431.558	0.00003
8	St Dev X	STDEV	0.509	(0.00000)
9	St Dev Y		65,244.957	0.00000
10	Covariance	COVAR	(22,122.645)	-
11	Correlation	CORREL	(0.685)	-
12	Slope	SLOPE	(87,890.928)	-
13	Intercept	INTERCEPT	683,738.117	-
14	Standard Error (SEE)	STEYX	48,201.166	-

Standard error

Standard deviation measures how the sample deviates from the mean. The standard error of the estimate (SEE) measures the uncertainty about the accuracy of the predicted variables due to using samples rather than the whole population (STEYX function). Sometimes the relationship is strong, whereas in other cases, such as stock returns and inflation, the relationship is usually much weaker. The SEE will be low if the relationship is strong and high if it is weak. The general equation for the predicted trend line as above is:

$$Y_i = mX_i + b_i$$

To calculate the SEE, first you need to calculate the sum of the squared errors (SSE):

$$SSE = \sum_{i=1}^{n}(Y_i - \hat{Y}_i)^2$$

This is the sum of the variables minus the predicted variables squared. The SEE is the degree of variability of the Y values relative to the estimated Y values. The standard error is a function of the SSE, as given below:

$$SEE = \sqrt{\frac{SSE}{N-2}}$$

Coefficient of determination

A further measure of fit is the coefficient of determination (R^2), which is the percentage of total variation in the dependent variable explained by the independent variable. If the value is 0.75, then it confirms that 75 per cent of the variation can be explained. A low value would signify that most of the variation is unexplained.

With one independent variable as above, you can find the R^2 value simply by squaring the correlation. The correlation is 0.6854 and the square is 0.4698 (46.98%).

Breakdown of variation

The total variation (SST) is the sum of the squared total variations:

$$SST = \sum_{i=1}^{n}(Y_i - \overline{Y})^2$$

The total variation is made up of the explained and the unexplained variation (see Figure 16.45). The unexplained variation is the sum of the squared errors (SSE):

$$SSE = \sum_{i=1}^{n}(Y_i - \hat{Y}_i)^2$$

The explained variation is the sum of the squared distances between the predicted Y values and the mean of Y. This is the sum of the squared regressions (SSR):

$$SSR = \sum_{i=1}^{n}(Y_i - \overline{Y})^2$$

Therefore SST = SSE + SSR and the coefficient of determination can be expressed as:

$R^2 = (total\ variation - unexpected\ variation)/total\ variation = explained$
$variation/total\ variation$
$R^2 = SSR/SST = 1 - (SSE/SST)$

SSE and SSR

Figure 16.45

	I	J	K	L	M
32					
33				SSE	SSR
34		Predicted Y	Y -Pred Y	(Y -Pred Y)^2	(Pred Y - Yy)^2
35		326,892.16	(20,039.09)	401,565,221.96	7,155,284,551.64
36		317,355.99	23,602.94	557,098,779.29	8,859,530,835.00
37		327,634.84	12,991.16	168,770,306.85	7,030,191,411.86
38		334,165.13	30,111.60	906,708,454.35	5,977,754,692.08
39		354,111.98	(48,050.18)	2,308,819,753.91	3,291,213,007.56
40		352,982.58	(7,691.85)	59,164,522.23	3,422,073,678.99
41		364,012.89	(19,717.29)	388,771,628.53	2,253,228,249.90
42		389,822.06	(24,449.73)	597,789,317.75	469,112,727.95
43		388,872.84	(68,121.64)	4,640,558,071.90	511,132,169.75
44		390,261.52	(33,455.99)	1,119,302,936.67	450,269,543.08
45		419,691.80	(60,695.06)	3,683,890,605.21	67,415,950.91
46		411,047.72	(16,435.92)	270,139,563.83	187,793.18
47		431,789.98	(96,720.45)	9,354,845,204.76	412,451,744.18
48		444,169.42	(61,516.82)	3,784,319,061.99	1,068,527,916.37
49		460,591.84	(74,686.91)	5,578,133,925.38	2,411,867,262.72
50		461,650.93	(38,395.86)	1,474,241,937.47	2,517,013,942.35
51		451,011.73	(85,980.39)	7,392,628,287.57	1,562,672,609.25
52		400,861.16	11,028.70	121,632,274.45	112,782,482.22
53		394,216.61	22,623.99	511,844,915.51	298,061,713.65
54		371,826.40	83,090.34	6,904,004,131.07	1,572,493,480.22
55		384,368.43	1,913.44	3,661,233.57	735,095,379.32
56		422,394.44	14,282.09	203,978,137.79	119,101,595.71
57		433,196.24	4,145.43	17,184,587.71	471,548,297.84
58		448,594.73	21,048.07	443,021,352.26	1,377,423,277.15
59		453,332.05	(39,022.18)	1,522,730,685.15	1,751,504,071.25
60		415,451.06	47,393.01	2,246,097,224.76	15,760,776.20
61		413,078.00	47,018.26	2,210,717,079.19	2,550,183.32
62		432,800.73	65,016.74	4,227,176,339.15	454,527,632.93
63		429,271.91	7,049.69	49,698,171.74	316,513,735.33
64		423,339.27	54,706.80	2,992,833,677.28	140,616,794.20
65		443,391.58	40,346.62	1,627,849,372.16	1,018,280,683.67
66		455,309.59	60,996.67	3,720,594,013.10	1,920,939,204.39
67		461,606.98	(11,745.11)	137,947,676.41	2,512,606,398.77

This is confirmed by the figures in Figure 16.46 where both methods produce an R^2 of 0.4698. In this example, 47 per cent of the variation in X is explained by the variation in Y. The balance is the unexplained variation.

Figure 16.46

Coefficient of determination (R^2)

⬚ A	B	C	D	E
15				
16	Coefficient of Determination: R2 = 1 - SSE / SST or SSR / SST			
17	SSE		78,993,982,236.949	(Y -Pred Y)^2
18	SEE		48,201.166	SQRT (SSE / n-2)
19				
20	SSR		69,997,672,867.592	(Pred Y - Yy)^2
21	SST (SSE+SSR)		148,991,655,104.540	(Y-Yy)^2
22				
23	R^2 = 1 - SSE / SST		0.470	
24	R^2 = SSR / SST		0.470	
25				
26	RSQ (R^2)	RSQ	0.470	

LINEST FUNCTION

The LINEST function provides a method of calculating the regression statistics dynamically. This is an array function and has to be entered as a matrix (with Control + Enter). You can enter one line only to derive the intercept and factor variables or as a grid and obtain further information as below:

- standard error values for the coefficients;
- standard error value for the constant;
- coefficient of determination;
- standard error for the y estimate;
- F-statistic, or the F-observed value;
- degrees of freedom;
- regression sum of squares;
- residual sum of squares.

The grid has to be as wide as the number of variables plus one for the intercept and at least five rows down. Example output is given in Figure 16.47.

The factors can be used for forecasting: the range C18:C21 provides the forecast factors for the next four periods. In the grid, the actual data are compared with the forecast to back-check the accuracy of the method. The regression equation is:

$$Y = Intercept + (A * x1) + (B * x2)$$

If you do not want dynamic output that will update every time the data changes, the simplest way to generate regression is to use the option in the Data Analysis ToolPak. You input the Y axis with its label and then the

LINEST function

Figure 16.47

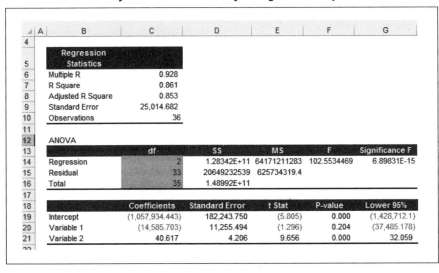

	B	C	D	E	F
4					
5	**Linest Coefficients**				
6	**Intercept**	**X Variable 1**	**X Variable 2**		
7	(1,057,934)	40.62	(14,585.70)		
8					
9	**Linest Stats - explanation below**				
10	Slope Factors		40.62	(14,585.70)	(1,057,934.44)
11	Standard Error Values		4.21	11,255.49	182,243.75
12	R2 and Std Error for Y		0.86	25,014.68	#N/A
13	F Stat and Degrees of Freedom		102.55	33.00	#N/A
14	Regression & Residual Sum of Squares		1.28E+11	2.06E+10	#N/A
15					
16	**Forecast**				
17	**Period**	**Variable 1**	**Variable 2**	**Forecast Sales**	**Error ^2**
18	37	2.355	40,464	551,256	
19	38	2.330	40,734	562,576	
20	38	2.300	41,006	574,043	
21	40	2.275	41,279	**585,510**	
22					
23	**Actuals**			**RMSE**	**15,266**
24	37			539,678	134,040,176
25	38			549,757	164,344,444
26	38			555,305	351,111,878
27	40			602,324	282,720,077
28					

X range (Variables 1 and 2) together with the label. The output is normally to a new sheet, and Excel will generate all the data provided by LINEST and more data together with the chart plots (see Figure 16.48).

Analysis ToolPak data analysis regression output

Figure 16.48

	B	C	D	E	F	G
4						
5	**Regression Statistics**					
6	Multiple R	0.928				
7	R Square	0.861				
8	Adjusted R Square	0.853				
9	Standard Error	25,014.682				
10	Observations	36				
11						
12	ANOVA					
13		**df**	**SS**	**MS**	**F**	**Significance F**
14	Regression	2	1.28342E+11	64171211283	102.5534469	6.89831E-15
15	Residual	33	20649232539	625734319.4		
16	Total	35	1.48992E+11			
17						
18		**Coefficients**	**Standard Error**	**t Stat**	**P-value**	**Lower 95%**
19	Intercept	(1,057,934.443)	182,243.750	(5.805)	0.000	(1,428,712.1)
20	Variable 1	(14,585.703)	11,255.494	(1.296)	0.204	(37,485.178)
21	Variable 2	40.617	4.206	9.656	0.000	32.059
22						

EXERCISE

The separate data file for this chapter (MFMath3e_16_Data) contains some excess return figures for an index and an individual stock. Produce the following from the data:

- Draw a frequency table and histogram chart.
- Produce full descriptive statistics using functions or the Analysis ToolPak.
- Find the correlation between the variables.
- Calculate the regression equation. Use the data to plot a scatter chart of the index as the X-axis and the stock as the Y-axis. A trend line through the data should prove the beta of the stock as the beta.

SUMMARY

This chapter has reviewed basic statistical concepts and shown how they can be applied to Excel. As a tabular method, Excel is more suited to building up the calculations and checking each stage than pocket calculators, where there is more chance of an error. Basic methods included:

- descriptive statistics such as the mean, mode, median range;
- variance and standard deviation;
- the shape of a data distribution with skew and kurtosis;
- probability distributions such as the uniform, binomial and normal distributions;
- sampling, large numbers and the Central Limit Theorem;
- hypothesis testing with two-tailed and one-tailed tests;
- the t-distribution for smaller samples;
- correlation, regression, standard errors and the coefficient of determination.

Appendices

Appendix 1

Appendix 1 contains:

Exercise answers
Useful Excel and Analysis ToolPak functions list by category
Software installation and licence
System requirements
Installation
Accessing the application files
Licence
File list

File: MFMaths3e_Exercises.xls

Appendix 2

Appendix 2 contains:

An introduction to Microsoft® Office

Appendix 1

EXERCISE ANSWERS

Chapter 2 – Interest rates

The answer (see Figure A1.1) uses the FV function to calculate the balance outstanding since a payment of 2,000 fails to write off fully the capital of 100,000 at the nominal rate of 10 per cent. At the future value of 5,000 the payment increases marginally to 2,060 per month. A specimen spreadsheet using the Comparison sheet as a template is given in Figure A1.1. The inputs change and the formula in C15 is changed to calculate the required future value.

Chapter 2

	B	C	D	E	F	G	H
5		Example 1			Example 2		Variance
6	N	60		N	60		
7	I	10.00%		I	10.00%		
8	PV	(100,000.00)		PV	(100,000.00)		
9	PMT	2,000.00		FV	5,000.00		
10	Periods per Annum	12		Periods	12		
11	Begin	0		Begin	0		
12							
13	Periodic Interest Rate	0.83%			0.83%		
14							
15	FV	9,656.75		PMT	2,060.14		
16							
17	Total Payable	129,656.75			123,608.15		6,048.59
18							
19	Net Advance	98,000.00			97,939.86		60.14
20							
21	Effective Period	5.00			5.00		-
22							
23	Charges	29,656.75			23,608.15		6,048.59
24							
25	Simple Interest Rate	6.05%			4.82%		1.23%
26							
27	Nominal Rate	10.00%			10.00%		-
28							
29	Effective Rate	10.47%			10.47%		-

Chapter 3 – Cash flows

The spreadsheet in Figure A1.2 sets out all the inputs for this semi-annual loan agreement. The cash flows use a simple IF statement to choose between the individual cash flows. While an IF statement can become over-complex, this method is often simpler than resorting to functions such as CHOOSE.

Figure A1.2

Chapter 3

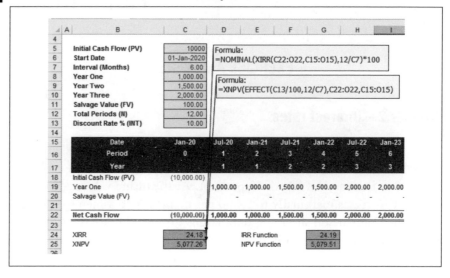

Chapter 4 – Fixed income products

Two bonds bear the characteristics below. Calculate the prices and using a data table in Excel check the relevant prices if the yield falls or rises by 1 per cent. This should confirm the bond which is more responsive to changes in yield (see Figures A1.3 and A1.4).

Period	6.0 yrs	10.0 yrs
Coupon Rate %	10.00	9.75
Redemption Value	100.00	100.00
Coupons per annum	1	1
Yield %	9.50	9.50

Figure A1.3

Chapter 4

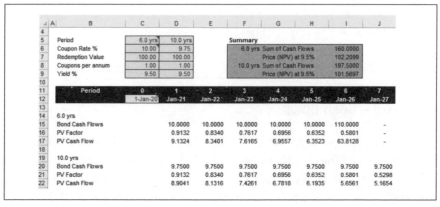

Chapter 4

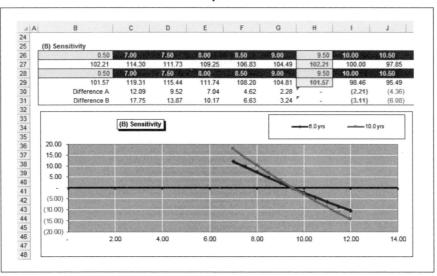

Chapter 5 – Bond risks

An amount of 100,000 is required in 3.25 years' time. Interest rates are currently 8 per cent and a company wishes to invest an amount in bonds, which will grow to 100,000 at the time of maturity (see Figures A1.5 and A1.6). The calculations for the two bonds are:

■ Price, duration and modified duration, and estimate the change in value if interest rates rise by 1 per cent.

■ Present value of 100,000 in 3.25 years at the input rate of 8 per cent as the amount to be invested now.

■ Proportion of the present value to be invested in each bond.

■ The amount divided by the price to find out how many bonds are required.

Figure A1.5

Chapter 5

	A	B	C	D	E	F
4						
5	Bond		A	B		C
6	Settlement Date		31/12/2020	31/12/2020		31/12/2020
7	Maturity Date		30/06/2024	31/05/2025		30/03/2024
8	Coupon		10.00	3.00		0.00
9	Coupons per Annum		1.00	1.00		1.00
10	Yield to Maturity		8.00	8.00		8.00
11	Redemption		100.00	100.00		100,000.00
12	Basis		0	0		0
13						
14	Price		105.8072	81.9615		
15	Period		3.50	4.42		3.25
16	Present Value					77,891.00
17	Duration		3.004 yrs	4.094 yrs		3.250 yrs
18	Modified Duration		2.782 yrs	3.791 yrs		
19						
20	% Change		1.00			
21						
22	(A) Simple Convexity		(2.8897)	(3.2581)		
23			102.9175	78.7034		
24						
25	(B) Price * Modified Duration * Δ Yield		(2.9432)	(3.1072)		
26			102.8640	78.8542		
27						
28	[C] Duration + Convexity Calculation					
29	Price plus 1%		102.7854	78.8644		
30	Price minus 1%		108.9521	85.2146		
31						
32	Lower - Difference to P		(3.0217)	(3.0970)		
33	Upper - Difference to P		3.1449	3.2532		
34						
35	(Upper price - lower price)/(2 * bond price*Δ `		2.9141	3.8739		
36	(UP - LP - 2 * Price) / (2 * Price*Δ Yield)^2		5.8201	9.5238		
37						
38	-D * Δ Yield + C * (Δ Yield) ^2		(2.8559)	(3.7787)		
39			102.7854	78.8644		
40						
41	Percentage A		77.45%			
42	Percentage B		22.55%			
43						
44	Actual Duration		3.25			100.00%

Figure A1.6

Chapter 5

	A	B	C	D	E	F
46						
47	Percentage A		77.45%		77,891.00	60,329.75
48	Percentage B		22.55%			17,561.25
49					Sum	77,891.00
50	No of Bonds A (Amount/Price)		570.19			
51	No of Bonds B (Amount/Price)		214.26			
52						

Chapter 6 – Forward rate agreements

This example extends the coupon stripping model to allow for up to 20 periods and calculates the profit or loss on the scenario, as in Figure A1.7.

Chapter 6

Period	0	1	2	3	4	5	6	7	8
	Jun-20	Dec-20	Jun-21	Dec-21	Jun-22	Dec-22	Jun-23	Dec-23	Jun-24

Coupon Rate %	10.00				Sum of Cash Flows				73.00	
Redemption Value	100.00				Price (NPV) at 9.0%				105.37	
Price	102.00				Yield				9.62%	
Settlement Date	30-Jun-20									
Maturity Date	31-Dec-27									
Coupons pa	2.00									
Yield %	9.00									

	0	1	2	3	4	5	6	7	8
Bond Cash Flows	(102.00)	5.00	5.00	5.00	5.00	5.00	5.00	5.00	5.00
		-	-	-	-	-	-	-	-
Sum	(102.00)	5.00	5.00	5.00	5.00	5.00	5.00	5.00	5.00
PV Factor	1.0000	0.9569	0.9157	0.8763	0.8386	0.8025	0.7679	0.7348	0.7032
PV Cash Flow	(102.00)	4.78	4.58	4.38	4.19	4.01	3.84	3.67	3.52
Individual Yield		8.00	8.00	8.00	8.00	8.00	8.00	8.00	8.00
PV Factor	1.0000	0.9615	0.9246	0.8890	0.8548	0.8219	0.7903	0.7599	0.7307
PV Cash Flow	(102.00)	4.81	4.62	4.44	4.27	4.11	3.95	3.80	3.65
PV Capital		-	-	-	-	-	-	-	-
Sum	(102.00)	4.81	4.62	4.44	4.27	4.11	3.95	3.80	3.65
Difference	-	0.02	0.04	0.06	0.08	0.10	0.11	0.13	0.14
Average Input Yield	8.98								
Total	106.70								
Profit / (Loss)	1.33								

Chapter 7 – Amortisation

The model in Figures A1.8 and A1.9 needs to calculate the present value of the future value in 67 periods. The present value of six payments of 1,000 with the six rentals of 1,000 on signing is also required. These two elements with the capital value add up to 76,701.44.

The factor is the present value of 60 payments of one further discounted for the initial period. The derived rental of 1,712.88 can then be tested in the cash flow.

Chapter 7

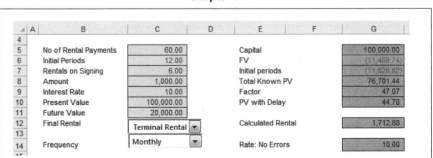

No of Rental Payments	60.00	Capital	100,000.00
Initial Periods	12.00	FV	(11,469.74)
Rentals on Signing	6.00	Initial periods	(11,826.82)
Amount	1,000.00	Total Known PV	76,701.44
Interest Rate	10.00	Factor	47.07
Present Value	100,000.00	PV with Delay	44.78
Future Value	20,000.00		
Final Rental	Terminal Rental ▼	Calculated Rental	1,712.88
Frequency	Monthly ▼	Rate: No Errors	10.00

Chapter 7

	Period	Rental	Int	Capital	Balance	Cash Flow
15						
16						
17						
18	0	6,000.00		6,000.00	(94,000.00)	(94,000.00)
19	1	1,000.00	783.33	216.67	(93,783.33)	1,000.00
20	2	1,000.00	781.53	218.47	(93,564.86)	1,000.00
21	3	1,000.00	779.71	220.29	(93,344.57)	1,000.00
22	4	1,000.00	777.87	222.13	(93,122.44)	1,000.00
23	5	1,000.00	776.02	223.98	(92,898.46)	1,000.00
24	6	1,000.00	774.15	225.85	(92,672.61)	1,000.00
25	7	1,712.88	772.27	940.61	(91,732.01)	1,712.88
26	8	1,712.88	764.43	948.45	(90,783.56)	1,712.88
27	9	1,712.88	756.53	956.35	(89,827.21)	1,712.88
28	10	1,712.88	748.56	964.32	(88,862.89)	1,712.88
29	11	1,712.88	740.52	972.36	(87,890.54)	1,712.88
30	12	1,712.88	732.42	980.46	(86,910.08)	1,712.88
42	24	1,712.88	629.75	1,083.13	(74,487.39)	1,712.88
54	36	1,712.88	516.34	1,196.54	(60,763.90)	1,712.88
66	48	1,712.88	391.04	1,321.84	(45,603.37)	1,712.88
78	60	1,712.88	252.63	1,460.25	(28,855.33)	1,712.88
79	61	1,712.88	240.46	1,472.42	(27,382.91)	1,712.88
80	62	1,712.88	228.19	1,484.69	(25,898.22)	1,712.88
81	63	1,712.88	215.82	1,497.06	(24,401.16)	1,712.88
82	64	1,712.88	203.34	1,509.54	(22,891.63)	1,712.88
83	65	1,712.88	190.76	1,522.12	(21,369.51)	1,712.88
84	66	1,712.88	178.08	1,534.80	(19,834.71)	1,712.88
85	67	20,000.00	165.29	19,834.71	-	20,000.00
86	68	-	-	-	-	-
87	69	-	-	-	-	-
88	70	-	-	-	-	-
89	71	-	-	-	-	-
90	72	-	-	-	-	-
102	84	-	-	-	-	-
114	96	-	-	-	-	-
126	108	-	-	-	-	-
138	120	-	-	-	-	-
139						
140	Sum	134,772.77	34,772.77	100,000.00	-	-
141						

Chapter 8 – Swaps

The model uses the valuation methodology in Chapter 8 except that the zero rate factors need to be derived from the interest rates. This is simply the $1 / (1 + \text{IntRate})$ ^ period, noting that these are annual cash flows. The forward rates are based on the change in the factor and are used in computing the interest out.

Based on the forward rates, there is a slight cost on the swap against the fixed interest payments (see Figure A1.10).

Chapter 8

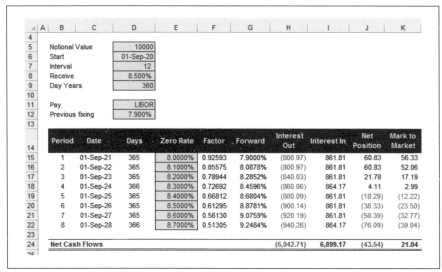

	A	B	C	D	E	F	G	H	I	J	K
4											
5		Notional Value		10000							
6		Start		01-Sep-20							
7		Interval		12							
8		Receive		8.500%							
9		Day Years		360							
10											
11		Pay		LIBOR							
12		Previous fixing		7.900%							
13											
14		Period	Date	Days	Zero Rate	Factor	Forward	Interest Out	Interest In	Net Position	Mark to Market
15		1	01-Sep-21	365	8.0000%	0.92593	7.9000%	(800.97)	861.81	60.83	56.33
16		2	01-Sep-22	365	8.1000%	0.85575	8.0878%	(800.97)	861.81	60.83	52.06
17		3	01-Sep-23	365	8.2000%	0.78944	8.2852%	(840.03)	861.81	21.78	17.19
18		4	01-Sep-24	366	8.3000%	0.72692	8.4596%	(860.06)	864.17	4.11	2.99
19		5	01-Sep-25	365	8.4000%	0.66812	8.6804%	(880.09)	861.81	(18.29)	(12.22)
20		6	01-Sep-26	365	8.5000%	0.61295	8.8781%	(900.14)	861.81	(38.33)	(23.50)
21		7	01-Sep-27	365	8.6000%	0.56130	9.0759%	(920.19)	861.81	(58.39)	(32.77)
22		8	01-Sep-28	366	8.7000%	0.51305	9.2484%	(940.26)	864.17	(76.09)	(39.04)
23											
24		Net Cash Flows						(6,942.71)	6,899.17	(43.54)	21.04

Chapter 9 – Forward rates

The December contract is priced at 6 per cent and the March contract at 6.10 per cent (see Figure A1.11). This can be multiplied out:

$$[1 + (6.0/4/100)] * [1 + (6.1/4/100)] = 1.015 * 1.01525 = 1.03048$$

From this you subtract one and multiply by two (two quarterly periods). The answer to the six-month period from December to March is 6.09575 per cent.

The same procedure can be repeated from the March to September period to produce the second rate of 6.19728 per cent (see Figure A1.12). Since the 45 days is halfway through the 90-day period, the derived price is prorated between the two dates. This is 6.14651.

Figure A1.11

Chapter 9

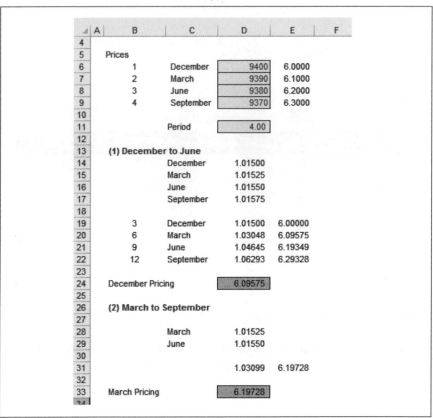

Figure A1.12

Chapter 9

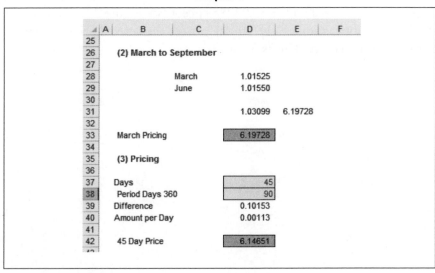

Chapter 10 – Futures

Figure A1.13 gives the initial data from Chapter 10.

Chapter 10 data

	A	B	C	D	E
4					
5		**(1) Prices**			
6				**Price**	**Interest Rate**
7			Spot	9,520.00	4.80
8		1	December	9,508.00	4.92
9		2	March	9,505.00	4.95
10		3	June	9,496.00	5.04
11		4	September	9,499.00	5.01
12					
13		Current Date		Sept	
14		Loan Required		March	
15		Payments per Annum		2.00	
16		Loan Amount		5,000,000.00	
17		Contract Size		1,000,000.00	
18					
19		Number of Contracts		5	
20					
21		Sell futures		9505	

The spot price in March is 9,505 on an interest rate of 4.95 per cent. The position on the futures contract is:

*Five contracts * (0.15%) * 1,000,000 contract size / payments per year = 3,750.*

Interest rates are lower than expected in that rates were expected at 4.95 per cent and have reduced to 4.80 per cent (see Figure A1.14).

Chapter 10 answer

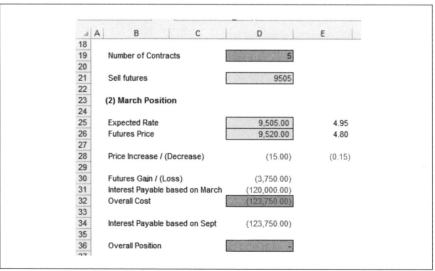

	A	B	C	D	E
18					
19		Number of Contracts		5	
20					
21		Sell futures		9505	
22					
23		**(2) March Position**			
24					
25		Expected Rate		9,505.00	4.95
26		Futures Price		9,520.00	4.80
27					
28		Price Increase / (Decrease)		(15.00)	(0.15)
29					
30		Futures Gain / (Loss)		(3,750.00)	
31		Interest Payable based on March		(120,000.00)	
32		Overall Cost		(123,750.00)	
33					
34		Interest Payable based on Sept		(123,750.00)	
35					
36		Overall Position		-	

On the loan you could have borrowed at 4.95 per cent but the price reduced marginally to 4.8 per cent in March. The model multiplies out 6 months' interest at the two rates and finds that the difference is 3,750. When the loss on the future is taken into account, there is no overall loss or gain.

Chapter 11 – Foreign exchange

A treasurer has the option of borrowing in dollars or euros and wants to know if there is a potential saving in one of the currencies over 91 days. The data are:

Spot EUR/USD	*1.4000*
Swap	*0.0100*
USD Interest	*3.000%*
EUR Interest	*5.000%*
EUR Margin	*0.500%*
Amount	*10,000,000.00*

Also, what is the break even exchange rate? The answer uses the same methodology as in Chapter 11 to show a slight saving for the covered borrowing (see Figure A1.15).

Figure A1.15 **Chapter 11 answer**

	A	B	C	D
4				
5		Spot EUR / USD	1.4000	
6		Swap	0.0100	
7		USD Interest	3.000%	
8		EUR Interest	5.000%	
9		EUR Margin	0.500%	
10		Period	91 days	
11		Days	360 days	
12		Amount	10,000,000.00	
13		Actual Days	365 days	
14				
15		EUR Amount	7,142,857.14	
16		Repayment	99,305.56	
17		Total	7,242,162.70	
18				
19		Rate	1.39	
20		Sell at 1.3900	10,066,606.15	
21		Extra	66,606.15	
22				
23		Yield	2.635%	
24		Formula	2.635%	
25				
26		USD Rate	3.000%	
27		Gain / (Loss)	0.365%	

The rate at which there is no variance can be found using `Data, Data Tools, Goal Seek` and the answer is 1.6045.

Chapter 12 – Options

Produce a spreadsheet to calculate the payoff from this strategy (see Figure A1.16):

(1) Purchased call options

Exercise price	25.0
Premium	0.5
Number of contracts	4
Minimum number	200
Share price at option expiration	30.0

(2) Purchased put options

Exercise price	30.0
Premium	4.5
Number of contracts	4
Minimum number	200.0

(3) Shares

Purchase price	25
Number of shares	500

Chapter 12 options payoff

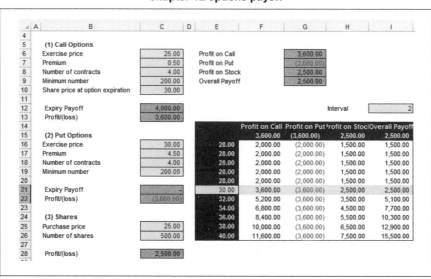

Figure A1.16

The layout calculates the payoffs on the call, put and share and summarises the position in cell G9. The data table is based on cell C10 and demonstrates the changing payoff with the rising share price on expiry. The chart plots each series on the data table with the overall payoff as a line chart (see Figure A1.17).

Figure A1.17

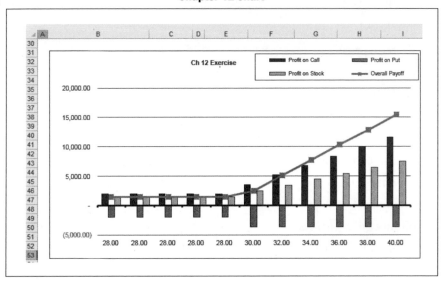

Chapter 12 chart

Chapter 13 – Real options

The put option values the option as in Figures A1.18 and A1.19 using the formula:

$$= (EXP((0 - Yield)*TR))*P*N(d1) - Salvage*(EXP((0 - Int)*N(d2)$$
$$-(EXP((0 - Yield)*TR))*P + Salvage*(EXP((0 - Int)*TR))$$

Figure A1.18

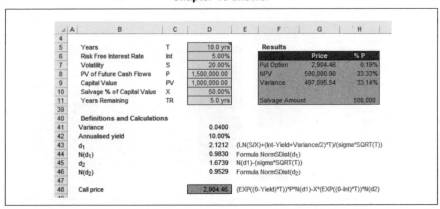

Chapter 13 answer

Sensitivity chart

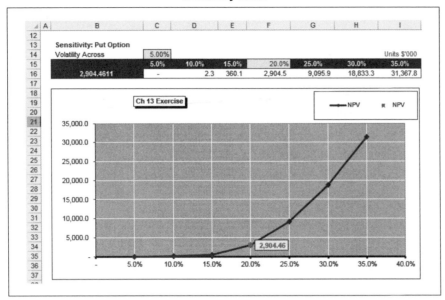

Chapter 14 – Valuation

The supplied data were:

WACC	*10.00*
Growth	*1.00*
Debt	*250.00*
Minority Interests	*100.00*

Year	1	2	3	4	5	6	7
Cash Flow	100.00	125.00	150.00	175.00	200.00	225.00	250.00

The terminal value is based on the perpetuity model and discounted along with the cash flows back at 10.0 per cent. Debt and minority interests are deducted from the enterprise value to form the equity value (see Figure A1.20).

Sensitivity is best achieved by two data tables for one and two dimensions. The answer uses indirect references between the tables and variables so that the tables automatically update when the variables in the input section are changed (see Figures A1.21 and A1.22). The tables are based on variables in cells B59 and B60 which also drive the valuation calculations. These cells are simply lookups of the inputs in cells C5 and C6. The variables in cells F26, F34 and B38 are derived from cells C5 and C6. The key point is that the variables on the axes of the data table and the data table itself cannot link to the same cells.

Figure A1.20

Valuation calculation

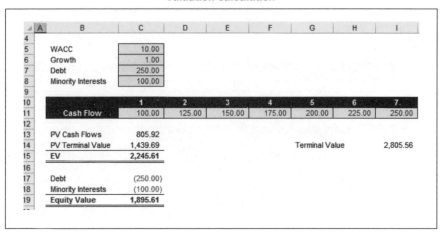

	B	C	D	E	F	G	H	I
4								
5	WACC	10.00						
6	Growth	1.00						
7	Debt	250.00						
8	Minority Interests	100.00						
9								
10		1	2	3	4	5	6	7
11	Cash Flow	100.00	125.00	150.00	175.00	200.00	225.00	250.00
12								
13	PV Cash Flows	805.92						
14	PV Terminal Value	1,439.69			Terminal Value		2,805.56	
15	EV	2,245.61						
16								
17	Debt	(250.00)						
18	Minority Interests	(100.00)						
19	Equity Value	1,895.61						

Figure A1.21

Sensitivity tables

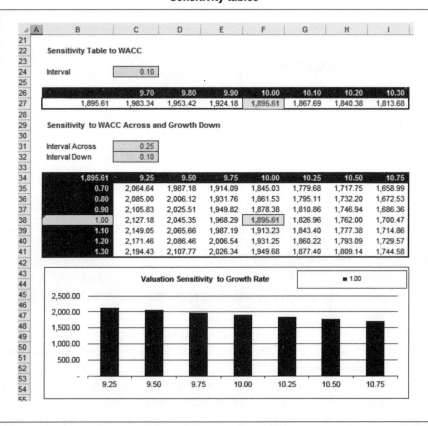

	B	C	D	E	F	G	H	I
21								
22	**Sensitivity Table to WACC**							
23								
24	Interval	0.10						
25								
26		9.70	9.80	9.90	10.00	10.10	10.20	10.30
27	1,895.61	1,983.34	1,953.42	1,924.18	1,895.61	1,867.69	1,840.38	1,813.68
28								
29	**Sensitivity to WACC Across and Growth Down**							
30								
31	Interval Across	0.25						
32	Interval Down	0.10						
33								
34	1,895.61	9.25	9.50	9.75	10.00	10.25	10.50	10.75
35	0.70	2,064.64	1,987.18	1,914.09	1,845.03	1,779.68	1,717.75	1,658.99
36	0.80	2,085.00	2,006.12	1,931.76	1,861.53	1,795.11	1,732.20	1,672.53
37	0.90	2,105.83	2,025.51	1,949.82	1,878.38	1,810.86	1,746.94	1,686.36
38	1.00	2,127.18	2,045.35	1,968.29	1,895.61	1,826.96	1,762.00	1,700.47
39	1.10	2,149.05	2,065.66	1,987.19	1,913.23	1,843.40	1,777.38	1,714.86
40	1.20	2,171.46	2,086.46	2,006.54	1,931.25	1,860.22	1,793.09	1,729.57
41	1.30	2,194.43	2,107.77	2,026.34	1,949.68	1,877.40	1,809.14	1,744.58

Data table extract to show linkages

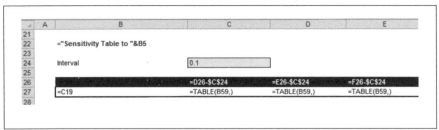

⊿	A	B	C	D	E
21					
22		="Sensitivity Table to "&B5			
23					
24		Interval	0.1		
25					
26			=D26-$C$24	=E26-$C$24	=F26-$C$24
27		=C19	=TABLE(B59,)	=TABLE(B59,)	=TABLE(B59,)
28					

Chapter 15 – Leasing

The answer plots all the cash flow and calculates a cost of capital using the leverage and individual costs of capital (see Figures A1.23–A1.25). The discount rate is used to present-value all the known cash flows and these are reduced to their post-tax cash values. The factor is five rentals in arrears and this is divided into the after-tax present value to derive the rental of 26,963. The inclusion of the costs and the effect of the tax rate increase the client interest rate to 13.10 per cent.

Lessor cash flows

⊿ A	B	C	D	E	F	G	H	I
4								
5		0	1	2	3	4	5	
6	Capital Cost	100,000.0						
7	RV	10.00%						
8	Period	5.0						
9	SG&A	-	(50.0)	(50.0)	(50.0)	(50.0)	(50.0)	
10	Bad Debt	-	(10.0)	(10.0)	(10.0)	(10.0)	(10.0)	
11	Other	(1,000.0)						
12								
13	Debt/Equity %	75.0%			WACC		9.750%	
14	Debt	10.0%						
15	Equity	15.0%			Calculated Rental		26,712.9	
16	Tax	20.0%			Client Rate		12.76%	
17								
18		0	1	2	3	4	5	0
19	Capital	(100,000.0)						
20	RV	-	-	-	-	-	10,000.0	-
21	SGA	-	(50.0)	(50.0)	(50.0)	(50.0)	(50.0)	-
22	Bad Debt	-	(10.0)	(10.0)	(10.0)	(10.0)	(10.0)	-
23	Other	(1,000.0)	-	-	-	-	-	-
24	Tax Depn	-	20,000.0	16,000.0	12,800.0	10,240.0	8,192.0	32,768.0
25								
26	Total	(101,000.0)	19,940.0	15,940.0	12,740.0	10,180.0	18,132.0	32,768.0

Figure A1.24

Lessor rental calculation

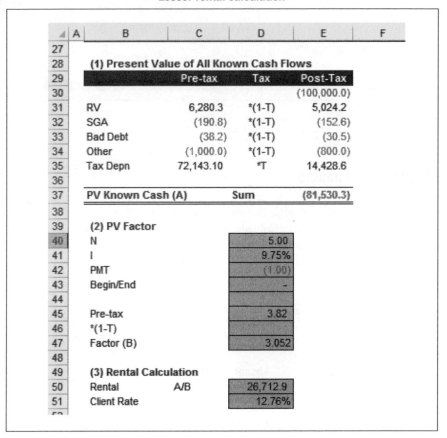

Figure A1.25

Sensitivity table

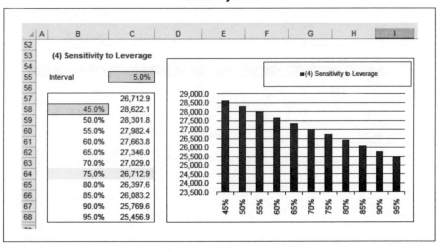

Chapter 16 – Statistics

The answer sheet contains the following:

- Draw a frequency table and histogram chart (see Figure A1.26).

- Produce the full descriptive statistics using functions or the Analysis ToolPak.

- Find the correlation between the variables (see Figure A1.27).

- Calculate the regression equation. Use the data to plot a scatter chart of the index as the X-axis and the stock as the Y-axis. A trend line through the data should prove the beta of the stock as the beta (see Figure A1.28).

Histogram

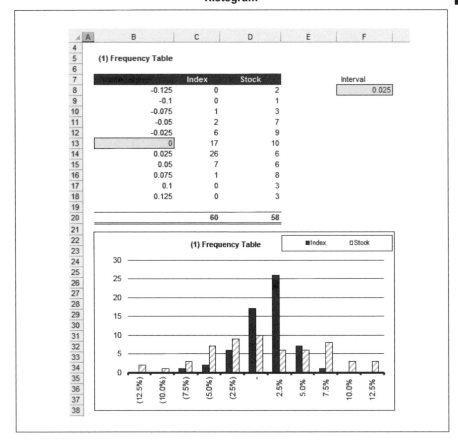

Figure A1.27

Correlation and descriptive statistics

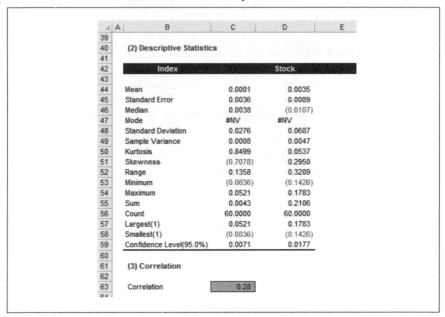

Figure A1.28

Regression equation–beta as a slope of the trend line

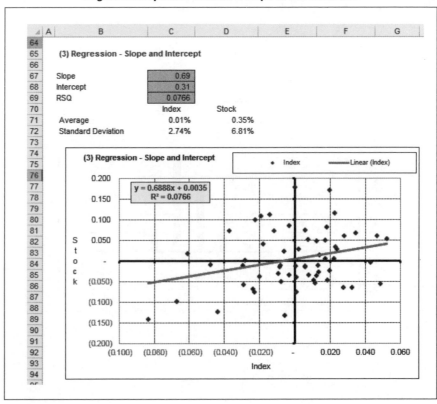

USEFUL EXCEL AND ANALYSIS TOOLPAK FUNCTIONS LIST BY CATEGORY

Function	Type	Analysis ToolPak	Description
DATE	Date/Time	–	Returns the serial number of a particular date
DATEDIF	Date/Time	–	Calculates the difference between two dates
DATEVALUE	Date/Time	–	Converts a date in the form of text to a serial number
DAY	Date/Time	–	Converts a serial number to a day of the month
DAYS360	Date/Time	–	Calculates the number of days between two dates based on a 360-day year
EDATE	Date/Time	Yes	Returns the serial number of the date that is the indicated number of months before or after the start date
EOMONTH	Date/Time	Yes	Returns the serial number of the last day of the month before or after a specified number of months
HOUR	Date/Time	–	Converts a serial number to an hour
MINUTE	Date/Time	–	Converts a serial number to a minute
MONTH	Date/Time	–	Converts a serial number to a month
NETWORKDAYS	Date/Time	Yes	Returns the number of whole workdays between two dates
NOW	Date/Time	–	Returns the serial number of the current date and time
SECOND	Date/Time	–	Converts a serial number to a second
TIME	Date/Time	–	Returns the serial number of a particular time
TIMEVALUE	Date/Time	–	Converts a time in the form of text to a serial number
TODAY	Date/Time	–	Returns the serial number of today's date
WEEKDAY	Date/Time	–	Converts a serial number to a day of the week
WEEKNUM	Date/Time	Yes	Converts a serial number to a number representing where the week falls numerically with a year

Function	Type	Analysis ToolPak	Description
WORKDAY	Date/Time	Yes	Returns the serial number of the date before or after a specified number of workdays
YEAR	Date/Time	–	Converts a serial number to a year
YEARFRAC	Date/Time	Yes	Returns the year fraction representing the number of whole days between start_date and end_date
ACCRINT	Financial	Yes	Returns the accrued interest for a security that pays periodic interest
ACCRINTM	Financial	Yes	
AMORDEGRC	Financial	Yes	Returns the depreciation for each accounting period by using a depreciation coefficient
AMORLINC	Financial	Yes	Returns the depreciation for each accounting period
COUPDAYBS	Financial	Yes	Returns the number of days from the beginning of the coupon period to the settlement date
COUPDAYS	Financial	Yes	Returns the number of days in the coupon period that contains the settlement date
COUPDAYSNC	Financial	Yes	Returns the number of days from the settlement date to the next coupon date
COUPNCD	Financial	Yes	Returns the next coupon date after the settlement date
COUPNUM	Financial	Yes	Returns the number of coupons payable between the settlement date and maturity date
COUPPCD	Financial	Yes	Returns the previous coupon date before the settlement date
CUMIPMT	Financial	Yes	Returns the cumulative interest paid between two periods
CUMPRINC	Financial	Yes	Returns the cumulative principal paid on a loan between two periods
DB	Financial	–	Returns the depreciation of an asset for a specified period using the fixed declining balance method
DDB	Financial	–	Returns the depreciation of an asset for a specified period using the double declining balance method or some other method you specify

Function	Type	Analysis ToolPak	Description
DISC	Financial	Yes	Returns the discount rate for a security
DOLLARDE	Financial	Yes	Converts a dollar price expressed as a fraction into a dollar price expressed as a decimal number
DOLLARFR	Financial	Yes	Converts a dollar price expressed as a decimal number into a dollar price expressed as a fraction
DURATION	Financial	Yes	Returns the annual duration of a security with periodic interest payments
EFFECT	Financial	Yes	Returns the effective annual interest rate
FV	Financial	–	Returns the future value of an investment
FVSCHEDULE	Financial	Yes	Returns the future value of an initial principal after applying a series of compound interest rates
INTRATE	Financial	Yes	Returns the interest rate for a fully invested security
IPMT	Financial	–	Returns the interest payment for an investment for a given period
IRR	Financial	–	Returns the internal rate of return for a series of cash flows
ISPMT	Financial	–	Calculates the interest paid during a specific period of an investment
MDURATION	Financial	Yes	Returns the Macauley modified duration for a security with an assumed par value of $100
MIRR	Financial	–	Returns the internal rate of return where positive and negative cash flows are financed at different rates
NOMINAL	Financial	Yes	Returns the annual nominal interest rate
NPER	Financial	–	Returns the number of periods for an investment
NPV	Financial	–	Returns the net present value of an investment based on a series of periodic cash flows and a discount rate
ODDFPRICE	Financial	Yes	Returns the price per $100 face value of a security with an odd first period

Function	Type	Analysis ToolPak	Description
ODDFYIELD	Financial	Yes	Returns the yield of a security with an odd first period
ODDLPRICE	Financial	Yes	Returns the price per $100 face value of a security with an odd last period
ODDLYIELD	Financial	Yes	Returns the yield of a security with an odd last period
PMT	Financial	–	Returns the periodic payment for an annuity
PPMT	Financial	–	Returns the payment on the principal for an investment for a given period
PRICE	Financial	Yes	Returns the price per $100 face value of a security that pays periodic interest
PRICEDISC	Financial	Yes	Returns the price per $100 face value of a discounted security
PRICEMAT	Financial	Yes	Returns the price per $100 face value of a security that pays interest at maturity
PV	Financial	–	Returns the present value of an investment
RATE	Financial	–	Returns the interest rate per period of an annuity
RECEIVED	Financial	–	Returns the amount received at maturity for a fully invested security
SLN	Financial	–	Returns the straight line depreciation of an asset for one period
SYD	Financial	–	Returns the sum-of-years' digits depreciation of an asset for a specified period
TBILLEQ	Financial	Yes	Returns the bond-equivalent yield for a treasury bill
TBILLPRICE	Financial	Yes	Returns the price per $100 face value for a treasury bill
TBILLYIELD	Financial	Yes	Returns the yield for a treasury bill
VDB	Financial	–	Returns the depreciation of an asset for a specified or partial period using a declining balance method
XIRR	Financial	Yes	Returns the internal rate of return for a schedule of cash flows that is not necessarily periodic

Function	Type	Analysis ToolPak	Description
XNPV	Financial	Yes	Returns the net present value for a schedule of cash flows that is not necessarily periodic
YIELD	Financial	Yes	Returns the yield on a security that pays periodic interest
YIELDDISC	Financial	Yes	Returns the annual yield for a discounted security; for example, a treasury bill
YIELDMAT	Financial	Yes	Returns the annual yield of a security that pays interest at maturity
ABS	Maths	–	Returns the absolute value of a number
ACOS	Maths	–	Returns the arccosine of a number
ACOSH	Maths	–	Returns the inverse hyperbolic cosine of a number
ASIN	Maths	–	Returns the arcsine of a number
ASINH	Maths	–	Returns the inverse hyperbolic sine of a number
ATAN	Maths	–	Returns the arctangent of a number
ATAN2	Maths	–	Returns the arctangent from x- and y-coordinates
ATANH	Maths	–	Returns the inverse hyperbolic tangent of a number
CEILING	Maths	–	Rounds a number to the nearest integer or to the nearest multiple of significance
COMBIN	Maths	–	Returns the number of combinations for a given number of objects
COS	Maths	–	Returns the cosine of a number
COSH	Maths	–	Returns the hyperbolic cosine of a number
COUNTIF	Maths	–	Counts the number of non-blank cells within a range that meet the given criteria
DEGREES	Maths	–	Converts radians to degrees
EVEN	Maths	–	Rounds a number up to the nearest even integer
EXP	Maths	–	Returns e raised to the power of a given number
FACT	Maths	–	Returns the factorial of a number

Function	Type	Analysis ToolPak	Description
FACTDOUBLE	Maths	Yes	Returns the double factorial of a number
FLOOR	Maths	–	Rounds a number down, towards zero
GCD	Maths	Yes	Returns the greatest common divisor
INT	Maths	–	Rounds a number down to the nearest integer
LCM	Maths	Yes	Returns the least common multiple
LN	Maths	–	Returns the natural logarithm of a number
LOG	Maths	–	Returns the logarithm of a number to a specified base
LOG10	Maths	–	Returns the base 10 logarithm of a number
MDETERM	Maths	–	Returns the matrix determinant of an array
MINVERSE	Maths	–	Returns the matrix inverse of an array
MMULT	Maths	–	Returns the matrix product of two arrays
MOD	Maths	–	Returns the remainder from division
MROUND	Maths	Yes	Returns a number rounded to the desired multiple
MULTINOMIAL	Maths	Yes	Returns the multinomial of a set of numbers
ODD	Maths	–	Rounds a number up to the nearest odd integer
PI	Maths	–	Returns the value of π
POWER	Maths	–	Returns the result of a number raised to a power
PRODUCT	Maths	–	Multiplies a series of arguments
QUOTIENT	Maths	Yes	Returns the integer portion of a division
RADIANS	Maths	–	Converts degrees to radians
RAND	Maths	–	Returns a random number between 0 and 1
RANDBETWEEN	Maths	Yes	Returns a random number between the numbers you specify

Function	Type	Analysis ToolPak	Description
ROMAN	Maths	–	Converts an Arabic numeral to a Roman one, as text
ROUND	Maths	–	Rounds a number to a specified number of digits
ROUNDDOWN	Maths	–	Rounds a number down, towards zero
ROUNDUP	Maths	–	Rounds a number up, away from zero
SERIESSUM	Maths	–	Returns the sum of a power series based on the formula
SIGN	Maths	–	Returns the sign of a number
SIN	Maths	–	Returns the sine of the given angle
SINH	Maths	–	Returns the hyperbolic sine of a number
SQRT	Maths	–	Returns a positive square root
SQRTPI	Maths	Yes	Returns the square root of (number * π)
SUBTOTAL	Maths	–	Returns a subtotal in a list or database
SUM	Maths	–	Adds the input parameters
SUMIF	Maths	–	Adds the cells specified by a given criterion
SUMPRODUCT	Maths	–	Returns the sum of the products of corresponding array components
SUMSQ	Maths	–	Returns the sum of the squares of the arguments
SUMX2MY2	Maths	–	Returns the sum of the difference of squares of corresponding values in two arrays
SUMX2PY2	Maths	–	Returns the sum of the sum of squares of corresponding values in two arrays
SUMXMY2	Maths	–	Returns the sum of squares of differences of corresponding values in two arrays
TAN	Maths	–	Returns the tangent of a number
TANH	Maths	–	Returns the hyperbolic tangent of a number
TRUNC	Maths	–	Truncates a number to an integer

Function	Type	Analysis ToolPak	Description
AVEDEV	Statistical	–	Returns the average of the absolute deviations of data points from their mean
AVERAGE	Statistical	–	Returns the arithmetic mean of a series of inputs
AVERAGEA	Statistical	–	Returns the arithmetic mean of a series of inputs, including numbers, text and logical values
BETADIST	Statistical	–	Returns the cumulative beta probability density function
BETAINV	Statistical	–	Returns the inverse of the cumulative beta probability density function
BINOMDIST	Statistical	–	Returns the individual term binomial distribution probability
CHIDIST	Statistical	–	Returns the one-tailed probability of the chi-squared distribution
CHIINV	Statistical	–	Returns the inverse of the one-tailed probability of the chi-squared distribution
CHITEST	Statistical	–	Returns the test for independence
CONFIDENCE	Statistical	–	Returns the confidence interval for a population mean
CORREL	Statistical	–	Returns the correlation coefficient between two data sets
COUNT	Statistical	–	Counts how many numbers are in the list of arguments
COUNTA	Statistical	–	Counts how many values are in the list of arguments
COVAR	Statistical	–	Returns covariance, the average of the products of paired deviations
CRITBINOM	Statistical	–	Returns the smallest value for which the cumulative binomial distribution is less than or equal to a criterion value
DEVSQ	Statistical	–	Returns the sum of squares of deviations
EXPONDIST	Statistical	–	Returns the exponential distribution
FDIST	Statistical	–	Returns the F probability distribution
FINV	Statistical	–	Returns the inverse of the F probability distribution

Function	Type	Analysis ToolPak	Description
FISHER	Statistical	–	Returns the Fisher transformation
FISHERINV	Statistical	–	Returns the inverse of the Fisher transformation
FORECAST	Statistical	–	Returns a value along a linear trend
FREQUENCY	Statistical	–	Returns a frequency distribution as a vertical array
FTEST	Statistical	–	Returns the result of an F-test
GAMMADIST	Statistical	–	Returns the gamma distribution
GAMMAINV	Statistical	–	Returns the inverse of the gamma cumulative distribution
GAMMALN	Statistical	–	Returns the natural logarithm of the gamma function, $\Gamma(x)$
GEOMEAN	Statistical	–	Returns the geometric mean
GROWTH	Statistical	–	Returns values along an exponential trend
HARMEAN	Statistical	–	Returns the harmonic mean
HYPGEOMDIST	Statistical	–	Returns the hypergeometric distribution
INTERCEPT	Statistical	–	Returns the intercept of the linear regression line
KURT	Statistical	–	Returns the kurtosis of a data set
LARGE	Statistical	–	Returns the kth largest value in a data set
LINEST	Statistical	–	Returns the parameters of a linear trend
LOGEST	Statistical	–	Returns the parameters of an exponential trend
LOGINV	Statistical	–	Returns the inverse of the lognormal distribution
LOGNORMDIST	Statistical	–	Returns the cumulative lognormal distribution
MAX	Statistical	–	Returns the maximum value in a list of arguments
MAXA	Statistical	–	Returns the maximum value in a list of arguments, including numbers, text and logical values
MEDIAN	Statistical	–	Returns the median of the given numbers
MIN	Statistical	–	Returns the minimum value in a list of arguments

Function	Type	Analysis ToolPak	Description
MINA	Statistical	–	Returns the smallest value in a list of arguments, including numbers, text and logical values
MODE	Statistical	–	Returns the most common value in a data set
NEGBINOMDIST	Statistical	–	Returns the negative binomial distribution
NORMDIST	Statistical	–	Returns the normal cumulative distribution
NORMINV	Statistical	–	Returns the inverse of the normal cumulative distribution
NORMSDIST	Statistical	–	Returns the standard normal cumulative distribution
NORMSINV	Statistical	–	Returns the inverse of the standard normal cumulative distribution
PEARSON	Statistical	–	Returns the Pearson product moment correlation coefficient
PERCENTILE	Statistical	–	Returns the kth percentile of values in a range
PERCENTRANK	Statistical	–	Returns the percentage rank of a value in a data set
PERMUT	Statistical	–	Returns the number of permutations for a given number of objects
POISSON	Statistical	–	Returns the Poisson distribution
PROB	Statistical	–	Returns the probability that values in a range are between two limits
QUARTILE	Statistical	–	Returns the quartile of a data set
RANK	Statistical	–	Returns the rank of a number in a list of numbers
RSQ	Statistical	–	Returns the square of the Pearson product moment correlation coefficient
SKEW	Statistical	–	Returns the skewness of a distribution
SLOPE	Statistical	–	Returns the slope of the linear regression line
SMALL	Statistical	–	Returns the kth smallest value in a data set
STANDARDIZE	Statistical	–	Returns a normalised value
STDEV	Statistical	–	Estimates standard deviation based on a sample

Function	Type	Analysis ToolPak	Description
STDEVA	Statistical	–	Estimates standard deviation based on a sample, including numbers, text and logical values
STDEVP	Statistical	–	Calculates standard deviation based on the entire population
STDEVPA	Statistical	–	Calculates standard deviation based on the entire population, including numbers, text and logical values
STEYX	Statistical	–	Returns the standard error of the predicted y-value for each x in the regression
TDIST	Statistical	–	Returns Student's t-distribution
TINV	Statistical	–	Returns the inverse of Student's t-distribution
TREND	Statistical	–	Returns values along a linear trend
TRIMMEAN	Statistical	–	Returns the mean of the interior of a data set
TTEST	Statistical	–	Returns the probability associated with a Student's t-test
VAR	Statistical	–	Estimates variance based on a sample
VARA	Statistical	–	Estimates variance based on a sample, including numbers, text and logical values
VARP	Statistical	–	Calculates variance based on the entire population
VARPA	Statistical	–	Calculates variance based on the entire population, including numbers, text and logical values
WEIBULL	Statistical	–	Returns the Weibull distribution
ZTEST	Statistical	–	Returns the two-tailed P-value of a z-test

SOFTWARE INSTALLATION AND LICENCE

The Excel files and templates accompanying this book are hosted on the website **www.financial-models.com**. The file names relate to their chapter numbers and you should refer to the file list. The file notation is MFMaths3e and then the chapter number. For your reference, the files for a particular chapter are quoted at the beginning of each chapter.

Follow the instructions below to install the files and create a program group using the simple SETUP command.

SYSTEM REQUIREMENTS

This section summarises the requirements for using the application.

- IBM-compatible personal computer
- Hard disk with 20Mb of free space
- Microsoft® Mouse or other compatible pointing device
- Microsoft® Windows 7 or above and Excel 2003 or later. The files have been developed using Excel 2003 and tested with Excel 2007 + for the widest compatibility.

INSTALLATION

- Download the files from the digital downloads section of www.financial-models.com
- Unzip the file to a temporary directory.
- Select and double click SetUp.
- The application will now install itself. Follow the instructions on screen to select a destination directory.
- If you are prompted, then restart Windows.

Important
When the installation has finished, open Excel and select **File, Excel Options** – Add-Ins (see Figure A1.29). Then press Go at the bottom to display a list of your current add-ins. You need to make sure that the Analysis ToolPak and Solver are selected. When you tick the boxes you may be prompted for your original Office install disk.

Excel options

This is because the files use some of the advanced functions from the Analysis ToolPak such as EDATE and XNPV or Solver routines. Analysis ToolPak is not installed using a typical Excel installation. If this is the case, use your original Office disks to install the option as you cannot simply copy the files from another location.

Analysis ToolPak contains extra statistical and financial functions needed by the applications (see Figure A1.30). Click it to select it and press OK. If you do not install it, you will encounter errors on opening certain files.

Analysis ToolPak

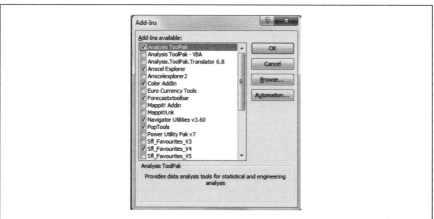

ACCESSING THE APPLICATION FILES

- You will see that a program group has been created for you. The application will also now appear under `Programs` on the `Start Menu`.

- When installed, the program group should include all the files on the accompanying file list.

- To access any of the files, simply double click the icons in the program group.

- You can also open a ReadMe file of installation instructions and a file list.

- Press OK to continue and the selected file will open.

- There is a master file list in the form of an Excel model and a list within the book.

LICENCE

This notice is intended to be a 'no nonsense' agreement between you ('the licensee') and Systematic Finance Ltd ('Systematic'). The software and associated documentation ('software') are subject to copyright law. They are protected by the laws of England. If you use this software, you are deemed to have accepted the terms and conditions under which this software was supplied.

Files accompanying *Mastering Financial Mathematics in Microsoft® Excel – Third Edition* are copyright 'Systematic Finance Ltd' ('Systematic').

The software has not been audited and no representation, warranty or undertaking (express or implied) is made and no responsibility is taken or accepted by Systematic and its directors, officers, employees, agents or advisers as to the adequacy, accuracy, completeness or reasonableness of the financial models and Systematic excludes liability thereof.

In particular, no responsibility is taken or accepted by Systematic and all liability is excluded by Systematic for the accuracy of the computations comprised therein and the assumptions upon which such computations are based. In addition, the recipient receives and uses the software entirely at its own risk and no responsibility is taken or accepted by Systematic and accordingly all liability is excluded by Systematic for any losses which may result therefrom, whether as a direct or indirect consequence of a computer virus or otherwise.

No part of the accompanying documentation may be reproduced, transmitted, transcribed, stored in a retrieval system or translated without the prior permission of the copyright holder. You have a limited licence to use the software for the period stated on the software copyright notice and to make copies of the software for backup purposes. This is a single copy software licence granted by Systematic. You must treat this software just like a book except that you may copy it onto a computer to be used and you may make an archival backup copy of the software for the purposes of protecting the software from accidental loss.

The phrase 'just like a book' is used to give the licensee maximum flexibility in the use of the licence. This means, for example, that the software can be used by any number of people, or freely moved between computers, provided it is not being used on more than one computer or by more than one person at the same time as it is in use elsewhere. Just like a book, which can only be read by one person at a time, the software can only be used by one person on one computer at one time. If more than one person is using the software on different machines, then Systematic's rights have been violated and the licensee should seek to purchase further single copy licences by purchasing further copies of the book. (In the case of multiple licences or network licences, then the number of users may only equal the number of licences.)

You may not decompile, disassemble or reverse-engineer the licensed software. You may not rent or lease the software to others or claim ownership. If you wish to pass the software onto another person, you may. However, you must provide all original disks, documentation and remove the software from your own computer(s) to remain within the single copy licence agreement. To do otherwise will violate the rights of Systematic.

Systematic does not warrant that the functions contained in the software will meet your requirements or that the operation of the software will be uninterrupted or error free. This warranty does not extend to changes made to the software by third parties, nor does it extend to liability for data loss, damages or lost profits due to the use of the software.

Systematic does not have any responsibility for software failure due to changes in the operating environment of the computer hardware or operating system made after delivery of the software.

Copyright © Systematic Finance Ltd

FILE LIST

Chapter	Topic	Items
1	Introduction and overview	MFMaths3e_01
2	Basic financial arithmetic	MFMaths3e_02
3	Cash flows	MFMaths3e_03
4	Fixed income products	MFMaths3e_04
5	Bond risks	MFMaths3e_05
6	Floating rate securities	MFMaths3e_06
7	Annuities	MFMaths3e_07
8	Swaps	MFMaths3e_08
9	Forward interest rates	MFMaths3e_09
10	Futures	MFMaths3e_10
11	Foreign exchange	MFMaths3e_11
12	Options	MFMaths3e_12
13	Real options	MFMaths3e_13
14	Equity valuation	MFMaths3e_14
15	Leasing	MFMaths3e_15
		MFMaths3e_16a
16	Basic statistics	MFMaths3e_16b
		MFMaths3e_16_Data
	Appendices	MFMaths3e_Exercises
		MFMaths3e_Functions

The above files comprise Excel templates for each chapter. The file names and sheets are referenced in the chapters.

Important
Make sure that you follow the installation instructions and ensure that the Analysis ToolPak and Solver are loaded into your version of Excel.

Systematic Finance Ltd is an independent company specialising in:

- Financial modelling and consulting – review, design, build, train and audit.
- Financial training – financial modelling techniques, credit analysis, leasing and corporate finance on an in-house and public basis.
- Leasing as a corporate lessor and arranger.

For further information and support, please go to <u>www.financial-models.com</u> or contact:

Alastair L. Day
Systematic Finance Ltd

Email: aday@system.co.uk
Web: www.system.co.uk and www.financial-models.com

Appendix 2

AN INTRODUCTION TO MICROSOFT® OFFICE

This appendix provides an introduction to Microsoft® Office to show the differences in the menus and commands. This appendix provides an overview and some screenshots of the menu ribbon at the top of the screen. There is also a function reference on the disk (MFMaths3e_Menus).

Microsoft® Office user interface overview

The whole Office interface was redesigned initially in Excel 2007 and amended in later editions to contain more features and new file formats. Microsoft explains that most Office users accessed around 10 per cent of the functions on the many toolbars and menus in previous versions of the applications, because most of the programs' features were buried in layers of menus and submenus. In response, Microsoft has placed the functions on a single, changeable ribbon to make them more visible, and thus more likely to be used. The result is a user interface that makes it easier for people to get more out of Office applications so they can deliver better results faster. Microsoft® Word, Excel, PowerPoint and Access feature a similar workspace to offer the same style across the Office family.

Key features

Prior to Office 2007 applications, people used a system of menus, toolbars, task panes and dialogue boxes to get their work done. This system worked well when the applications had a limited number of commands. Now that the programs do so much more, the system of menus and toolbars does not work as well. Too many program features are said to be too hard for many users to find. For this reason, the overriding objective for the user interface is to make it easier for people to find and use the full range of features these applications provide. The result is better performing applications in Word, PowerPoint, Access and Excel.

The Ribbon

The previous menus and toolbars have been replaced by the Ribbon, which presents commands organised into a set of tabs. The tabs on the Ribbon display the commands that are most relevant for each of the task areas in Office Word, Office PowerPoint, Office Excel and Office Access.

Figure A2.1 **File screen**

Contextual tabs

Certain sets of commands are only relevant when objects of a particular type are being edited. For example, the commands for editing a chart are not relevant until a chart appears in a spreadsheet and the user is focusing on modifying it. In earlier versions of Office, these commands could be difficult to find. In Excel, clicking a chart causes a contextual tab to appear with commands used for chart editing. Contextual tabs appear only when they are needed and make it much easier to find and use the commands needed for the operation at hand.

Galleries

Galleries provide users with a set of clear results to choose from when working on their document, spreadsheet, presentation or Access database. By presenting a simple set of potential results, rather than a complex dialogue box with numerous options, Galleries simplify the process of producing clear output. The traditional dialogue boxes are still available for those wishing a greater degree of control over the result of the operation.

Live Preview

Live Preview shows the results of applying an editing or formatting change as the user moves the pointer over the results presented in a Gallery. This new capability simplifies the process of laying out, editing and formatting so users can create excellent results with less time and effort.

Migration

Home screen

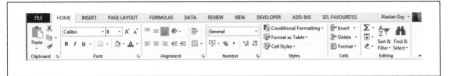

Office now uses file formats different from Office 2003 primarily due to the switch to XML file formats as the defaults in Word, Excel and PowerPoint. Office applications can open and work on files created in previous releases back to Office 97, and you can create files in all existing Office formats. However, to take full advantage of the smaller file sizes and other benefits of the latest Office, you must use the new XML formats: .docx/docm in Word; .xlsx/xlsm in Excel; and .pptx/pptm in PowerPoint.

1. Office Menus – Home

Figure A2.3 shows the difference in the menu commands starting with Home. To open, modify or print a document you click the Office icon at the top left. Home provides all cell formatting currently on the Formatting toolbar and under Edit. The elements on the right, such as conditional formatting, tables and styles, are currently found under Format.

Insert

2. Insert

This screen combines further toolbars and options. These commands all insert objects on the spreadsheet so the Office Ribbon brings them together here. Where you see a triangle on the Ribbon item, further menus open out with options. When you click these buttons, they open to reveal further options. For example, Recommended Charts opens further choices or you can click the different types of charts.

Submenu

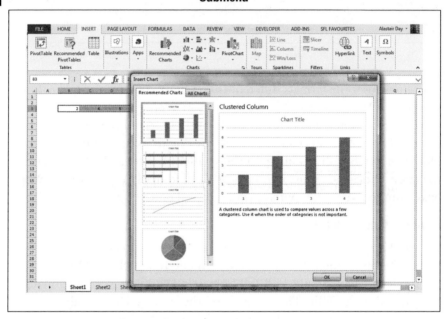

3. Page Layout

The menu brings together all the layout commands. These relate to the layout (margin, orientation, size, etc.) and printing setup of individual sheets.

Page Layout

4. Formulas

Inserting formulas in Excel can be complex when you need to find one of the 300+ different functions. This menu helps with functions arranged in categories with names and formula auditing. Names allow you to name individual cells and ranges to make the code easier to understand. Commands such as Evaluate Formula and Watch Window allow you to trace commands and understand the process of calculation and result. Calculation options allow you to switch between the manual and automatic calculation states.

Formulas

Figure A2.6

5. Data

The Data menu contains commands such as Connections and Data Validation. Sorting and Filtering are also on Data. What-If analysis such as Data Tables, Scenarios and Goal Seek are also shown here. These are key commands for risk and variance analysis in Excel. The commands for linking data and workbooks are also here since Excel works well with Access databases and other external sources.

Data

Figure A2.7

6. Review

Review includes options such as spelling and protection together with comments. The idea is to use this set of commands when the initial workbook has been written and needs to be checked. Good practice includes annotating and commenting cells, together with protecting formula cells against unauthorised changes.

Review

Figure A2.8

7. View

There are a number of tools for changing the appearance of Excel such as Gridlines, Formula Bar, Freezing and Splitting Panes, etc., which can be found in View. These are all the commands that control the appearance of Excel on the screen.

Figure A2.9   **View**

8. Developer

The Developer options are not available unless you click the box using the Options tab as shown below. This allows you to record macros and make use of extended possibilities in Visual Basic. You also get access to forms and controls for convenient data entry, for example scroll bars and combo boxes.

Figure A2.10   **Developer**

Figure A2.11   **Options**

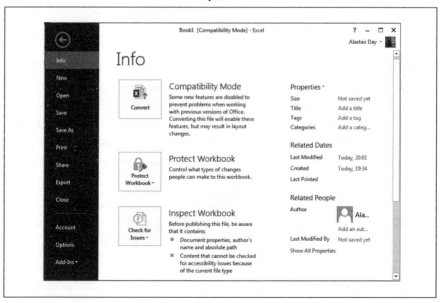

You need to tick the box below and the extra option appears on the Ribbon.

Show Developer: Excel Options, Customize Ribbon, Developer

9. Add-Ins

In Office, Add-Ins are a separate option and you choose the add-ins with the options below. You can load add-ins manually or allow them to open with Excel using Options.

Add-Ins

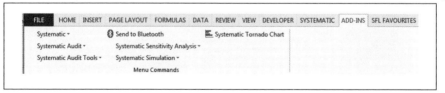

10. Options – General

There are a number of options in General and this section is the equivalent of setup, for example, the default number of sheets in an Excel workbook. You can personalise colours, fonts and author names by default.

General

11. Options – Formulas

These options determine the automation of calculation and the error checking options. Iterations options are set here together with calculation options and error checking rules.

Formulas

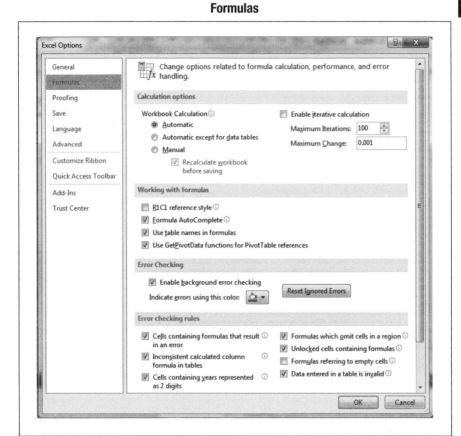

12. Options – Proofing

This option is common to other parts of Office and chooses how proofing is carried out and how Excel seeks to correct potential errors. The AutoCorrect and dictionary options are also here.

Figure A2.16

Proofing

13. Options – Save

Here you set up file locations, the auto-save interval and the visual appearance. You can also define the default Excel file type, for example xls (Excel 2003), xlsm (with macros) and xlsx (without macros).

Save

14. Options – Advanced

This section deals with advanced options for editing and other actions. This includes the controls for editing options such as AutoComplete together with editing and display options.

Advanced

15. Options – Customize Ribbon

You can customise the Ribbon by adding and subtracting controls or insert your own items on the Ribbon. This is a big advantage over Excel 2007 which did not allow any customisation, and this option reinstates the flexible toolbar possibilities in Excel 2003.

Customisation

Figure A2.19

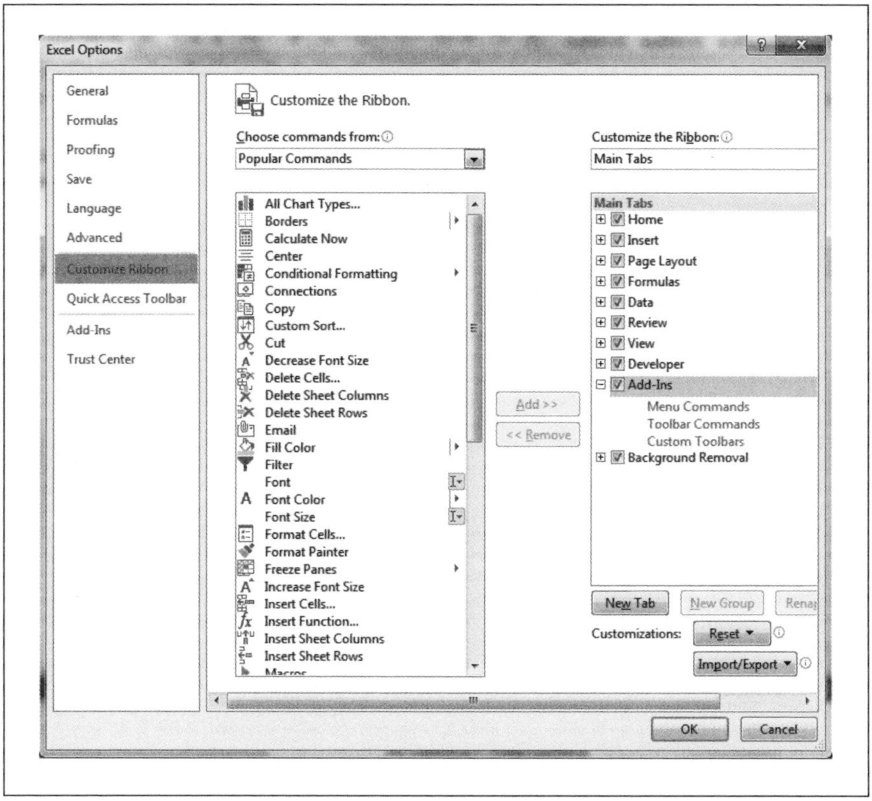

16. Options – Quick Access Toolbar

You can customise toolbars with quick commands and this menu option allows you to select commands for the Quick Access Toolbar. The Quick Access Toolbar is visible at the top left of the Ribbon.

Quick Access Toolbar Customisation

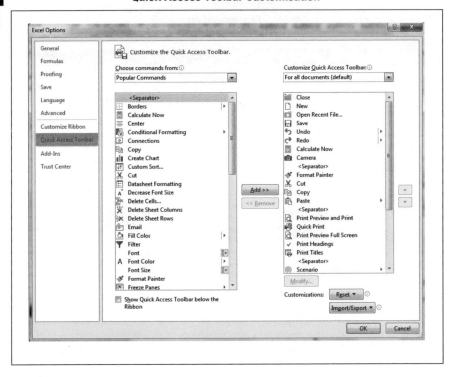

17. Options – Add-Ins

You can add these resources to the list to allow Excel to open them every time you start Excel. Clicking the box 'Add' at the bottom brings up a dialogue box similar to Excel 2003 and you can browse or pick items from the list.

Add-Ins

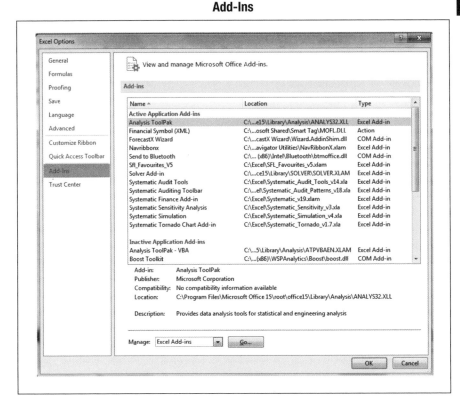

18. Options – Trust Center

This section on security provides tools for securing documents and privacy. The Trust Center setting include the security settings for Visual Basic and document access.

Trust Center

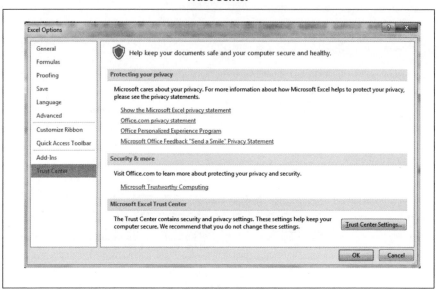

What did you think of this book?

We're really keen to hear from you about this book, so that we can make our publishing even better.

Please log on to the following website and leave us your feedback.

It will only take a few minutes and your thoughts are invaluable to us.

www.pearsoned.co.uk/bookfeedback

Index